BEING HUMAN IN STEM

Advance Praise for *Being Human in STEM*

"Throughout my career, I have taken on many roles—faculty member, faculty developer, and institutional leader—and I wish this book had been available to guide me. Many faculty want to work with their students to change STEM fields collaboratively, and the authors demonstrate a compelling, flexible model of how to achieve those goals. This resource sheds light on ways to enlist colleagues in an ongoing, constructive institutional dialogue on difficult topics. Across higher education, we need to bring more folks into the HSTEM movement."—***Becky Wai-Ling Packard****, Professor of Psychology and Education, Mount Holyoke; Author of* Successful STEM Mentoring Initiatives

"Faculty often ask me how they can make students feel like they really belong in STEM and excel in courses. After reading this book, the answer is crystal clear—allow them to bring their whole selves to the environment thereby eliminating the need to ignore any part of their humanity. This book is a treasure trove of information for making STEM (or any environment) more inclusive by partnering with students to make it happen."—***Saundra Y. McGuire****, Director Emerita, Center for Academic Success; Former Assistant Vice Chancellor and Professor Emerita of Chemistry, Louisiana State University*

"This book chronicles a remarkable project that began with three sophomores planning a sit-in that ultimately transformed how their campus supports student belonging and understanding in STEM. Sarah Bunnell, Sheila Jaswal, and Megan Lyster share the compelling story and a wealth of guidance, inviting us to adapt what they learned within our own disciplinary and campus contexts. In the end, though, this book is so much more than course design: It's a roadmap for what higher education should be in the 21st century."—***Nancy Chick****, Director of the Endeavor Foundation Center for Faculty Development, Rollins College*

"*Being Human in STEM* is a welcome addition to the field of higher education that addresses how to unveil the curtain in STEM fields and embrace diversity. The authors describe a course with clear learning outcomes that directly confronts humanity in STEM. They describe its successful implementation at multiple institutions. The course counters the narrative that inclusivity cannot be directly addressed in undergraduate STEM education. I encourage all who want to provide exceptional learning experiences for their STEM students to consider how this course could be offered at their institution. There is a place for *Being Human in STEM* at colleges and universities of all types from community colleges; historically Black colleges and universities; minority serving institutions; tribal colleges and universities; public universities; private universities; master's colleges and universities; small, private liberal arts colleges, to K-12 schools. The course is relevant to any institution educating students in STEM disciplines.

For those ready to explore an avenue for supporting diversity in STEM, the book provides a helpful roadmap for developing a *Being Human in STEM* course within any context. More than just the syllabus, the authors describe their experiences building the course and growing it into a community spanning several institutions, provide recommendations for implementation, give sample activities, assignments, and inclusive teaching approaches, and present feedback from students who completed the course. It's all here.

Perhaps this book interests you for a variety of reasons—being human in STEM is an intriguing concept, you want to learn more detail about the course, you are interested in how such a course could fit in with the existing curriculum at your institution. Whatever your reasons, I hope you'll consider utilizing the precious content to make STEM education more inclusive at your college, university, or K-12 school. Now is the time to stop hiding our identities behind the curtain. We need to embrace our humanity in STEM."—*From the Foreword by* **Tracie Marcella Addy**, *Lafayette College*

"By centering the voices and agency of students, this book offers a significant and new approach to making any—and every—course, program, and institution a more inclusive learning environment. Although the book's four-step change process emerges from STEM disciplines at one college, the authors give us concrete advice about and vivid examples of how we can adapt that model across fields and contexts. This is a guide all of us in higher education can and should use to make our classrooms and campuses more humane and equitable."—**Peter Felten**, *Professor of History, Executive Director of the Center for Engaged Learning, Elon University*

BEING HUMAN IN STEM
Partnering With Students to Shape Inclusive Practices and Communities

Sarah L. Bunnell, Sheila S. Jaswal, and Megan B. Lyster

Foreword by Tracie Marcella Addy

Routledge
Taylor & Francis Group
NEW YORK AND LONDON

First published in 2023 by Stylus Publishing, LLC.

Published in 2023 by Routledge
605 Third Avenue, New York, NY 10017
4 Park Square, Milton Park, Abingdon, Oxon OX14 4RN

Routledge is an imprint of the Taylor & Francis Group, an informa business.

© 2023 Taylor & Francis Group

All rights reserved. No part of this book may be reprinted or reproduced or utilised in any form or by any electronic, mechanical, or other means, now known or hereafter invented, including photocopying and recording, or in any information storage or retrieval system, without permission in writing from the publishers.

Trademark Notice: Product or corporate names may be trademarks or registered trademarks, and are used only for identification and explanation without intent to infringe.

Cover photo by Hanaa Charania. Pictured (from left): Amherst HSTEM students Sam Young, Lauren Ju, Jorge Rodas, and Alexa Augustine.

Library of Congress Cataloging-in-Publication-Data
Names: Bunnell, Sarah L., author. | Jaswal, Sheila S., author. | Lyster, Megan B., author. | Addy, Tracie Marcella, author of foreword.
Title: Being human in STEM : partnering with students to shape inclusive practices and communities / Sarah L. Bunnell, Sheila S. Jaswal, and Megan B. Lyster ; foreword by Tracie Marcella Addy.
Description: First edition. | Sterling, Virginia : Stylus, 2023. | Includes bibliographical references and index.
Identifiers: LCCN 2023001599
  ISBN 9781642672282 (cloth) | ISBN 9781642672299 (paperback)
Subjects: LCSH: Science--Study and teaching (Higher)--United States. | Technology--Study and teaching (Higher)--United States. | Engineering--Study and teaching (Higher)--United States. | Mathematics--Study and teaching (Higher)--United States. | Science--Study and teaching (Higher)--Social aspects--United States. | Inclusive education--United States.
Classification: LCC Q181 .B86
DDC 507.1/073--dc23/eng20230415
LC record available at https://lccn.loc.gov/2023001599

ISBN: 9781642672282 (hbk)
ISBN: 9781642672299 (pbk)
ISBN: 9781003443216 (ebk)

DOI 10.4324/9781003443216

This book is dedicated to the nine students who founded the first "Being Human in STEM" course at Amherst College: Doyin Ariyibi, Louise Atadja, Ashley Bohan, Ruth Manzanares, Gaby Mayer, Chelsea Nkansah-Siriboe, Emma Ryan, Sanyu Takirambudde, and Olivia Truax. Your collective vision of who we can be, as fellow humans in STEM, remains the North Star of our work.

CONTENTS

	LIST OF FIGURES AND TABLES	ix
	FOREWORD *Tracie Marcella Addy*	xi
	PREFACE	xiii
	ACKNOWLEDGMENTS	xxi
1	THE AMHERST UPRISING	1
2	THE HSTEM COURSE	16
3	A PROCESS FOR PARTNERSHIP	36
4	TEACHING WITH AND FOR EMPATHY	54
5	PRACTICES FOR BUILDING COMMUNITY IN STEM CLASSROOMS AND LABS	67
6	TELLING YOUR HSTEM STORY	95
7	BRINGING ABOUT CHANGE	111
8	MEASURING THE IMPACT OF INCLUSIVE EFFORTS	128
9	GROWING THE HSTEM NETWORK Adapting the HSTEM Course Across Institutions	141
10	CONCLUSIONS	165

APPENDICES 173

APPENDIX A: SELECTED HSTEM COURSE READINGS AND REFLECTIONS 175

APPENDIX B: FACILITATOR GUIDE: HUMANIZING THE PROFESSOR 183

APPENDIX C: FACILITATOR GUIDE: AIRPLANE GAME 185

APPENDIX D: FACILITATOR GUIDE: THIS I BELIEVE 187

APPENDIX E: FACILITATOR GUIDE: DISCUSSING CLASS EXPECTATIONS 189

APPENDIX F: FACILITATOR GUIDE: DESIGNING SUCCESS AND HOW TO ACHIEVE IT 191

APPENDIX G: FACILITATOR GUIDE: COMMUNITY AGREEMENTS 193

APPENDIX H: FACILITATOR GUIDE: MINUTE PAPER 195

APPENDIX I: FACILITATOR GUIDE: UTILITY VALUE WRITING 197

APPENDIX J: FACILITATOR GUIDE: EXAM WRAPPERS 199

APPENDIX K: FACILITATOR GUIDE: MIDSEMESTER FEEDBACK 201

APPENDIX L: FACILITATOR GUIDE: SCIENTIST TRADING CARDS 203

APPENDIX M: FACILITATOR GUIDE: COMMUNITY ANNOUNCEMENTS 205

APPENDIX N: FACILITATOR GUIDE: GROUP WORK REFLECTIONS 207

APPENDIX O: FACILITATOR GUIDE: TELLING YOUR HSTEM STORY 209

ABOUT THE AUTHORS 213

INDEX 215

LIST OF FIGURES AND TABLES

Preface

Figure P.1.   Sarah Bunnell. *Photo credit.* Maria Stenzel, Amherst College Office of Communications.

Figure P.2.   Sheila Jaswal. *Photo credit.* Laura Quinlan, Amherst College Office of Communications.

Figure P.3.   Megan Lyster. *Photo credit.* Maria Stenzel, Amherst College Office of Communications.

Chapter 1

Figure 1.1.   The Amherst Uprising. *Photo credit.* Kaelan McCone. Permanently stored in the Amherst College Archives & Special Collections.

Figure 1.2.   Timeline of police violence.

Figure 1.3.   Sit-in leaders. *Photo credit.* Kaelan McCone. Permanently stored in the Amherst College Archives & Special Collections.

Chapter 2

Figure 2.1.   The HSTEM course model.

Table 2.1   HSTEM Collective List of Unfamiliar Words

Figure 2.2.   Common action project themes.

Chapter 3

Figure 3.1. The HSTEM process model.

Table 3.1 How Student Partnership Compares to Other Forms of Collaboration With Students

Chapter 4

Table 4.1 Comparing the Roles of Educators and Medical Practitioners

Chapter 5

Figure 5.1. Brief history of a human in STEM.

Chapter 6

Figure 6.1. Cy's HSTEM story.

Chapter 7

None

Chapter 8

None

Chapter 9

Table 9.1 Early Adopters of HSTEM: Institutional Profiles

Figure 9.1. Timeline of HSTEM course offerings.

Chapter 10

Figure 10.1. Individual and collective change in the HSTEM course.

FOREWORD

Several years ago I attended a notable summit. The event, described by the authors of *Being Human in STEM: Partnering With Students to Shape Inclusive Practices and Communities*, involved undergraduates from three colleges and universities showcasing action projects they designed for an institutional course. The atmosphere was inviting as the keynote speaker shared aspects of her humanity and her path as a scientist. Her compelling talk was not structured with scientific methods, data analyses, results, and conclusions, but focused on her journey in a field often centered on neutrality and objectivity. I recall feeling affirmed that the speaker spoke from this perspective and embraced her humanity in science.

Later I had the opportunity to hear students from their Being in Human in STEM courses present action projects designed to advance inclusivity in STEM more broadly at their institutions. Their energy was evident and they were excited to share their proposals. This was not a traditional STEM poster session. The projects involved student-led inquiry and explorations at the intersection of science and identity. The students' engagement highlighted the positive outcomes of well-crafted courses supporting diverse students in undergraduate STEM education.

The major STEM challenge these students tackled through their coursework was the dissonance that sometimes occurs—the sense that one has to "turn off" their social identities to effectively "turn on" their scientific, design, and mathematical ways of thinking and doing. However, one's humanness and ability to perform STEM work do not exist as a dichotomy, but are interconnected. For too long there has been pressure placed on those in STEM disciplines to hide their social identities behind a curtain so that no one can view them, a deficit-minded perspective. We can see the harmful impacts of such suppression—exclusion, imposter phenomenon, lack of a sense of belonging, diverse individuals leaving STEM fields, and other problematic issues left unaddressed.

Being Human in STEM is a welcome addition to the field of higher education that addresses how to unveil the curtain in STEM fields and embrace diversity. The authors describe a course with clear learning outcomes that directly confronts humanity in STEM. They describe its successful implementation at multiple institutions. The course counters the narrative that inclusivity cannot be directly addressed in undergraduate STEM education. I encourage all who want to provide exceptional learning experiences for their STEM students to consider how this course could be offered at their institution. There is a place for Being Human in STEM at colleges and universities of all types from community colleges; historically Black colleges and universities; minority serving institutions; tribal colleges and universities; public universities, private universities; master's colleges and universities; small, private liberal arts colleges, to K–12 schools. The course is relevant to any institution educating students in STEM disciplines.

Inclusivity within STEM education requires the collective efforts of students, instructors, and staff members to make disciplines more welcoming and equitable. The value of student partnership through co-creation is strongly interwoven throughout the book. Students' perspectives matter, and co-creating courses with learners enables students to have a voice, providing opportunities to reveal gaps and needs. The design of the Being Human in STEM course includes ways of being and knowing in STEM disciplines, lived experiences, and action projects within the institution that can advance inclusivity. The course cultivates empathy development and helps students build important skills such as active listening and validation. This dynamic approach can lead to significant, meaningful learning experiences for diverse students in STEM fields that they can take with them wherever their paths lead.

For those ready to explore an avenue for supporting diversity in STEM, the book provides a helpful roadmap for developing a Being Human in STEM course within any context. More than just the syllabus, the authors describe their experiences building the course and growing it into a community spanning several institutions, provide recommendations for implementation, give sample activities, assignments, and inclusive teaching approaches, and present feedback from students who completed the course. It's all here.

Perhaps this book interests you for a variety of reasons—being human in STEM is an intriguing concept, you want to learn more detail about the course, you are interested in how such a course could fit in with the existing curriculum at your institution. Whatever your reasons, I hope you'll consider utilizing the precious content to make STEM education more inclusive at your college, university, or K–12 school. Now is the time to stop hiding our identities behind the curtain. We need to embrace our humanity in STEM.

Tracie Marcella Addy
Lafayette College

PREFACE

When did you first experience a sense of belonging—that you were enough, that you were with your people, that you felt comfortable expressing yourself in the space and with others? For many of us, this feeling emerges when we are with our friends, family, neighbors, and other social networks that affirm our identities. Professionally, however, a sense of belonging may be more fleeting or nonexistent, particularly for scientists who may not fit the stereotypical mold of what a scientist should look like, how they should act, and the training, skills, and values they should hold. We may go to great efforts to minimize aspects of our identity that do not conform to the stereotypical scientist ideal. On top of this, many of us have been trained to believe that science seeks objective scientific truth, a truth that is not impacted by who we are as humans and social agents. By the time we complete our training and are educating the next generation of emerging scientists in the classroom, how we present ourselves to our students, how we design and deliver our courses, and the values we convey to our students have been deeply ingrained in our daily practice.

This book presents the "Being Human in STEM" initiative, or HSTEM, as a model for challenging those assumptions and how we communicate to students about who belongs and who can thrive in STEM (science, technology, engineering, and mathematics fields). This work arose out of a time of conflict at Amherst College—a 4-day sit-in protest to support the Black Lives Matter movement and bring attention to related experiences of exclusion and marginalization that minoritized students experienced on campus. What emerged from that conflict has been transformative for our institution, for our students, and for ourselves. In this book, we share how HSTEM came into being, resources and recommendations for building and evaluating the multilevel impact of HSTEM, and models of how the HSTEM course has been adapted at colleges and universities across the country.

Our Goals for This Book

In writing about our experiences and the experiences of the students, faculty, and staff who have been a part of the HSTEM initiative, we had two key goals:

1. Provide resources, recommendations, and reflective questions that will help more individuals adapt the HSTEM course to their particular institutional contexts. Again and again, we hear about the transformative nature of HSTEM as a space where students experience a sense of community and validation, where faculty and staff establish meaningful relationships with students and deeper understandings of themselves as teachers, and where the seeds of inclusive change are sown. As you read this book, we hope that you are inspired to bring HSTEM to your own campus community.
2. Articulate ways that you can make *any* course or institutional structure more inclusive. We strongly believe that conversations about equity in STEM should not occur merely in the one "diversity" course that students complete at their institution, but rather we hope that in reading this book, you can identify ways to make small, sustainable changes in any course or program with which you are involved. The lasting impacts of HSTEM are seen in the students, faculty, and staff who, following participation in the initiative, have refined their skills of active listening, reflective practice, and inclusive partnership and are now applying these skills outside of the course, as engaged citizens in the world.

The HSTEM Process Model

As you read through this book, you will encounter the HSTEM process model. This process consists of four interrelated steps: listening, validating, reflecting, and partnering. We discuss this model in detail in chapter 3. Engaging in a cycle of listening, validating, reflecting, and then partnering is critical for both identifying specific disconnects that are impeding inclusivity within a local STEM community and for collaboratively bridging those disconnects in a way that is effective and inclusive of the needs and ideas of relevant community members. What are some of the disconnects that working through this model can reveal? One such common disconnect is that while we recognize the value of having a diversity of learners and viewpoints in our classrooms, we may not be teaching in ways that actually invite a range of viewpoints and experiences into classroom discussions. Relatedly, while we may hold an awareness that students' backgrounds, educational preparation, and early experiences contribute to their advantages in STEM, we may actually be constructing curricula, grading schemas, and selection criteria for career-advancing opportunities, such as research positions and internships, that operate from a deficit model, penalizing our less well-resourced students. By listening for and naming these and other disconnects, we can engage in a process of reflecting on how we may be contributing to the challenge and then how we may partner with others to bridge the disconnect and create a more inclusive learning environment.

Who Are We?

As we have learned from our work with students, it is important to ground ourselves in our own lived experiences and recognize the backgrounds and lenses that we bring to the table. These positionalities inherently contribute to our subjective experiences and how we see and are seen by the world. Throughout the book, you'll hear us refer to Sarah, Sheila, and Megan. Here is a little context about who we are and how we got involved in this work.

Figure P.1. Sarah Bunnell.

Photo credit. Maria Stenzel, Amherst College Office of Communications.

Sarah is a developmental and cognitive psychologist by training, now working full time in faculty development. Early in her graduate studies, she became involved in partnering with students in course design. As a psychologist whose work has explored meaning-making and psychological well-being in children and adolescents with a range of traumatic life experiences, her pedagogy recognizes the cognitive and affective dimensions of learning, and thriving, in the classroom. As a white woman in STEM, she navigates hierarchical dynamics and cultures that both raise and lower barriers for her. As a mother in academia, she chases a seemingly elusive work–life balance. Since arriving at Amherst College in 2018, she has been deeply involved in codesigning, assessing, and supporting the HSTEM initiative.

Figure P.2. Sheila Jaswal.

Photo credit. Laura Quinlan, Amherst College Office of Communications.

Sheila is a biophysical chemist who teaches in the Chemistry Department and the Biochemistry & Biophysics program. She leads a team of undergraduate researchers in applying experimental and computational approaches to study protein folding at Amherst College. Over her educational and professional career navigating STEM and academia as a queer biracial woman, she has been involved in building community, leading and participating in a variety of mentoring models, and sharing her experiences. After accepting the invitation from students to codesign the founding HSTEM course in 2016, she has stewarded the Amherst course as it has evolved through 10 iterations, involving many cofacilitators and more than 180 students. She continues to cofacilitate the HSTEM course and serves as the informal director of the broader HSTEM initiative, including supporting the national network of more than a dozen institutions now offering their own HSTEM courses.

PREFACE   *xvii*

Figure P.3. Megan Lyster.

Photo credit. Maria Stenzel, Amherst College Office of Communications.

Megan is an experiential educator with a background in supporting students, faculty, and staff in designing and implementing project-based learning experiences across a range of contexts. She has partnered with Sheila (and later, Sarah) on the development of the HSTEM initiative since its inception, and served as a codesigner and coinstructor for seven iterations of the HSTEM course, with a focus on the development and implementation of student-led projects. Her experience as a cofacilitator has been an opportunity to productively grapple with her own identity and positionality as a white woman working within institutions of higher education. Megan now works at Smith College and continues to serve as an advisor to the HSTEM initiative.

Together, we see ourselves as a three-legged stool, bringing distinct contributions to our shared work in HSTEM. Sarah helps us to ground our work in the pedagogical and psychological literatures and ensures that we collect meaningful evidence to explore and learn from the impact of our inclusive practices on student learning, while also helping to make this work public to a range of institutional, national, and international audiences. Sheila is the visioner, both in articulating what a truly inclusive STEM environment can be and how partnerships can be forged to better leverage the power and potential for change in higher education STEM spaces. She also is the individual who consistently ensures we are bringing the work of inclusion back to a focus on students—that student voices are included and that students are partners in our efforts. Finally, Megan's keen understanding of human-centered design and organizational change makes it all possible. She keeps us focused on what is core and what is realistic. Further, given her knowledge of how to help students successfully navigate community-based learning opportunities, she is able to support students in articulating their goals, collaborating with stakeholders, and identifying practical, concrete action steps for successful partnerships.

How the Book Is Structured

Each chapter includes a set of guiding reflective questions, to help you identify connections between these ideas, frameworks, and strategies and your own teaching and institutional context. While we have written each chapter to build on the previous ideas and frameworks, we also recognize that reading this book from front to back may not be possible for you at this moment. Instead, you may be coming to this text because of a specific question or issue you are facing—looking for a just-in-time strategy or framework for informing your approach. We therefore offer a road map for navigating the book.

From Protests to Partnerships (Chapters 1–3)

In chapter 1, we describe the historical context of our own institution and the protest that brought about the HSTEM initiative. We highlight student voices and experiences, many of which are likely shared by students on your own campuses. If your institution is currently in a position of unrest or protest, we encourage you to start with this chapter to help place your experience in context. In chapter 2, we present a detailed description of the HSTEM course that emerged as a response to the Amherst Uprising. The goals of this course include exploring the literature on diversity and inclusion in STEM, reflecting on our own and others' personal narratives of their experiences in STEM, and developing action projects to enhance inclusive efforts at the institution and beyond. We present an overview of the course structure and guidelines for creating your own HSTEM course; more than a dozen institutions in the United States have already adapted our course materials and framework to teach HSTEM courses on their campuses, and we encourage you to do the same. And in chapter 3, we provide recommendations and a framework for building more inclusive partnerships and collaborations, with students within a course, between students and campus partners, and across larger campus and cross-institutional settings. If you are working to bring more individuals into collaboration, you may wish to start there.

Inclusive Practices (Chapters 4–6)

In this section of the book, we present a number of concrete, evidence-based activities that you can embed into your STEM classrooms and laboratory spaces to foster a sense of belonging and community. Throughout all of these activities and practices, we emphasize a strong need for empathy and active listening; see chapter 4 for a discussion of how to incorporate empathy-building activities into your classrooms. Chapter 5 presents a large number of inclusive practices designed for the first day of class and for across the semester in your classroom, as well as strategies for increasing a sense of community and belonging in your labs. In the description of each practice described in chapter 5, we also provide a discussion of *why* you might choose to incorporate this practice into your tool kit, depending upon your pedagogical context and goals, as well as the evidence you may look for that this practice is successful. Finally, we have created facilitator guides for each of these practices, summarized in the appendices and available in the online resources for this book. And, in chapter 6, we discuss the impact of our flagship course assignment, the HSTEM story, in which students, staff, and faculty craft their own story of their experiences in STEM and share these narratives with others. This chapter provides guidelines for constructing your own HSTEM story and shares examples of the kinds of rich narratives and varied experiences that we, as humans in STEM, bring into community with each other. We encourage you to start with this chapter if you are working to increase identity awareness in your teaching.

Making and Measuring Inclusive Change (Chapters 7–9)

The last section of the book considers the broader factors that contribute to and hinder institutional change, articulates how we can look for evidence that change is happening, and features a discussion of the 10 colleges and universities who were early adopters of the HSTEM course to their own institutional setting. In chapter 7, we describe the institutional conditions that allow for inclusive institutional change to occur and what to consider as you seek to enhance inclusivity and impact on your campuses. We also present a range of narratives about the kinds of changes, both personal and collective, that have emerged as a result of the HSTEM initiative. If you are working on organizational questions and facilitating diversity, equity, and inclusion (DEI) leadership, you may wish to start with this chapter. Building on the frameworks presented in chapter 7, chapter 8 then describes the process of applying a scholarly approach to identifying obvious and less obvious measures of impact. How do we know that our inclusive efforts are making a difference, and for whom? We describe a number of assessment approaches that you may employ to look for change, and we also seek to challenge the assumption built into many models of DEI work in STEM that persistence, or retention, should be the primary measure of success for our inclusive efforts. Finally, chapter 9 describes how faculty and staff have modified the HSTEM course structure and activities to align with their own institutional values, structures, and limitations, and also describes a number of the student action projects that have emerged at those institutions as a result of the HSTEM experience. If you are looking to adapt the HSTEM course to your own campus community, you may wish to start here for inspiration.

A Final Note of Welcome

We appreciate your commitment to learning with us and with your students about pathways toward more inclusive STEM classrooms, laboratories, and culture. We're happy to be on this journey with you, fellow human in STEM!

ACKNOWLEDGMENTS

First and foremost, we want to express our most sincere gratitude to the nine HSTEM cofounders—Doyin Ariyibi, Louise Atadja, Ashley Bohan, Ruth Manzanares, Gaby Mayer, Chelsea Nkansah-Siriboe, Emma Ryan, Sanyu Takirambudde, and Olivia Truax. All of this work builds on their efforts, their voices, and their vision for what is possible. They approached the development of HSTEM, coming on the heels of the Amherst Uprising, with a love for their community and a belief and need for it to do better.

We are also grateful to Kristen Greenland, who helped anchor Megan and Sheila as the third HSTEM cofacilitator from 2017–2019. Kristen provided invaluable guidance as the course evolved from an independent study project to a full-credit course. Her partnership enabled us to adapt the course to a new generation of students, while maintaining the original ethos and core HSTEM values of the founders. She has committed to remaining an active thought partner at the network level from the University of California, Berkeley.

Each time the HSTEM course is offered, it expands and improves in unpredictable and fantastic ways. Thank you to each of the cofacilitators at Amherst who have brought their expertise, their curiosity, and their commitment to being in authentic, brave conversations with students and with each other to this course: Stephanie Capsuto, Sony Coráñez-Bolton, Jeffers Engelhardt, Kristen Gardner, Jyl Gentzler, Thea Kristensen, Tanya Leise, Shu-Min Liao, Leah Schmalzbauer, and Josef Trapani.

We also appreciate all of the student HSTEMbassadors, who have taken HSTEM and then taken off with it. Nicole Chung and Ji Chung, your ability to speak about student experiences at Amherst, and to connect them with the larger literature and institutional context, is stunning. We have watched repeatedly as your voices and your contributions allow faculty, staff, and administrators to see a better, more collaborative way forward. To our early HSTEM postbac fellows, Ashley Bohan, Michaela Ednie, and Minjee Kim, your efforts to archive, document, and pull together threads of the early years of HSTEM are deeply appreciated. Thanks also to Kevin Zhangxu for originating the peer cofacilitator role, and Aidan Park for further developing the leadership aspect of that role alongside Nicole and Ji, which was crucial to the success of the inaugural virtual January term HSTEM course. A core mission of this work is to keep the voices and experiences of students active in our minds, to ensure that our efforts honor and attempt to do justice to the students who have come before and asked more of us. Thank you.

We'd like to extend a special thank you to Jeanne Weintraub, whose often behind-the-scenes work of supporting the HSTEM initiative infrastructure, including securing funding from the National Science Foundation, made many things possible that seemed impossible. Hosting a conference of all of the institutional leads for HSTEM across the country, in the middle of a pandemic, happened because of your indefatigable efforts. Thank you.

To Riley Caldwell-O'Keefe, who is a constant champion of HSTEM and a stalwart friend, advocate, and thought partner to each of us, for bolstering us, supporting us, and for all of the moves that you have made behind the scenes to smooth a way forward for this work—thank you.

Thanks also to Sarah Buhl and Jess Martin, who continue to commit Science Center funds and labor to support the HSTEM student magazines, swag, and salons; integrate the HSTEM values of equity, inclusion, and community into all of the programming that they do; and participate as thought partners in our mission to diffuse HSTEM beyond the boundaries of STEM and Amherst.

We are lucky to work with an incredible array of departmental partners at Amherst College, all of whom hold deep professional expertise and institutional insight. To the Amherst College Department of Chemistry: In addition to the important structural support for HSTEM that you have provided, thank you for committing to being in partnership with our students, especially Ji and Nicole, as they have led us in conversations about who we want to be as a community of teachers and learners. To the Amherst College Library and the Center for Community Engagement: Thank you for providing structural support, expertise, and partnership as the HSTEM course has evolved and expanded through the years. Thank you, also, to the other departmental partners who have supported HSTEM events, workshops, salons, and institutes over the years—the Center for Humanistic Inquiry, the Office of the Provost and Dean of Faculty, and the Office of Diversity and Inclusion.

To the students: For showing up as your full, brave, human selves and allowing us to do the same, in partnership with you, thank you.

To the member institutions of the growing HSTEM network: For your partnership, your perspectives, and your energies to expand HSTEM and give it new life on your campuses, thank you.

And finally, to our families: Through the late nights, the early mornings, the rushed meals, you help us see the light when things feel dark. You remind us that we are loved and we are enough. You make it all worth it.

I

THE AMHERST UPRISING

In this chapter, we first reflect on the intentional diversification efforts made by undergraduate colleges in the United States over the past 50 years. What is clear from our vantage point is that while many of these initiatives have focused on diversifying the enrolled student body, less attention has been paid to proactively creating inclusive systems and practices to support students once they arrive at our institutions. We then present the "Amherst Uprising" in 2015 as a case study to illustrate how the disconnect between efforts focused on diversity, relative to those efforts focused on inclusion and equity, can lead to moments of intense challenge at our higher education institutions. During this 4-day sit-in at Amherst College, minoritized students expressed their frustrations with the current college climate and shared personal experiences of exclusion and discrimination while at the college. During this protest, students asked for validation, solidarity, and immediate responses from faculty, staff, and administrators; in response, many departments and offices wrote letters of support. In the final section of this chapter, we share a thematic analysis of these departmental and administrative letters, in order to explore commonalities in institutional responses to protest, as well as disciplinary differences in both the interpretation of protest as an appropriate mechanism for institutional change and the locus of responsibility for change.

In each chapter of this book, we provide a set of reflective questions for you to consider as you engage with that section of the text. Here is the first set of guiding questions:

Guiding Questions

- As you reflect on your institution's diversity, equity, and inclusion (DEI) mission, where do you see opportunities for better alignment between efforts of diversification and efforts of inclusion?

- While you may not have experienced or participated in student protests firsthand, there are likely parallels between the tensions illustrated by the Amherst Uprising and points of challenge in your own institutional context. What lessons can be learned from this case study to apply to your own educational setting?
- In what ways do your disciplinary assumptions about how arguments are engaged, and what evidence "counts," influence your reactions to student protests or bottom-up demands for change?

The Changing Demographics of Undergraduate Colleges and Universities: A Push for Diversification

An examination of national patterns of demographic changes in the United States over the last 4 decades reveals dramatic shifts in the relative representation of white, Asian American, Hispanic, and Latino persons in the population (Frey, 2020). In 1980, close to 80% of the U.S. population was white, non-Latino and non-Hispanic. Around 11.5% of the population identified as Black, with Latino or Hispanic individuals representing 6.5% of the population and Asian Americans representing 1.8%. Forty years later, these figures have shifted in important ways—the white population declined 20%, the Latino and Hispanic population increased 12%, and Asian Americans now represent nearly 6% of the U.S. population. Interestingly, the percentage of Black and Indigenous individuals in the United States has remained fairly constant across this time period.

Echoing the national data, demographics have shifted in parallel ways at our undergraduate institutions. In 2010, close to 40% of students enrolled in undergraduate colleges and universities were Asian, Black, Hispanic, or Indigenous individuals, whereas this number was only 17% in 1980 (Tienda, 2013). During this same period, the U.S. population also grew over 50%, resulting in many more nonwhite students seeking undergraduate degrees at our institutions. Coupled with population demographic shifts, many colleges and universities have engaged in intentional recruitment strategies and changes to their institutional practices in order to recruit a more diverse student body. A recent U.S. Department of Education report, titled *Advancing Diversity and Inclusion in Higher Education* outlines many of these approaches (Office of Planning, Evaluation, and Policy Development, 2016). One example this report describes is that of the University of Colorado-Boulder; drawing on a national data set from the Education Longitudinal Study conducted in 2002, the institution created a model for admissions that includes a "disadvantage index" and an "overachievement index." These indices allow their admissions officers to factor in the socioeconomic disadvantages that students, many of whom belong to minority demographic groups, may have faced and how they have succeeded in their academic pursuits in spite of these setbacks.

In terms of socioeconomic challenges and impact on college admissions, the cost of attaining an undergraduate degree has also increased dramatically during this time. From 1985 to 2018, the average combined cost of tuition, fees, room, and board, per student, rose by 117%, after adjusting for inflation. In addition to these rising costs impacting all students, minoritized students, on average, have fewer family resources to contribute to paying college tuition and incur more debt than their white peers (Office of Planning, Evaluation, and Policy Development, 2016). Per a 2016 Brookings report on Black–white disparity in student loan debt, Black bachelor degree graduates carry an average of $52,726 in debt, 4 years after college graduation, compared to $28,006 for white bachelor degree graduates across the same time period (Scott-Clayton & Li, 2016). In the face of these financial limitations to diversifying the student body, a handful of institutions across the country, including our home institution of Amherst College, has adopted an admissions policy that admits U.S.-based and international students on a need-blind basis and provides scholarships to every student based on their level of financial need, with the intention that no student graduates with tuition-based debt. Since the enactment of this admissions approach, the percentage of domestic nonwhite students enrolled at Amherst College has risen. In 2003, the percentage was 34%; in contrast, the admitted class of fall 2021 was 50.2% domestic nonwhite (Jaschik, 2021).

As we discuss in the next section, however, diversity ensures representation, but it is not the same thing as inclusion (Barkas et al., 2020; Tienda, 2013). Inclusive higher education asks us to create spaces, once students enroll at our institutions, in which they feel respected and supported in their pursuit of their academic and cocurricular goals. Bryan Dewsbury (2020) describes an inclusive classroom as "one where all voices, regardless of background have equal opportunity to contribute to and shape the community dialogue" (p. 173). Many of our institutions have a long way to go from diversification to inclusion. We present our own institution, and the Amherst Uprising (see Figure 1.1), as a case study illustrating this challenge.

The Amherst Uprising as a Case Study

In the late hours of Wednesday, November 11th, 2015, Amherst College sophomores Sanyu Takarimbudde, Katyana Dandridge, and Lerato Teffaro had gathered to complete their homework assignments for the day. Instead,

Figure 1.1. The Amherst Uprising.

Note. Students holding signs at the student sit-in that grew to become the 4-day Amherst Uprising protest.

Photo credit: Kaelan McCone. Permanently stored in the Amherst College Archives & Special Collections.

they found themselves discussing images of student protests from across the world that were ubiquitous on their Facebook feeds. Campuses around the United States had been experiencing unrest following a string of high-profile killings of Black men by police (see a timeline of these events in Figure 1.2); these events had brought to public awareness the fatal toll racial injustice takes on the Black community.

A national Black Lives Matter movement calling for accountability was growing, and students across the country were joining these efforts. Two U.S. campuses in particular were simmering during the first 2 weeks of November. After several "Racism Lives Here" rallies and a student hunger strike at the

Figure 1.2. Timeline of police violence.

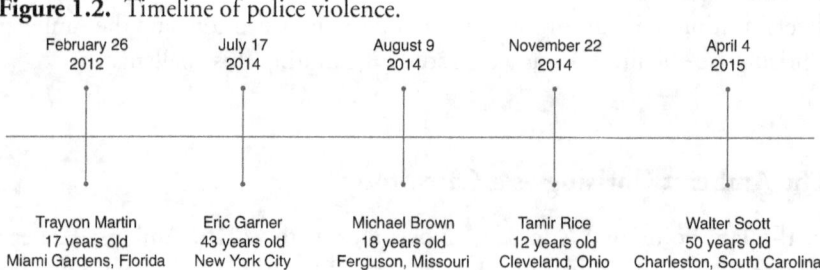

University of Missouri-Columbia, the president of the university stepped down in response to calls for his resignation. Soon, student protesters were also marching at Yale University, following a series of administrative communications related to cultural sensitivity when choosing Halloween costumes (Friedersdorf, 2016). University administrators sent a letter recommending that students not wear Halloween costumes that could be offensive or harmful, such as donning blackface or Indigenous headpieces, prompting a lecturer at Yale to write an open letter challenging the university's stance (Christakis, 2015); students on campus protested in response. In reflecting on these incidents, the friends talked about how inspiring the student action was to them, and Lerato and Sanyu, who both hail from South Africa, also discussed the parallel actions of students in South Africa protesting massive tuition hikes.

At that moment, how could these students simply focus on conjugating French verbs and pushing electrons around in Organic Chemistry when their peers were leading important fights around the globe? In a moment of inspiration, they set up a Facebook event for the following day calling for students to join a 1-hour sit-in in the college library, stayed up late into the night making signs in the art building, and sent personal invitations to the college president and dean of the faculty. They also asked that the invitation be shared with faculty and that faculty be encouraged to attend the sit-in the following afternoon.

Word quickly spread among students through social media and hundreds of students streamed into the Amherst College Frost Library. After Lerato, Ketyana, and Sanyu opened the sit-in with a call for solidarity with other campuses (Figure 1.3), it evolved to a spontaneous moment of truth-telling by Amherst students. One after another, they began sharing their experiences of racism and marginalization at the institution. As one person after another rose to speak, their statements full of pain and raw vulnerability, those in the library were compelled to remain and bear witness, listening in silence.

The dean of the faculty stood listening to students as they shared their stories into the early evening hours. At times, over a thousand students, staff, and faculty were crowded into the space. The president of the college had been about to board a plane bound for Japan when the sit-in began; she canceled her trip and arrived at the library around midnight, as the sit-in was still ongoing. Senior leadership, through their willingness to listen and validate the experiences of each student, sent a clear message of how the college would respond; they were taking the moment, and the students, seriously.

Figure 1.3. Sit-in leaders.

Note. Lerato Teffaro, Katyana Dandridge, and Sanyu Takirambudde (left to right).

Photo credit. Kaelan McCone. Permanently stored in the Amherst College Archives & Special Collections.

Cullen Murphy, Amherst college class of 1974 and chairman of the Board of Trustees from 2012 to 2018, described the Amherst Uprising in an article for the Amherst alumni magazine:

> Students talked about their lives at Amherst but also their lives before and outside of Amherst. They said out loud what they had perhaps never said before, or had said individually to one another or to trusted advisers but not in such a large setting. They talked about the relatively small number of faces like theirs among the ranks of faculty and staff. About feeling excluded at social events. About distinctions of class that are all too visible when seen from one side but may be given little thought by those on the other. About casual remarks and behaviors that cause anger and pain, and whose residue inexorably accumulates. About the widespread ignorance of the path that many students of color travel as they make their way to Amherst. About legacies of personal history that other students can scarcely imagine and could never infer. About the exhaustion sometimes involved in juggling college life and family needs at home. About the utter disorientation that may occur when arriving at an idyllic spot with alien folkways that others take for granted. About having few people to talk with about any of this, and classmates who may be unaware that these issues loom as large as they do. (Murphy, 2016, para. 8)

The sit-in continued for 4 days. During this same time, Sheila collected direct, anonymized information from STEM students, asking them what they wished their STEM professors knew about their experiences at Amherst. In part, the prompt read,

> We are collecting feedback from STEM students who would like to share anything about their experiences in STEM classes that would help STEM faculty understand how our classes, office hours, labs and approach to curriculum and students are contributing to the feelings of severe alienation and marginalization that have been voiced by so many students over the past 4 days. Anything you feel is important for us to know is welcome.

Almost 30 students responded to this request. Many students shared frustrations about curricula that did not directly address the benefits of diversity in science or the history of harms inflicted on underrepresented groups by scientists. Others wrote about instances in which they felt that they experienced differential treatment by an instructor or peer because of their group membership or identities. For instance, one student wrote, "I've had a specific professor who has allowed women to ask questions, sort of answer/ignore them, only to be asked something very similar by a man in the class and praise him for his good question." Another student wrote, "As one of the few Black women in STEM classes and on campus, I often feel that some people think I am not smart enough to handle the workload."

> Students' letters were consistently pointing to a painful disconnect:
> They had been invited into the institution to contribute their diverse strengths and experiences to the learning environment, but there were many ways in which they were not yet being included or able to thrive in these diverse spaces.

Another prevailing theme that emerged from students' responses was a sense that STEM curricula assume such a high level of entering background disciplinary knowledge that those students who did not have the option to complete advanced scientific coursework in high school were at a disadvantage right from the start of their higher education journey. Given that student income levels correspond closely with available high school resources such as advanced placement courses, laboratory equipment, research opportunities, and field trips (e.g., Nathan, 2017), students from greater economic means are likely to enter into their first-year collegiate STEM classrooms with more expansive scientific preparation. One student's statement remarked, "Professors of intro[ductory] classes here will from the very beginning assume that everyone in the class has taken that science before. This automatically alienates students from low-income backgrounds from the very first lecture, already putting them at a disadvantage." Another student asked of STEM faculty: "Please don't assume we know how to set up experiments in the same way more privileged students do. Include detailed pictures of every piece of equipment we're using. If students already know how to use something, great! But don't assume we do."

Conversely, a student who self-identified as being from a high socioeconomic status family wrote, "Never once have I hesitated on study methods for a chem[istry] or bio[logy] exam; never once have I thought twice about attending office hours. I've been doing this kind of work since I was 13 or 14. It comes naturally to me. The same cannot be said for my peers—most of color, but some not—who have come to Amherst with far less academic and social preparation than I."

This student noted that "these students do not always advocate for themselves with faculty . . . because they do not know that they have the ability to do so" and that when students from less well-resourced backgrounds struggle on exams, it is "not because they do not study, but because they have not been taught to study effectively."

As Anthony Jack (2019), Amherst College class of 2007, notes in his book *The Privileged Poor: How Elite Colleges Are Failing Disadvantaged Students*, students from lower socioeconomic backgrounds often do not have the cultural capital to understand the unwritten rules and norms of academia, such as how to maximize one's use of office hours, communicate requests for extensions, and seek out additional support services at their institutions. One statement from a student letter mirrored this point: "Different students have different backgrounds in terms of student–teacher relationships and some students lack the ability or knowledge to directly interact with professors. For example, in my previous schooling, meetings with professors were only encouraged when you were really struggling with a class." This same student described their hesitancy in requesting one-on-one time with their professors because the student was aware that there were "other students who needed to meet with teachers more than [I] did."

On a related note, many students bemoaned the lack of diversity in the STEM faculty. Students spoke about the importance of increasing visual representation in the faculty; learning from scholars who hold similar identities as their own would provide a powerful message to underrepresented students that they too could be successful in the academy. Students also discussed the importance of faculty members' awareness of pedagogical approaches aimed at teaching and supporting diverse students. For instance, one student shared their desire for more faculty of color in the STEM majors who can "teach to a group in a particular way that they can understand the material . . . and understand that not all of us came from privileged backgrounds." The needs articulated by students correspond with the larger literature on the benefits of diversification of students, faculty, and staff (Cook, 1991; Goethe & Colina, 2018; Hurtado, 2007; Hurtado & DeAngelo, 2012; Packard, 2013). As Cook (1991) writes, "A diverse student body is only part of the equation. A diverse faculty and staff provide role models for minority and majority students, enriches the curriculum, and better reflects the reality which most students will face when they graduate" (p. 4).

Finally, student reflections indicated a sense that not only did these inequities manifest in classroom spaces, they also influenced opportunities for career development and advancement in the sciences. One student described how high school science preparation again hinders lower-resourced students in their pathways toward STEM careers, saying, "[Undergraduate] lab[oratory] research positions go to the students who have the best grasp of the lab techniques or chemical/biological/physics concepts, and rarely consider the fact that some students are encountering these things for the first time." Undergraduate research experiences, and increasingly, undergraduate coauthorship on research manuscripts, play an outsized role in the likelihood of acceptance into graduate training programs and medical school; as such, students not selected for undergraduate research and mentoring opportunities, because of their lack of preparation and background knowledge in the discipline, are then doubly disadvantaged when they apply for graduate study or other career opportunities in the sciences.

Exploring Responses to Student Protest

Many college departments, student service offices, and student groups wrote public letters of support in the days following the protest; some of these letters emerged independently while others were written in response to a plea for statements of support by students. We have gathered as many of these letters as were available, which included letters of support from senior administration, almost half of all of the academic departments on campus, and 10 student-focused offices and resource groups. What we present in the following is a description of the ways in which these institutional and departmental constituencies framed their responses. We don't seek to present a generalizable claim as to how institutional leadership groups respond to student protest broadly, but rather our goal is to share the patterns that emerged in our context and reflect on how these response patterns may help us to better understand the institutional dynamics around inclusive efforts at our institution since the Amherst Uprising occurred.

To this aim, we applied an emergent thematic coding approach to the content of these letters. In this analysis, we noted commonalities across statements of support in the types of sentiments that were shared:

- *Protest support.* These statements articulated support for the students' protest and related actions.
- *Emotional validation.* Distinct from expressing support for the protests themselves, these statements acknowledged students' emotional experiences and/or the vulnerability that engaging in the Amherst Uprising required of students.
- *Connection to educational mission.* These statements were reflections on how the protests served as a reminder or recommitment to a departmental or institutional mission.
- *Taking of responsibility.* These statements, though rare, articulated having failed students in the past and an acceptance of responsibility for the actions that caused harm.

Three distinct themes for discussing change were also present in these letters:

- *A call for action.* These statements called on institutional leadership to act in support of student needs.
- *A commitment to change.* Statements of this nature expressed a general support for change to happen on campus.
- *A specification of action steps.* Statements of this kind described particular steps individuals or departments were committing to take in the future to increase student support.

Most commonly, letters expressed support for the protest. For example, one letter stated, "Today we stand in solidarity with Amherst College's students, staff, and faculty of color and all students of color at colleges and universities across the nation that have felt threatened on campus. We are humbled by the strength and courage of those individuals who have spoken, and continue to speak." There was also a general commitment to change. One departmental letter said, "As a department, we will renew our efforts to provide an environment that welcomes and enables the success of all students." Further, many campus entities reflected how the student protest had reaffirmed their disciplinary or institutional mission. One such response stated, "We heard those demands as a department and we are reminded of how central they are to our mission. Your words remind us of our purpose here as teachers, fellow campus citizens, as a department, and comrades in the struggle for racial justice here at the College and in the wider world from which we all come." Another department, in which only a small number of minoritized students declare a major each year, reflected on how their field "is a field in which students of color are underrepresented, both here and nationally. This is a great loss, because our field needs all the talent that it can find." In this response, the department is recognizing their commitment to increased diversity in the field and making the connection between on-campus student experiences and how they align with the failure of their discipline to support diverse scholars.

A smaller number of letters attempted to explicitly validate the emotions of student protesters. One such letter wrote, "The depth and intensity of [students'] pain and exhaustion are evident. That pain is real. Their expressions of loneliness and sense of invisibility are heartrending. No attempt to minimize or trivialize those feelings will be convincing to those of us who have listened." Others expressed a call for institutionally led action, with responses such as "We recognize that the administration must aid our efforts to improve in ways that will allow us to best support you. Support mechanisms for students, faculty, and staff need to be improved if we are all to accomplish the difficult task of removing racism and discrimination from our campus, community, and beyond." These calls for institutional change were more commonly expressed by untenured faculty groups and student affinity groups; indeed, individuals holding vulnerable positions on campus may be positioned to more readily recognize the need for institutional change.

Finally, a small subset of letters of solidarity articulated specific actions to address the issues raised by the student protesters. One such letter said, "For our part, the recent events have already caused us to bring a more critical eye to the materials and methods with which we teach, to acknowledge and incorporate a greater multiplicity of experiences, perspectives, histories, and practices." Least commonly, letters acknowledged past failures and responsibility. One departmental letter that took responsibility for past harm said, "We are passionately committed to creating a safe and nurturing environment for every one of our students. We also understand that we have failed in this commitment in the past, and we promise to listen and respond to the concerns of every one of our students."

Interestingly, these responses to student concerns map onto the aspects of the HSTEM process model that we describe in detail in the next chapter. Specifically, responses of emotional validation indicate the powerful initial response of actively *listening* to students. Secondly, expressions of support for students' efforts demonstrate that departments were working to *validate* students' concerns and the reality of their emotional experiences. Third, themes of calling for institutional change and acknowledging personal responsibility for past failures to act indicate departmental attempts at *reflection*, and finally, expressing general and specific commitments to change, in response to and in partnership with students, initiates the process of active *partnership* in addressing ways departments could do better.

How Did Disciplinarity Relate to the Nature of Departmental Response?

In examining letters from academic departments in response to the student protests, we were interested in exploring whether particular themes, as described previously, were more likely to be present in letters from STEM departments than from non-STEM departments. Did disciplinary lenses or perspectives correspond to how faculty and staff expressed support for students during moments of protest? To pursue this question, we tallied the number of sentences that aligned with each of the seven themes and calculated proportional variables based on the number of sentences each letter contained. For instance, in a letter from one of the humanities (i.e., non-STEM) departments, seven sentences out of the total of 15 sentences were coded as expressing support for the student protest, resulting in a proportional value for the category of protest support of 47%. This letter included statements such as "[W]e want to recognize, applaud, and express the deepest respect for the courage it took to say all of that" and "Your demands to be seen and heard are righteous."

When we examine differences in each of these thematic proportional variables between STEM and non-STEM department letters, we find that while the two do not differ in terms of sentence number ($t(15) = .098$, $p = .923$), letters from STEM departments were significantly *less likely* to explicitly articulate support for students' protest actions than were letters from non-STEM departments ($t(14.63) = 2.17, p = .047$). From the student perspective, this difference in departmental letters' expressions of support for the protest was consistent with many students' feelings that STEM faculty did not stand in solidarity with their actions. To this point, one student wrote in their comments to STEM faculty, "After taking science classes for three semesters at Amherst, I did not see any of my nine past and present professors at the library. This is extremely troubling and makes me wonder if they care about my livelihood and makes it very difficult for me to go back to my normal life and continue doing my work. It also makes me wonder if my involvement in a movement like this makes myself a target to professors who don't care about racial issues on campus or who take a stance against what Amherst Uprising stands for."

However, we think that a separate dynamic is at play, such that this difference likely points to a disconnect between *how* faculty across disciplines conceive of protest as an appropriate or effective mechanism for change, rather than *whether* they support students. STEM departmental letters demonstrated a tremendous level of support for their students, although the form that this expression took differed in important ways from non-STEM departmental letters. The STEM departmental letters commonly and explicitly focused on particular action steps that their own departments would take to improve their support of students.

How might we understand this differential response to students' use of protest as a mechanism for demanding change? Work by Hoffman et al. (2016) argues that individuals who have benefited from existing structures and hierarchies may feel uncomfortable with the notion of protest as an appropriate avenue for systemic change. They write, "Many people who have privilege are critical of the protest movements for causing disruption and engaging in civil disobedience. A frequent assertion is that it would be better to utilize the usual channels to advocate for change" (p. 601). To those of us for whom the "usual channels" have worked smoothly, protest may seem impolite or aggressive. This discomfort with protest may be further escalated for many of us trained as scientists, a domain in which the employment of emotional and inherently subjective narratives as pieces of evidence, as in the case of protests, can seem disciplinarily inconsistent with the scientific, objective worldview (e.g., Longino, 1990). Therefore, it is our belief that the letters written by STEM departments in response to the Amherst Uprising reflect not a difference in levels of support for students, but rather differences in how faculty and staff conceptualized the process by which these changes should occur.

What lessons are we taking from this analysis? First, our case study of the Amherst Uprising provides a powerful demonstration of the importance of responding to moments of student protest and uprising with a stance of openness that includes intentional listening and emotional validation. How can we work to ensure that students feel listened to during these moments of intense emotion and vulnerability? How can we hold back our own urges toward defensiveness and justification so that we can truly hear what is needed and felt in that moment? Second, we see that our disciplinary perspectives may influence how we interpret and respond to protest as a form of discourse or argument; how can we attend to our biases in how change "should" occur? And finally, we want to caution each of us against the immediate urge to fix the problem. Students are saying that they are in pain, and that they are feeling like they are not being included in our learning spaces and communities. At these moments, can we slow down our desire to urgently respond with action and instead, as we describe in the next chapters, invite students to partner with us to intentionally cocreate change?

References

Barkas, L. A., Armstrong, P.-A., & Bishop, G. (2020, June 15). Is inclusion still an illusion in higher education? Exploring the curriculum through the student voice. *International Journal of Inclusive Education*. Advance online publication. https://doi.org/10.1080/13603116.2020.1776777

Christakis, E. (2015, October 30). Email from Erika Christakis: "Dressing yourselves," email to Silliman College (Yale) students on Halloween costumes. *Fire: Foundation for Individual Rights in Education*. https://www.thefire.org/email-from-erika-christakis-dressing-yourselves-email-to-silliman-college-yale-students-on-halloween-costumes/

Cook, J. (1991, April 11–14). *Recruiting is only the beginning: Strategies for retaining diverse students on the small, liberal arts college* [Paper presentation]. Annual Convention of the Central States Communication Association, Chicago, IL, United States.

Dewsbury, B. M. (2020). Deep teaching in a college STEM classroom. *Cultural Studies of Science Education, 15*(1), 169–191. https://doi.org/10.1007/s11422-018-9891-z

Frey, W. H. (2020, July 1). *The nation is diversifying even faster than predicted, according to new census data.* Brookings. https://www.brookings.edu/research/new-census-data-shows-the-nation-is-diversifying-even-faster-than-predicted/

Friedersdorf, C. (2016, May 26). The perils of writing a provocative email at Yale. *The Atlantic*. https://www.theatlantic.com/politics/archive/2016/05/the-peril-of-writing-a-provocative-email-at-yale/484418/

Goethe, E. V., & Colina, C. M. (2018). Taking advantage of diversity within the classroom. *Journal of Chemical Education, 95*(2), 189–192. https://doi.org/10.1021/acs.jchemed.7b00510

Hoffman, L., Granger, N., Vallejos, L., & Moats, M. (2016). An existential–humanistic perspective on Black Lives Matter and contemporary protest movements. *Journal of Humanistic Psychology, 56*(6), 595–611. https://doi.org/10.1177/0022167816652273

Hurtado, S. (2007). Linking diversity with the educational and civic missions of higher education. *The Review of Higher Education, 30*(2), 185–196. https://doi.org/10.1353/rhe.2006.0070

Hurtado, S., & DeAngelo, L. (2012). Linking diversity and civic-minded practices with student outcomes. *Liberal Education, 98*(2), 14–23. https://www.heri.ucla.edu/PDFs/Linking-Diversity-and-Civic-Minded-Practices-with-Student-Outcomes.pdf

Jack, A. A. (2019). *The privileged poor: How elite colleges are failing disadvantaged students*. Harvard University Press.

Jaschik, S. (2021, June 7). Amherst College attracts diverse students. *Inside Higher Ed*. https://www.insidehighered.com/admissions/article/2021/06/07/amherst-college-attracts-diverse-students

Longino, H. E. (1990). *Science as social knowledge: Values and objectivity in scientific inquiry*. Princeton University Press.

Murphy, C. (2016, August 1). *Home: Some thoughts on the Frost Library protest*. Amherst College. https://www.amherst.edu/amherst-story/magazine/issues/2016-summer/home

Nathan, L. (2017). *When grit isn't enough: A high school principal examines how poverty and inequality thwart the college-for-all promise*. Beacon Press.

Office of Planning, Evaluation, and Policy Development. (2016). *Advancing diversity and inclusion in higher education: Key data highlights focusing on race and ethnicity and promising practices*. U.S. Department of Education. https://www2.ed.gov/rschstat/research/pubs/advancing-diversity-inclusion.pdf

Packard, J. (2013). The impact of racial diversity in the classroom: Activating the sociological imagination. *Teaching Sociology*, *41*(2), 144–158. https://doi.org/10.1177/0092055X12451716

Scott-Clayton, J., & Li, J. (2016, October 20). *Black-white disparity in student loan debt more than triples after graduation*. Brookings. https://www.brookings.edu/research/black-white-disparity-in-student-loan-debt-more-than-triples-after-graduation/

Tienda, M. (2013). Diversity ≠ inclusion: Promoting integration in higher education. *Educational Researcher*, *42*(9), 467–475. https://doi.org/10.3102/0013189X13516164

2

THE HSTEM COURSE

I wanted to be sure that Amherst was left better than I found it. That things were not going to carry on business as usual but that the momentum we gained during Amherst Uprising could be put and funneled in some way. (L.A., HSTEM student)

In this chapter, we describe the HSTEM course, developed through student, faculty, and staff partnership in response to the Amherst Uprising. As an overarching framework for the HSTEM course, there are four core components that we believe are crucial to its ability to enact change: (a) building community; (b) engaging in iterative reflection upon our own and others' personal experiences in STEM while, at the same time, grounding oneself in relevant scholarship; (c) developing and presenting action plans for change informed by synthesis of the literature with lived experiences; and (d) joining larger conversations around equity and inclusion in STEM beyond one's local campus context.

Guiding Questions

- Where are the opportunities in your own institutional setting to incorporate aspects of the HSTEM course structure?
- How can you incorporate students' lived experiences, and the lived experiences of others, into your classroom context? How might the climate of STEM teaching and learning at your institution shift as a result?

Building a Robust HSTEM Course Model

In spring 2016, the semester following the Amherst Uprising, Sheila, Megan, and nine students (including one of the three organizers of the Uprising) partnered to delve more deeply into the lived experience of students, faculty, and staff in STEM at Amherst College. To contextualize their findings, the group also wanted to engage with secondary research on diversity in STEM and best practices for STEM inclusion in higher education. Most of all, given the momentum of the Uprising and the public pledges of STEM departments to invest in the student experience, participants wanted their research to provide a strong foundation to inform proposals for enacting changes to move the campus toward more inclusion and equity. The students proposed a special topics course (i.e., a seminar primarily designed by students, with faculty mentorship) as the locus of their work, which had several benefits over a more informal structure. Operating under a course format provided needed structure, routine, and recognition, in the form of course credits, for their work; the independent study nature of the course allowed the group to be flexible and dynamic in the nature of the work they pursued together across the semester.

As liberal arts students, making a plan of action for doing the research portion of their plan was relatively straightforward. They gathered narratives from students, alumni, faculty, and staff at the college to better understand their experiences over their STEM journeys. They read and compiled an annotated bibliography of peer-reviewed articles, opinion pieces, and news reports about STEM and its intersection with diversity and identity, to place these personal narratives in a broader context. They delved into college archives to uncover a timeline of previous efforts at the college to bring attention and resources to the needs of marginalized students in STEM. They reached out to departments at peer institutions to find out about inclusive STEM practices that Amherst could learn from.

What was more of a struggle for students to conceptualize was something that has continued to be a threshold concept (Meyer & Land, 2005) for students in subsequent offerings: how to synthesize these many strands of information into concrete action projects for change. While the students had a lot of enthusiasm and ideas for projects that could make a difference on campus, they faced challenges connecting them to the research and harnessing those ideas into discrete actions that could be reasonably accomplished by the group in the time available. The project topics that felt most urgent to this first group of HSTEM students included

- making the experiences of marginalized students in STEM classrooms more visible to faculty members
- sharing effective practices for inclusive pedagogy and connecting those practices to the lived experiences of students
- creating publicly accessible pathways to encourage others at Amherst and beyond to grapple with these difficult topics and be empowered to take action within their own sphere of influence

At the end of the semester, the students launched a website to share their findings (www.beinghumaninstem.com) with others at Amherst and encourage other institutions to engage in the process of critically considering the lived experiences of their diverse community members. The students also hosted an interactive salon for the Amherst College community designed to share their findings and encourage dialogue among attendees. Over 70 students, faculty, and staff from across campus participated and left with resources and recommendations for next steps to maintain the momentum generated by the course.

That first course in spring 2016 revealed the importance of maintaining a consistent, structured framework to continue building on the work of the founding cohort, so Sheila made the commitment to offer an HSTEM course at least once each academic year. Each iteration of the Amherst College HSTEM course is structured around the same core elements that were established by the HSTEM founders in the spring of 2016—reflection on the lived experiences of oneself and others in STEM, engagement with the literature on STEM equity and inclusion, and the development of action projects that integrate these aspects of learning into a proposal for change that is publicly shared as HSTEM students contribute to driving the campus conversation on inclusion and equity. As shown in Figure 2.1, two additional components have revealed themselves as critical to supporting the transformational potential of the course for individuals and their impact on our STEM community: starting the course with building internal community

Figure 2.1. The HSTEM course model.

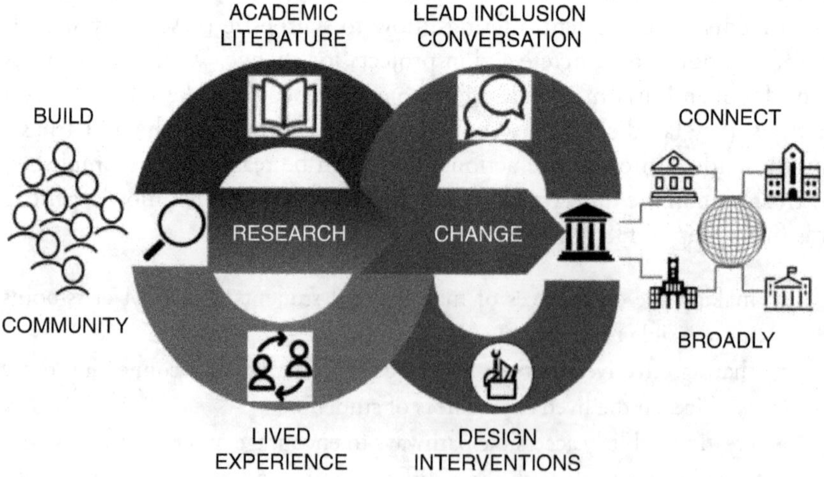

and ending the course with connecting to the broader community, outside of our campus context. This basic structure allows the HSTEM facilitators to maintain a consistent and recognizable format across course sections, while leaving room for the emergence of new ideas and the integration of new perspectives and directions that students and cofacilitators bring into the shared learning space.

As represented in Figure 2.1, engagement with the literature and the exploration of lived experience in STEM happen almost simultaneously over the first half of the course, following intensive community building. In the second half of the semester, the course pivots toward designing student-led interventions to share with the campus community. There is not a perfectly clean delineation between these components, however, as the process of collective inquiry is fairly cyclical. Connecting with the larger STEM community ("Connect Broadly" in Figure 2.1) is more flexible and often takes place through a summit with participants from other HSTEM courses at the end of the semester, or through students sharing their HSTEM-related work at scholarly conferences and with other institutions.

Creating a Brave and Inclusive HSTEM Community

While the HSTEM founders came into the course already bonded through the experience of having participated in the campus-wide Uprising, it quickly became clear that subsequent HSTEM classes needed to experience intentional community building in the beginning of the course. The cultivation of trust and care within each cohort of students, staff, and faculty is crucial to the group's ability to engage in deep and authentic questioning together. It is critical, then, that facilitators carefully and intentionally incorporate community-building activities to establish psychological safety (Edmondson & Lei, 2014) through the collaborative construction of a "brave space" (Arao & Clemens, 2013). Such a brave space, Arao and Clemens (2013) state, is one in which a number of community ground rules are upheld:

1. There is "controversy with civility," where varying opinions are accepted.
2. Individuals demonstrate an "owning [of] intentions and impacts," in which participants acknowledge and discuss instances where a dialogue has affected the emotional well-being of another person.
3. Individuals can "challenge by choice," such that participants have an option to step in and out of challenging conversations as they choose.

4. Dynamics are guided by the principle of "respect," where individuals show respect for one another's basic personhood.
5. The group agrees to a value of "no attacks," where participants agree not to intentionally inflict harm on one another. (pp. 143–149)

In the HSTEM classroom, we integrate a number of practices that are intended to help cultivate a brave space for our work together. At the beginning of each course, as discussed in chapter 5, we dedicate time to developing community agreements that are grounded in the values and intentions that each member of the cohort brings to the course. The agreements serve to establish shared expectations within the group about how important issues such as confidentiality and moments of conflict will be managed. Other early activities emphasize active listening, followed by reflection on how active listening skills might support discussion about difficult topics we may encounter. In chapter 4, we discuss these practices and provide guidelines for how and why these activities can help to support the early building of inclusive communities in our classrooms. Further, all cohort members spend time throughout the course reflecting on, documenting, sharing, and revising their own stories of being a human in STEM (see chapter 6 for an in-depth discussion of this practice). And, as we discuss in chapter 3, a critical component in the efficacy of these activities and building community throughout the course is that faculty and staff facilitators model curiosity, humility, and vulnerability as partners in learning alongside the students as fellow human beings, rather than as experts. The shared vulnerability of discussing the course material with colearners who are all experiencing a growing awareness of the interplay between identity, lived experience, and barriers and privileges in their own trajectory supports the fostering of community.

Early intensive connecting efforts in the first few class sessions are then reinforced by the cultivation of rituals throughout the course. Educators of younger learners have been thinking and writing for a long time about the importance of ritual in establishing a sense of community and shared identity in the classroom (e.g., Howell & Reinhard, 2015). We draw on this insight by inviting students to add music choices to a shared class playlist, asking each student to take turns leading the group in a welcome or warm-up activity at the start of each class, and establishing set times before or after class meetings as focused time for informal conversation. As you reflect on your own communities, what consistent practices have allowed you to feel welcomed into the space? Could you incorporate those rituals into your teaching as well?

Engaging With the Scholarship on Inclusion and Diversity in STEM

The shared engagement with empirical articles and other sources focused on the DEI landscape in STEM, such as podcasts, essays, and newspaper articles, serves several purposes. Students arrive as learners in the HSTEM classroom holding a wide variety of disciplinary expertise and frameworks; some are majoring in a STEM discipline while others are not, some are engaged already as change agents on campus or in other community spaces while others are not, and some have firsthand experience with identity-based discrimination and harassment while others do not. By starting the course with a set of core readings, this diverse group is able to both explore the different perspectives they bring to the course and begin to develop some common frameworks, language, and tools. These readings are intentionally chosen to highlight diverse ways of thinking and knowing and to challenge some commonly held assumptions in STEM and in the academy more generally. By doing so, we are setting an early stage that invites critique and questioning—both of STEM disciplines and of ourselves as having full expertise. Additionally, the written reflections on, and in-class discussions of, the readings provide an early opportunity for facilitators and students to step into vulnerability with each other, admitting to "not knowing," and when disagreements arise, approaching them with curiosity and the goal of seeking understanding. Some guidelines for structuring students' reflections on the readings are offered in the following section.

Suggested Prompts for Student's Written Reflections on Readings

Students in the HSTEM course commonly complete written reflections in advance of each class session to help them prepare for discussion of the readings and other assignments for the day. Here is one approach, codesigned by HSTEM facilitators Jyl Gentzler, Sheila Jaswal, and Leah Schmalzbauer, that you might consider for structuring an HSTEM reading reflection assignment:

> *Part 1: Summary.* Please capture, using bullet points, your top two to three key points per assigned reading. The summary helps develop your ability to engage with the material and concisely summarize information.
> *Part 2: Reflection.* Please respond to the material with two paragraphs, one which adopts a "Believing Approach" and one which adopts a "Skeptical Approach."

Believing Approach
Take a welcoming stance toward the arguments and evidence presented. Describe what meaning the material had for you. Find intersections between your own lived experience and the material. You might consider the following prompts:

"Before doing this reading, I didn't know about . . . [some significant new insight]." Why is this insight significant to you?

or

"Before doing this reading, I wasn't familiar with the concept of . . . [some illuminating new concept]." In what ways does this concept illuminate a new understanding for you?

or

"Before doing this reading, I wasn't able to understand my experience of . . . [some personal experience that you thought was idiosyncratic, but now you see it as part of a larger pattern]." How has your understanding of your experience changed?

Skeptical Approach
Try to challenge the arguments or interpretations (but not the human lived experiences). What did you find puzzling or confusing? Were any claims inconsistent with your own experience or understanding of STEM? Can you propose alternative interpretations?

Part 3: Invitation to Engage in Discussion. Please choose a passage in the reading that you would like to discuss with the HSTEM community. Why did you pick this passage? What question does it raise for you that you would like to discuss with the rest of us?

Scholarship Modules

The specific reading list for the course changes each semester based on the disciplinary expertise of the facilitators, students' interests and courses of study, recommendations and discoveries from previous cohorts, and attentiveness to current events and prominent conversations that are occurring both within and outside our campus community (see Appendix A for a selection of readings and resources from the Amherst College HSTEM course). When selecting readings, some questions we consider are whose voices are represented, how are we challenging existing systems of who, and whose ideas, are valued and excluded, and where can students have agency to bring materials, perspectives, and new questions into the course? Student agency can take the form of choosing a preferred topic or perspective from a larger set of materials we have previously curated, or students might identify and introduce novel resources within the context of their course projects. Creating room in the syllabus for students to select and facilitate topics that are of interest to them is in keeping with the HSTEM ethos of colearning and cofacilitation, and it keeps the course feeling dynamic and responsive. That being said, there are a few core modules that are always included, due to their ability to successfully set the stage for the rest of the course. We describe the learning goals and approaches for each of these three core modules in the following section.

Scholarship Module 1: Being Human
As a new cohort of facilitators and students start off on their HSTEM journey, one of our first aims is to develop a shared sense of purpose and introduce ourselves to some of the frameworks that might allow us to discover our shared goals for our work. The "Being Human" module includes resources about being in an intentional community with others; these resources discuss calling people in versus calling them out (e.g., Bennett, 2020), normalizing and understanding conflict, and talking together about difficult things. For both facilitators and students, talking in depth about how you will work to cocreate a sense of belonging in an academic space is often new territory, so it is worth the expense of time and energy to explore these topics together.

After these initial discussions about building a brave community, this module then becomes more focused on what it means to engage in the work of creating inclusive STEM spaces, and inclusive spaces more broadly, in the context of a specific institutional dynamic. At Amherst, that context is one where individuals navigate how to bring our whole human selves into a space that has historically served white, privileged elites (until 1975, the college enrolled predominantly white elite males). Anthony Jack's (2019) *The Privileged Poor: How Elite Colleges Are Failing Disadvantaged Students* has become one of our staples in this module. Jack's text is based on his research exploring the experiences of disadvantaged students who attend elite colleges and universities. Through his sociological research he describes how three groups of students navigate elite institutions—disadvantaged students who attended preparatory high schools (whom Jack refers to as "privileged poor" students), disadvantaged students who attended local, often underresourced public schools (whom Jack refers to as "doubly disadvantaged" students), and students from upper-income families. Jack explores and exposes the ways in which institutional policies and cultural norms can "exacerbate social difficulties that cause structural exclusion: pushing poor students to the margins, thereby reminding them of their difference—often in ways that connect to racial inequalities on college campuses and in the nation as a whole" (p. 135). As a Black male Amherst alum, Jack weaves stories of his own experience as an undergraduate member of the "privileged poor"; the combination of personal campus experience and sociological analysis is particularly impactful for Amherst HSTEM students. While there may not be resources as closely linked to your immediate context as Jack's book is to Amherst, we encourage you to locate opportunities, ideally in partnership with your students, to engage with an analysis of power and privilege in campus dynamics similar to your own.

Toward the end of this first module, we turn our attention to the more general literature on diversity and inclusion in STEM: What is the demographic makeup of scientific fields and disciplines? How have demographic trends shifted over time? Who is overrepresented in STEM spaces, and which identities are somewhat invisible in STEM? The goal for this aspect of the module is to provide students with empirical evidence related to the scope of the challenge of diversification of STEM and where change has and has not been made. Note that while this component of module 1 has traditionally focused on representation and exclusion across all areas of STEM, there is a substantial body of work that dives into the nature of unequal representation within a number of individual STEM careers (e.g., geology and other field sciences, computer science, mathematics), and facilitators could readily adapt the module readings to attend to an individual field or subset of disciplines.

Scholarship Module 2: Interrogation of Ways of Knowing in STEM
This next module shifts to readings that invite students and cofacilitators to analyze a number of commonly held assumptions about scientific knowledge and practices. One such assumption we seek to critically examine is the assumption that science is a fully objective enterprise and that the identities and biases of individuals doing the science do not influence the scientific process or conclusions that are drawn. Another assumption is that of prioritizing Western scientific theory over Indigenous, feminist, and humanistic forms of inquiry.

The content of Scholarship Module 2 tends to be where cofacilitators outside of STEM bring their disciplinary expertise to bear, incorporating key texts and concepts from their field that can help the cohort analyze and "trouble" some of what we may take for granted in STEM. To this point, inviting individuals who identify as experts in fields other than STEM to serve as cofacilitators of this kind of course plays an important role in shedding light on the blind spots in our ways of thinking and operating that we may hold as scientists. In this second module, students and facilitators often find it helpful to start a collective list of terms that are new or unfamiliar to them. Table 2.1 shows a recent list of unfamiliar terms cocreated by cofacilitators and students.

As you review the list of words, you may notice terms about which you believe your students already hold deep knowledge as well as terms that may be less familiar to your students and, indeed, to you. Talking together as a class about the content you have jointly added to the collective document allows for a conversation about shared knowledge and individual differences in understanding; in this way, the list serves as a shared resource for navigating complex scholarship. More than that, however, it is an important space to normalize not knowing with students and to remind students that the course facilitators are colearners too. As one student reflected, "I came to class every day with questions about some weird word that I found that I knew nothing about, or I just couldn't make sense of. And at first, it was a little bit scary. . . . But I would say, as we grew to know each other, I would find that, almost always, someone had a similar question to me, and I wasn't the only person that didn't know what that word meant. . . . And that was a really validating experience."

TABLE 2.1
HSTEM Collective List of Unfamiliar Words

Animacy	Eugenic science	Pathologization
Aporia	Fungible	Personhood
Autarchy	Grievability	Pluralistic positionality
Axiological	Hegemonic	Polygenesis
Biomedicalization	Humanism	Posthumanist
Biopolitical	Ideology	Positivist
Body politic	Imbrication	Praxis
Colonialism	Infrahuman	Protectionism
Confirmation bias	Inhere	Racialized gender
Crip theory	Lag	Sociogenesis
Disenfranchise	Liminal	Solipsistic
Dysgenic	Manichean	Speciation
Enlightenment	Modernity	Teleology
Embodied	Necropolitics	Transversality
Epistemologies	Ocular anthropomorphism	WEIRD (acronym)
Essentialism	Ontology	Western empiricism

Scholarship Module 3: Humanizing STEM
This final core module works to integrate the learning that has occurred in previous modules. In this module, we continue to explore personal narratives and reflections about the subjective experience of being a human in STEM while considering avenues for reshaping STEM. We read and discuss the complex personal narratives of scientists who have navigated the academy while holding intersectional and often marginalized identities, as well as narratives about scientists whose work integrates scientific and humanistic methodologies. We also begin to adopt a future-focused mindset at this point in the course, as students start to conceptualize the shape and focus of their applied action projects.

Exploration of Lived Experiences in STEM

It is our goal to help students recognize that the lenses granted by their personal experiences, as well as the perspectives of others, are assets, not deficits, for both the doing of science and the process of shaping what a future, inclusive STEM community could be. To this end, one student reflected on their experience in HSTEM, saying, "Before HSTEM, I saw science as an objective field of study where you leave your background and identity at the door. . . . After studying the literature on the benefits of diversity in science, I know now that the intersectionality of my background, my trials and tribulations, [and] my struggles bring fresh/innovative ideas to the table." The validation and exploration of the lived experiences of local community members was the driving impetus behind the first iteration of HSTEM, and it continues to be a critical component of the course.

There are several learning goals that are accomplished by including a unit in the course focused on personal narratives and storytelling about ourselves and other scientists. First, many students come to the HSTEM course because they are seeking a space for having conversations about the difficult topics, such as experiences of exclusion, harassment, and imposter syndrome, that resonate with their personal experience. While many disciplines outside of STEM tackle these topics in depth, this unit allows students to explore experiences of racism, misogyny, ableism, and other forms of oppression as they manifest in STEM spaces, their home discipline. Importantly, many white students are motivated to take the HSTEM course because they understand in an abstract sense that structural racism and other forms of oppression exist in society, academia, and STEM, and seek to better understand their own experiences alongside those of classmates holding different identities. As students reflect on their experiences and the experiences of others in STEM, they are gaining the skills of telling their story from a place of deep understanding of the many different journeys of their classmates. They are learning how to communicate their experiences in STEM with nuance and context in ways that will resonate with others, and with the pressing issues at the institution. This is a key mechanism for driving inclusive change forward. Students have found that despite initial discomfort, expanding their learning beyond the classroom in this way often leads to rewarding connections with others, including peers with whom they thought they had nothing in common, faculty and staff with whom they have had minimal prior contact, and senior administrators at the institution.

How can we incorporate the lived experiences of others in STEM into our courses? The Amherst HSTEM course emerged from the power of student testimonials during the Amherst Uprising. Their voices and experiences were the critical triggers for change. We continue to honor and draw on this practice by integrating a range of assignments and events into the HSTEM course that engage stories from the campus community. One such assignment is to ask students to conduct interviews and oral histories with faculty, staff, current students, and alumni about their experiences in STEM. Through these interviews, students hear from others about what has helped them succeed in STEM, what barriers they have experienced, and what opportunities they see for a more inclusive STEM community. One interview subject reflected on the importance of representation in STEM, saying, "Not every person who has the same skin tone as you or looks like you is going to have the same experiences . . . but race is part of your lived experience. And being able to have someone who you can talk to about that lived experience is really, really important. Having allies who have lived through it, and have fought through it, and have succeeded: That's a game changer."

A consistent theme that emerges in these interviews is that of imposter phenomenon or imposter syndrome (Clance & Imes, 1978; Lindemann et al., 2016). For instance, one interviewee shared, "Female CS [computer science] majors have really bad imposter syndrome. . . . I think part of that has to do with having this preconceived notion of who a good coder is." Relatedly, another interviewee worried that if they did not perform at a high level, their failures would be attributed to their gender: "I don't want this person to think I'm stupid. I don't want them to be like, 'Why the hell does she not understand?'" Listening to these reflections from their peers, from alumni, and from staff and faculty members at the college serves an important function of normalizing students' experiences in STEM and helping them reflect on how their own journeys have paralleled those of others. Again and again, students express relief in knowing that they are not alone.

Other approaches that students have chosen to meet the goals of this unit include creating a documentary about the experiences of themselves and others in STEM or facilitating a discussion panel, open to the full campus community, in which they ask a small group of faculty and staff to share their background and experiences in STEM. A question students posed to the panelists that resonated especially strongly with students was one that asked them to reflect on the nonlinear components of their development as a scientist, including the challenges that they have faced and how they have sought to overcome those challenges. Finally, in some versions of the course, students have conducted historical and archival research into the institutional history of students, faculty, and staff in STEM. As students spend a relatively short period of time at our institutions, compared to most faculty and staff, this research can provide them with a grounding in the work that has been done and the strides that have already been made. In a related project, several years ago an HSTEM postbaccalaureate fellow led a group of students in creating a visual timeline of the first female scientists to earn tenure in each department. This inquiry project, and the visual installation that resulted, planted seeds for many productive conversations. Students were asking a variety of questions: "Is the trend in this department consistent with the field more broadly?" Or, "Just because women are tenured in this department, have they been held to an equal standard in terms of their teaching, scholarship, and service as their male colleagues?" Finally, "What does it mean that this department tenured its first female-identified scientist only a few years ago?"

Facilitating Campus Change Through Student-Led Action Project Proposals

As we noted previously, the second half of the course is focused on small-group work, in which students develop project proposals that identify and test an idea that addresses a need or opportunity for inclusion on campus. Groups ideally identify at least one department or office with which their project idea aligns, and then further refine their idea with feedback from that constituency. At the end of the semester, we host an event (called the "HSTEM Salon," described in the next section of this chapter) where students share their project proposals. Framing this culminating assignment as a proposal, as opposed to a fully developed project ready for implementation, helps to keep students focused on community-identified needs and community action. The proposals allow students to learn about a challenge and explore possible interventions while maintaining a sense of shared agency and responsibility among the various stakeholders. This framing also keeps the work manageable and achievable within a single semester, and helps set realistic expectations for students in terms of the outcomes that are possible in that short time frame.

The selection of project topics starts with a guided reflection on what the group has learned from both their review of the literature and exploration of lived experiences, to critically consider what they have come to understand about needs and opportunities on campus, as well as effective strategies for intervention. To structure this reflection, we ask students to conduct a thematic analysis of the written reflections that students generated in response to each of the resources we engaged across the scholarship modules (see chapter 4 for a detailed discussion of this Meta-Reflection activity). Small groups are each assigned to read a subset of their peers' reflections and to synthesize the themes and patterns that emerge. Following that synthesis, students are then well positioned to identify challenges and opportunities for their project proposals.

Doing the work of institutional inclusive change also requires personal investment and connection to the issue at hand, so we encourage students to consider the contexts in which they operate and where they might make meaningful change in those spaces. Examples include cultural competency training for the student-led campus emergency medical responders, workshops or initiatives focused on a student's departmental major, and resources for navigating specific preprofessional pathways. Focusing their proposals within familiar contexts can help students feel more confident and more invested in their project work, but it also generates some challenges. For one, students' deep-lived familiarity with a context can result in their overprivileging their own lived experience as being true for others in that space, and students often need to be encouraged to mindfully consider any assumptions or preconceptions about the challenge they may hold, and to check the generalizability of those assumptions with other stakeholders. See Figure 2.2 for a visual representation of common project topics that students have explored in the course over the years.

Planning an Action Project

Planning an action project requires asking questions about both the context for the work and the stakeholders involved in the work. Who are the people who are both invested in and impacted by this issue? What has already happened at the institution around this issue? Where have interventions previously gained traction, where have they gotten stuck, and why? Recently, we have also asked students to more explicitly consider the multiple contextual layers to the issue they seek to address through their project proposal. Informed by the micro-level, meso-level, and macro-level features of strategic,

Figure 2.2. Common action project themes.

- Raising Awareness of DEI Issues
- Information Gathering About Equity-Related Experiences
- Developing New Inclusive Programming, Seminars, and Workshops
- Supporting STEM Self-Efficacy in K–12 Educational Settings
- Creating Guides for Navigating Opaque Systems

Common Action Project Proposal Themes

inclusive leadership as articulated by Kathy Takayama, Matthew Kaplan, and Alison Cook-Sather (Takayama et al., 2017), we scaffold students in consideration of the interactive nature of top-down administrative initiatives (the macro level), departmental and divisional initiatives (the meso level), and work led by individual faculty, staff, and students (the micro level) to identify how their project can draw on and integrate these energies into more inclusive change at the institution.

One of the perennial challenges of approaching inclusion in STEM through the structure of a semester-long course is the enforced timescale that it provides. A single term limits how far students can move their projects forward. And we don't want to rush into the project proposals before we work as a community to ground ourselves in the literature, reflect on our own experiences in STEM, and intentionally listen and validate the experiences of other scientists. Indeed, we have seen too many instances at our institution and others where, in the rush to *do something*, these steps have been skipped. Especially in the work of inclusion, these rushed efforts often result in more harm than good, as they provide another venue where underrepresented voices are likely to be excluded from consultation and decision-making. All that being said, the shortened timescale creates a tension between product and process, between what is most beneficial as a learning experience for students and feeling that progress is being made at our institutions.

The restructuring of this assignment to take the form of a project proposal rather than expecting that the project will be implemented within the same semester as its conception helps to address this challenge, and we try to encourage students to build on previous students' project proposals, to help them connect their work to ongoing institutional efforts rather than starting from scratch whenever possible.

Inviting the Campus Community to Join the Conversation

An enduring component of the HSTEM course is the Being Human in STEM Salon, during which student teams share their project proposals with the local campus community. The salons are open to all members of the institution, with targeted invitations to the campus departments or offices that have been identified as potential partners for each proposal. The salon serves several purposes as the culminating event for each HSTEM cohort. From the beginning of the term, it establishes a deadline for accountability, generates a motivational push for students to keep the work moving forward, and sets the expectation of a public audience for students' work. The event is also a means to continue the campus conversation that was initiated during the Amherst Uprising; it serves to preserve the energy and urgency of the sit-in. Finally, the salons create an avenue for potential campus partners to learn about and build on the ideas brought forward by the students, which ideally helps to move the projects forward toward implementation.

The course dedicates significant time to the development of the salon, with students and facilitators working together to refine presentations, design the structure of the event, and participate in a full "dress rehearsal." As a result, the salon becomes part of what the cohort has created together, with a shared sense of ownership and a unique structure that reflects the community they have worked together to build. One component of the project proposal presentations that we have found requires substantial scaffolding, even after spending most of the semester focused on developing our skills of active listening and collaboration, relates to helping students structure these presentations in such a way that they are inviting partnership and feedback from stakeholders, rather than serving as a platform solely to present a critique. In formative feedback sessions, we encourage students to consider how they present their perception of an issue on campus and how their presentation is likely to be heard and received by the audience. As we discuss in chapter 4, "Teaching With and for Empathy," drawing on our skills of active listening and empathy is particularly important in this step of the process.

As more institutions have developed HSTEM courses on their own campuses (see chapter 9 for an in-depth discussion of how HSTEM has been adapted across multiple institutional contexts), we now have opportunities for student cohorts at different institutions to gather together, either in face-to-face or digital sessions, to share their final project proposals. At these cross-institutional gatherings, student teams gain insights into challenges that are shared across institutions and the factors that influence nuanced differences in how those challenges manifest. Attending a salon also serves to welcome students and facilitators into a broader community of inclusive practice where they can be inspired, supported, and celebrated together.

Reaching Beyond the Local STEM Community

The founding Amherst HSTEM students were invited to present about the course at Yale University in spring of 2016; although they didn't know it at the time, this half-day event was the original "HSTEM Summit." The following fall, Amherst hosted the first official regional HSTEM Summit with 18 attendees from Amherst and Yale. The regional HSTEM summits in 2018 and 2019 then further expanded to include members of Brown University's Race & Gender in the Scientific Community course (http://racegenderscience.weebly.com/), a remarkably similar course to HSTEM that was created by students at Brown in 2014. The original Race & Gender in the Scientific Community course drew on the expertise of several faculty members at Brown, including Cornelia Dean, who served as the faculty advisor to the students who first created the course syllabus as a group independent study project. After a group of these students advocated for the course to be institutionalized, Björn Sandstede, an applied mathematics faculty member, facilitated the first regular course in the spring of 2017 (Silber, 2018). The convergent evolution of these courses at Amherst and at Brown demonstrates the power and need for such a course in the curriculum.

The summit structure includes a subset of students from each participating institution, who share about their experiences in the HSTEM course, present a range of action projects that they have developed across the semester, and with facilitators, reflect on opportunities and challenges of creating more inclusive STEM communities on their campuses. The summit is an invigorating experience, because it provides attendees with a sense of validation and renewed energy for their efforts. Of particular importance is the fact that students and instructors are able to experience themselves as members of a larger scholarly community, all of whom are working with a shared purpose and vision. Our students often feel frustrated at the slow pace and small scale of change on campus. It can be challenging for them to invest so much of their time and energy into their action projects, only to see minimal shifts or experience resistance to their efforts. Many times, these responses can feel personal and painful. Connecting with students, staff, and faculty who have also been working to create inclusive change in their home contexts reveals that slow, nonlinear change and active resistance are common and transcend any local context. Normalizing this experience can help restore students' belief in the importance and worthiness of sustaining their efforts.

In addition to the summit, we encourage students to present on their research and institutional leadership work as invited speakers at other campuses and at scholarly conferences. When invited to share the HSTEM model with a new institution, we consistently seek to include students in these presentations. They have spent a full term working to build their expertise and knowledge about inclusion and equity in STEM, and they have reflected deeply on their own lived experiences as a student in STEM. And yet these same students often do not recognize that they hold substantial expertise from which others can benefit. Inviting students to step into these experiences helps them to embrace their identity as active scholars with something important to contribute to discussions of equity. In addition, for those who hold identities previously excluded from research opportunities, these opportunities can facilitate connections with others who are navigating similar challenges of being underrepresented in STEM.

Conclusions

The HSTEM course provides one model of how to teach about, and with, inclusion in STEM. It brings together elements of scholarly engagement, reflection on personal experience, and the process of identifying ways to improve the inclusive landscape of STEM. Action project proposals allow students to seek across-campus collaborations, practice active listening and partnership, and feel empowered to make changes happen in their spheres of influence on campus. Through these action project proposals, it is our hope that students are gaining transferable skills that they will bring with them into their future communities and workspaces in STEM. And finally, connecting students with other scholarly communities also working for equity in STEM helps to build their networks, sense of self efficacy, and understanding that they are contributing to an issue that transcends their home institution.

A frequent question we hear from folks who are interested in talking with their students about DEI in STEM is, "This sounds good, but does it have to be a course? Could these goals be accomplished using a different structure?" We appreciate this question, as it raises important questions about institutional context and what frameworks are most impactful on each of our campuses. The HSTEM model is designed to be flexible and to adapt to a range of structures and applications. In our context, we have found that a credit-bearing course structure provides several important signposts. For students, the course structure signals that this kind of learning bears equal worth to the other academic training that they receive; this is an important aspect of higher education. For faculty and staff, engaging this work through a course structure provides a familiar avenue for recognizing and providing credit for their work. Additionally, as we offer this course as an elective, students who are not yet ready to reflect on their own lived experiences in community with others are not pressured or required to do so. While students who take HSTEM often argue for making this course an institutional requirement, the fact that students opt in to this experience plays a critical role in establishing a community of trust and mutual support.

Be that as it may, the course-structured design to inclusion in STEM also presents some challenges, because it doesn't actually function like other courses in the sciences. The student-driven design process, the community engagement expectations, and the outcomes are likely all quite different from STEM courses that students take at the institution. It is not uncommon for students to feel a little out of place in the early days of the course, as they navigate these new ways of being invited to learn and contribute. And most disruptive, we find, is the question of how to approach assessment of student learning in a course focused on inclusion and reflection.

The question of how to evaluate student learning in the HSTEM course is a tricky one, as it highlights the ways that despite the dynamic of students serving as colearners and codesigners in the course, faculty still hold power over students' grades. We return often to the question of what exactly we hope to accomplish with students through the course, and what they themselves hope for their learning through this course. We have settled on a model of assessment that prioritizes sustained effort and reflective engagement. Have students stayed "in the arena," so to speak, throughout the course? Not only did they complete the assigned readings, assignments, and project proposal, but did their reflections demonstrate how their thinking about themselves and about issues of DEI in STEM has shifted over the course of the semester? Importantly, our model of assessment does not adopt an expectation of mastery, but rather of ongoing reflection and self-learning. A student has been successful in HSTEM if they have developed an action-oriented approach to inclusion, guided by an ongoing cycle of listening, validation, and partnership. In the next chapter, we describe this process in more detail and with a specific focus on the fourth component, that of partnership.

References

Arao, B., & Clemens, K. (2013). From safe spaces to brave spaces: A new way to frame dialogue around diversity and social justice. In L. M. Landreman (Ed.), *The art of effective facilitation: Reflections from social justice educators* (pp. 135–150). Stylus.

Bennett, J. (2020, November 19). What if instead of calling people out, we called them in? *The New York Times.* https://www.nytimes.com/2020/11/19/style/loretta-ross-smith-college-cancel-culture.html

Clance, P. R., & Imes, S. A. (1978). The imposter phenomenon in high achieving women: Dynamics and therapeutic intervention. *Psychotherapy: Theory, Research & Practice, 15*(3), 241–247. https://doi.org/10.1037/h0086006

Edmondson, A. C., & Lei, Z. (2014). Psychological safety: The history, renaissance, and future of an interpersonal construct. *Annual Review of Organizational Psychology and Organizational Behavior, 1,* 23–43. https://doi.org/10.1146/annurev-orgpsych-031413-091305

Howell, J., & Reinhard, K. (2015). *Rituals and traditions: Fostering a sense of community in preschool.* National Association for the Education of Young Children.

Jack, A. A. (2019). *The privileged poor: How elite colleges are failing disadvantaged students.* Harvard University Press.

Lindemann, D., Britton, D., & Zundl, E. (2016). "I don't know why they make it so hard here": Institutional factors and undergraduate women's STEM participation. *International Journal of Gender, Science & Technology, 8*(2), 221–241.

Meyer, J. H. F., & Land, R. (2005). Threshold concepts and troublesome knowledge (2): Epistemological considerations and a conceptual framework for teaching and learning. *Higher Education, 49*(3), 373–388. https://doi.org/10.1007/s10734-004-6779-5

Silber, M. (2018, June 1). *Race and gender in the scientific community.* Siam News. https://sinews.siam.org/Details-Page/race-and-gender-in-the-scientific-community

Takayama, K., Kaplan, M., & Cook-Sather, A. (2017). Advancing diversity and inclusion through strategic multilevel leadership. *Liberal Education, 103*(3/4).

3

A PROCESS FOR PARTNERSHIP

Student protests provide the opportunity to make obvious the ways that student voices and experiences are being excluded from institutional decision-making and policy. In this way, the Amherst Uprising provided a clear demonstration of a need to modify students' experiences in their classes and on campus more broadly. One way that HSTEM has helped contribute to moving from student protest to institutional progress at Amherst has been through forging partnerships with students and elucidating opportunities for other partnerships to emerge across campus. Partnerships differ from other ways in which you may already work with students, as they disrupt traditional notions of expertise; they seek to more evenly distribute power and responsibility across faculty, staff, and students; and they work toward outcomes that are emergent and jointly defined.

The founding HSTEM partnership between students and cofacilitators established a process model, introduced in the book's preface, that is critical for guiding how students navigate their work throughout the course while also providing important signposts for how other partnerships across campus can operate in more inclusive and effective ways. In this chapter, therefore, we describe how this HSTEM inclusive partnership process of listening, validating, reflecting, and partnering structures how facilitators and students initially build community, how facilitators work collaboratively, and how students engage with campus partners as they propose and present action projects that seek to integrate the goals, values, and perspectives of all stakeholders involved. Finally, we share firsthand accounts from students, staff, and faculty whose conceptions of themselves and the enterprise of teaching and learning have been transformed by the power of partnership.

Guiding Questions

- Derived from our early days of partnering with students, a model of listening, validating, reflecting, and partnering emerged. How might you apply this framework to your work of institutional change? In particular, how might we adopt this model at our institutions in proactive ways, such that change need not be predicated on protests or other large points of conflict?
- What are some key recommendations and challenges, from the literature and our lived experiences, for sustaining partnership efforts in higher education? What features of partnership seem most important to emphasize in your own work?

A Note About HSTEM Facilitators

Throughout this book, you have already seen us reference HSTEM course "facilitators" or "cofacilitators." Course facilitators are individuals who partner with enrolled students in the course. They hold particular responsibility for shepherding the course design process and overseeing the logistical course structures and daily operations. Across campuses within the HSTEM network, multiple models of facilitation exist, with some HSTEM courses led by a single facilitator, others led by multiple cofacilitators who may come to the course with different disciplinary expertise, and finally, some HSTEM courses that also include student cofacilitators. The choice of the word *facilitator* is an intentional one, selected to reflect the nature of partnership and colearning that HSTEM seeks to foster in the classroom community.

Exploring the HSTEM Process Model

The choice of codesigning the spring 2016 course with students was an in-the-moment, organic response to students' desires to process their experiences of the disconnects surfaced through the Uprising in community; students were calling for acts of solidarity and shared commitment. The founding cofacilitators, Sheila and Megan, were equally invested and interested in having meaningful conversations with students, wanting to share their own experiences and explore the academic literature together. In addition to fulfilling a need for community, this initial semester with student partners also illuminated the ways in which the partnership orientation to learning and action was key to engaging and sustaining this kind of

Figure 3.1. The HSTEM process model.

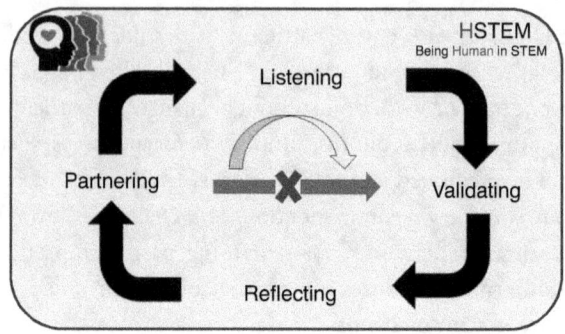

work. This insight led to the development of the HSTEM process model. This cyclical process (see Figure 3.1), is affectionately called the "HSTEM Central Dogma" by students and consists of four steps: listening, validating, reflecting and partnering.

Originally useful as the HSTEM founders sought to investigate and attempt to bridge (represented by the curved arrow) disconnects (represented by the broken arrow) underlying the experiences of students that led to the Amherst Uprising, this framework has also proven to be broadly applicable. In the next part of this chapter, we describe the first three steps in the model (listening, validating, and reflecting) in terms of how you can use them to foster inclusive partnerships and relationships on your campuses in general. We then illustrate how the cycle represented in this model allows specifically for three forms of partnership within the HSTEM course: (a) partnerships between facilitators and students, (b) partnerships between cofacilitators across disciplinary expertise, and (c) partnerships between students and campus community members in their shared work of developing and implementing their HSTEM action projects. In the final section of this chapter, we provide testimonials from individuals who have been impacted by approaching their efforts toward inclusive change using this framework for partnership.

Listening

As you approach partnering with students and other members of the campus community to create more inclusive practices and policies, the process of listening sets the stage for the identification of shared motivations and values as well as underlying gaps and disconnects that exist on campus. We encourage you to listen for the experiences and values that serve as individuals' motivations and goals for partnership. Further, from their perspective, what are meaningful outcomes or markers of success, and what would indicate that the work has not been successful? It may seem odd that we explicitly teach listening skills, one of the basic actions of humans as social beings, in a college setting (see the "Practicing Active Listening Exercise" in chapter 4). We listen all day long, don't we? Why would we need to practice? We have found, however, that for many of us, the approaches that we take to listening can actually undermine our attempts at inclusive partnership. It is common for all of us to adopt a stance of listening for what is self-relevant to us. In listening for what we deem as interesting or important to *us*, however, we can undermine our ability to actively listen for what our partner is saying is important to *them*.

Validating

The process of active and inclusive listening is only successful when it occurs in a relationship where trust is established, such that we trust that our partners will listen for and engage with what we have to share, and that we will do the same for them. How do we establish trust in partnership? The research suggests that one such way that we develop trust is through establishing an understanding that partners are working in the protected confidence of each other (e.g., Cook-Sather et al., 2019). What is shared in partnership is done so with the knowledge that it will not be shared with others without explicit permission. Your role as a partner, regardless of your positionality, is to affirm and validate others' perceived realities, both the challenges and the successes. Someone's experience may be counterintuitive or even counter to your own; that does not make their experience any less true for them.

Finally, the literature indicates that the establishment of trust and emotional validation is more likely to occur when partners have explicitly acknowledged that, due to their differential positions of power, authority, and autonomy, each will reap distinct outcomes from the partnership (Mercer-Mapstone et al., 2017). Much has been written about democratizing student partnership and why this is a worthy goal (e.g., Deeley & Bovill, 2017; Meinking & Hall, 2020). At the same time, individuals engaged in students-as-partners work commonly report that a truly equal partnership, in terms of equal risks born and benefits gained, is not a common reality of this work. When we think about students relative to faculty, in STEM or not, it's important to recognize that students bear a greater amount of risk in partnership in some domains and less risk in partnership in others (e.g., Cook-Sather, 2006; Mercer-Mapstone & Abbot, 2020). Students may have less institutional-level professional risk through partnership than do nontenured faculty. For instance, faculty partners' teaching reviews may be substantially impacted by the success of their work partnering with students in and alongside the classroom. In other cases, their research productivity (if they are not engaged in research on student partnership per se) may be impacted by the time that partnership work takes away from the pursuit of other tasks relevant to their review and promotion.

In terms of interpersonal-level risk, students may carry *more* risk than faculty as they navigate the student–faculty partnership relationship. Given the well-established dynamic of unidirectional feedback in education, in which faculty and staff provide feedback (often in the form of grades) to students much more frequently than students are invited to share feedback with faculty and staff, students may be uncomfortable with being asked to provide authentic critique and validation to their faculty and staff partners. Often students worry that critique of an instructor's pedagogical practice or decisions will not be received positively, and this may have limiting consequences for the student's ability to pursue additional educational and research opportunities, letters of recommendation, and the like. At the same time, it is not the case that the interpersonal risk for faculty and staff undertaking partnership work is negligible; faculty and staff partners may feel uncomfortable being asked to adopt a stance of openness to the receipt of that feedback, especially if students' feedback reveals an area of weakness or lack of expertise. Naming and validating these distinct and sometimes imbalanced risks is a critical step toward creating more inclusive teaching and learning spaces.

Reflecting

Listening and validating are then followed by the third step in the HSTEM process model, self-reflection. What am I hearing from others, and how does that connect with my own lived experience? What patterns do I observe, and what insights might these patterns provide? On the other hand, where are the disconnects between the experiences of others and myself? Why might those disconnects exist, and how may those differential experiences have contributed to biases or blind spots that I hold? In addition to these reflective prompts, we also encourage students, staff, and faculty to consider the role of structural and historical factors. What are the institutional efforts and barriers, as well as larger systemic inequities, that have impacted someone's personal journey through, and current relationship to, STEM?

Self-reflection can be emotionally challenging, as this process asks participants to be vulnerable, to acknowledge the limits of their understanding, and to inhabit spaces of discomfort. These spaces of discomfort call on us to admit to ourselves and others that we may have benefited from systems that have harmed others, that we may have acted in ways that caused harm or did not address harm done to others appropriately, and that we frequently struggle to understand the perspective of another and what they consider to be right and true.

Partnering

Too often we respond to the urgency of an interaction, conflict, or need by rushing to say the first thing on our mind or take immediate individual action. Without having the full story or fully understanding our motivations, we leap to a response. Taking the steps of listening, validating, and reflecting circumvents this habit. This process forces us to take in information and perspectives from others, confirm what we have heard, and carefully consider what this has to do with us and how (if at all) we want to engage in light of this more complete understanding and consideration. Framing the engagement—be it a conversation, an intervention, or a longer-term plan of action—as a partnership shifts our sense of agency and responsibility. We are not reacting; we are partnering. We are not telling our side of a story; we are partnering to come to an understanding of each other. We are not sharing a list of demands for change; we are partnering to create change together.

Although there are many ways we collaborate with students, it is helpful to explicitly consider collaboration with which students (and faculty and staff) may be more familiar. Table 3.1 articulates the points of overlap and distinction that we see between more common models of working with students and the student partnership model. Note here that the category of student partner refers both to the partnership work that happens with students within the context of the HSTEM course, as well as emerging partnerships that they forge with campus community members to enact inclusive action projects.

The Early Days of Partnership

As one might imagine, the emphasis on partnership and shared responsibility was quite strong in the first iteration of the course, since Sheila, Megan, and the students were embarking on a new enterprise together, full of exploration and experimentation. We learned several key lessons from our

TABLE 3.1
How Student Partnership Compares to Other Forms of Collaboration With Students

Student Role	Expectations of Student in This Role	Expectations of Faculty/Staff in This Relationship	Evidence Used to Inform This Work	Anticipated Outcomes
Student Partner	Willingness to be equally responsible for the work and process Colearner Openness to providing and receiving constructive feedback Equally prioritizes faculty/staff partners', peers', and own goals for the work	Willingness to be equally responsible for the work and process Colearner Openness to providing and receiving constructive feedback Equally prioritizes student partners', peers', and own goals for the work	Student lived experience, expertise, and observations Faculty/staff lived experience, expertise, and observations Course material	Codesigned brave space and/or product All partners responsible for the thriving and inclusion of all in learning community Reciprocal relationships among students and faculty/staff partners
Teaching Assistant	Responsible for implementing faculty/staff intentions Learner Openness to receiving constructive feedback Prioritizes faculty/staff goals for the work	Responsible for design and majority of implementation Expert Openness to providing constructive feedback Prioritizes faculty/staff goals for the work	Primary: Faculty/staff lived experience, expertise, and observations Minimal: Student lived experience, expertise, and observations	Faculty/staff-designed product Faculty/staff members responsible for success of product Hierarchical relationship between faculty/staff and student

Research Assistant	Responsible for implementing faculty/staff intentions

Learner

Openness to receiving constructive feedback

Prioritizes faculty/staff goals for the work | Responsible for design and majority of implementation

Expert

Openness to providing constructive feedback

Prioritizes faculty/staff goals for the work | Primary: Empirical literature, faculty/staff expertise

Observations and results of research conducted by assistant (in the lab) | Faculty/staff-designed product

Faculty/staff members responsible for success of product

Hierarchical relationship between faculty/staff and student |
| Mentee or Advisee | Responsible for reflecting on and implementing (some) faculty/staff recommendations

Learner

Openness to receiving constructive feedback

Prioritizes student goals | Responsible for providing sound recommendations

Expert

Openness to providing constructive feedback

Prioritizes student goals | Student lived experience, expertise, and observations

Faculty/staff lived experience, expertise, and observations | Codesigned product

All partners responsible for success of product

Reciprocal relationship between student and faculty/staff partner |

work with these remarkable founding student partners. First, our partnership work highlighted the importance of an *intentional, backward design* (Wiggins & MacTighe, 2006) approach to change. We began by coidentifying our goals for this work before articulating the metrics that would tell us that we had met or progressed toward those goals and developing a plan for how we would approach our collaborative endeavor. The second lesson we learned through this partnership was the *value of shared ownership*, particularly in higher education. Academic structures are hierarchical, and the traditional classroom is no exception. Students-as-partners work disrupts the model of a single authority figure in the classroom, through a recognition that students, staff, and faculty all hold important, distinctive expertise. Partnering with students means intentionally relinquishing some instructor-held control in order for meaningful collaboration to occur. The third lesson we gleaned from working with the inaugural cohort of student partners in HSTEM was the *importance of sharing personal stories and narratives and then putting them into conversation with empirical research*. We recognize that as scientists, we have been trained to privilege empirical research over personal experience. However, we have found that it is the hearing of an individual's story, especially one that highlights that our own lived experiences have not been the same as others, that can often serve as a catalyst for action and change. Listening to these student partners share their experiences of bias, exclusion, roadblocks, and pain made stagnation unconscionable. Equally important was hearing their strength, their resilience, their joy, and their agency in bringing their identities and full selves into STEM. By listening and sharing in partnership, we changed the script from traditional efforts to "help disadvantaged students" succeed and persist in STEM, to helping students and ourselves learn how to embrace our full human selves in the context of STEM. In this way, we experienced our own growth as humans and as educators.

Finally, we learned from our student partners about the *importance of thinking broadly and creatively about who else could and should serve as partners in this work*. Regardless of our positions at our institutions, we tend to operate in fairly insular and siloed ways, drawing on our direct departmental or divisional colleagues for collaboration. Students, on the other hand, move more fluidly through institutional spaces and can provide invaluable insight into a wider range of institutional expertise and potential change agents. They take coursework with faculty across divisional divides, build relationships with staff members in residential and cocurricular spaces, and, through their work in leadership roles and as members of student interest groups at the institution, interface with multiple members of senior administration. In fact, Megan was invited into the founding HSTEM class by one of the students! Students weave expansive webs of relationships during their time in higher education; we encourage you to partner with students to expand your reach on campus and invite more voices into collaboration.

We now turn to three contexts in which these lessons of partnership—the benefits of intentional, goal-driven design; the need for shared ownership; the equal value of research and experience; and the importance of thinking broadly about the nature of collaboration—contribute to the success of (a) partnering between students and facilitators, (b) partnering across facilitators, and (c) partnering with campus stakeholders.

Partnering With Students in the HSTEM Course: Creating Vulnerable, Brave Spaces

While the initial approach to partnering with students in shared colearning following the Amherst Uprising was not intentionally grounded in the students-as-partners framework, we have found that the initial and ongoing success of the partnership is attributable to aspects of the partnership that are consistent with the lessons learned by others working in partnership with students. As described by Cook-Sather et al. (2014), partnership is "a collaborative, reciprocal process through which all participants have the opportunity to contribute equally, although not necessarily in the same ways, to curricular or pedagogical conceptualization, decision making, implementation, investigation, or analysis" (pp. 6–7). Partnerships, these same authors argue, should be guided by three principles: respect, responsibility, and reciprocity.

How do these three tenets appear in our HSTEM partnership work? In terms of respect, faculty, staff, and students develop a deep sense of mutual esteem as they build connections and learn about each other as full people; this is why community building and the foregrounding of personal narrative is so critical. The community-building activities described in chapter 5 create the conditions necessary for students and facilitators to move from being strangers who share good intentions to members of a community open to being disrupted, destabilized, and in partnership together. With this preparation, students and facilitators can now partner in the creation of what journalist Jad Abumrad characterizes as a "third space" (Zomorodi, 2020). Abumrad argues that in order to have dialogue across differences, individuals must create something new—the third space—that only exists when both sides commit to formulating a new understanding, not by seeking preexisting commonalities and shared ground, but by listening and allowing each person to show up as their full self without bending and squeezing to fit into some imagined intersecting area. Secondly, participants recognize that we are responsible to each other, such that we all depend upon each other to give and receive support as well as to jointly contribute to the changes we wish to see in our STEM communities and larger institutional structures. And finally, there is an important level of reciprocity between faculty, staff, and students, which occurs in several dimensions. Collaborating with students highlights the fact that they bring the valuable insights of being a student on our campus who moves between many departments, offices, and social communities. Faculty and staff, on the other hand, bring their own valuable insights into departmental practices and institutional history. In this way, all participants are recognized as holding and contributing expertise.

Engaging in partnership work around issues of identity, privilege, individual bias, and systems of oppression requires a stance of vulnerability—a recognition that for a respectful, responsible, and reciprocal partnership to thrive, we all have to be willing to engage with points of discomfort, articulate what we do and do not know, and seek and provide support from and to each other. All individuals in the partnership must be willing to step into difficult dialogues and self-reflection. A critical component in building trust across the power differentials and different identities that faculty, students, and staff hold in the class is the active participation of faculty and staff facilitators as colearners. During community-building activities, facilitators take the lead in sharing with vulnerability and embracing their own identity as human beings who, despite being experts in their disciplines, are not experts in the scholarship of diversity, equity, and inclusive pedagogy. When facilitators openly share feelings of trepidation and concerns about being wrong or making mistakes in class discussions, they can decrease the distance between themselves and the students and allow students to see themselves as equally valuable members of the same learning community.

About this process, one facilitator reflected that while they were enjoying being with students in the classroom in this way, they also worried, "I don't know enough—Am I doing enough? Is this okay?" The questioning of oneself in the learning journey is a process that students constantly experience; when we share our own experiences of destabilization and doubt with our students, we can create space for relating to our students in the classroom in a different way. By modeling curiosity, humility, and vulnerability, facilitators shift from being presented as a "sage on the stage" (King, 1993, p. 30) to human beings who are colearners, shoulder-to-shoulder with their students. What emerges is a sense that the community is in a reciprocal relationship, a partnership with each other, and that this community is built on a foundation of trust, mutual respect, and shared responsibility. This foundation allows deeper learning about oneself and one's community, and greater potential for inclusive, collaborative change efforts to succeed.

Partnering Across Cofacilitators: Expanding Ways of Knowing

As expert scholars in our disciplines, we are commonly in positions of transmitting that knowledge to others, in our classrooms, laboratories, and professional communities. In the process of developing our disciplinary expertise, we have also developed an internalized set of values and assumptions about the nature of knowing. As scientists, how do we construct an argument? How do we know that a claim is valid? Whose views are important? Whose views are not? Partnering with facilitators across disciplinary boundaries allows us to unearth some of these biases and consider new or alternative ways of knowing and thinking. These partnerships create the context for us to listen to and validate the disciplinary values of others and to reflect on how these values and approaches align with, differ from, and help us understand our own disciplinary assumptions in a different way. At that point, we can then partner to construct interdisciplinary teaching and learning spaces that bring this range of perspectives into dialogue with each other.

Here's a concrete example of the impact of cross-disciplinary cofacilitation: In Scholarship Module 2 (described in detail in chapter 2), we work to place our lived experiences into the broader academic literature. In past versions of the course, the discussion focused on articles addressing specific aspects of identity in STEM. When Leah Schmalzbauer, a cofacilitator with disciplinary expertise in sociology joined the teaching partnership, she recognized that we could broaden the frame to include classic sociological and feminist texts to further contextualize these issues. In response, we have since included readings like *The Sociological Imagination* by C. Wright Mills (1959), *Science as Social Knowledge: Values and Objectivity in Scientific Inquiry* by Helen Longino (1990), and "Rethinking Standpoint Epistemology: What Is Strong Objectivity" by Sandra Harding (1992). These are frameworks that are typically brand new to STEM facilitators and students, and they provide the basis for expansive reconsideration of how we think about ourselves as scientists and about the scientific enterprise more broadly. (See Appendix A for a selected set of readings across each of the scholarship modules of the HSTEM course).

Cofacilitation partnerships across disciplines and roles on campus also have more practical benefits. Facilitating the HSTEM course requires faculty to be attentive to the full breadth of the student experience, including their learning, their emotional well-being, and their sense of community and safety. The intensive work of active partnership with students also means that facilitators are constantly making just-in-time decisions to manage the emergent design of both curricular elements and project work, while also engaging with stakeholders across campus. While many facilitators find this work exhilarating and rewarding, it can also be fatiguing and destabilizing. Being part of a group of HSTEM facilitators, both on your own campus and across other networks of inclusive practitioners, means having access to a support network of thought partners and practitioners. Having others who can serve as cheerleaders and sounding boards as you navigate this new dynamic can go a long way in sustaining energy and hope. These cross-disciplinary partnerships also strengthen an institution's HSTEM course over time by folding in new ideas and perspectives, making each iteration unique and creating opportunities to address new questions and develop new ideas. And including staff members as facilitators (e.g., at Amherst, our science librarian, Kristen Greenland, who cofacilitated HSTEM with Megan and Sheila from 2017 through 2019) both serves to highlight and activate their professional and academic expertise, while also integrating important and sometimes overlooked perspectives in understanding campus-based challenges.

Partnering With Campus Stakeholders: Codesigning for Change

Following an event such as a student protest, we are justifiably in a rush to act, to do something, to fix the problem. As we have previously mentioned, we have watched action steps taken without the foregrounding of listening, validating, and reflecting, commonly resulting in the exclusion of important voices and a less good solution. Drawing from the field of human-centered design (IDEO, 2015), we support students in partnering with campus offices and other stakeholders to codevelop action-oriented project proposals that are rooted in the needs and desires of the community that they seek to serve. The human-centered design process can be distilled into three phases that resonate with the centrality of partnership in HSTEM (and the scientific method): inspiration (conducting observations and research to develop an understanding of a challenge through the perspectives and desires of the communities impacted by the challenge), ideation (making sense of the data we've collected and identifying opportunities to intervene in the challenge, then testing those ideas by sharing them with community members), and implementation (bringing the most promising ideas to fruition, either through students' own efforts or by sharing their findings and recommendations with campus stakeholders). The resonance we see between the HSTEM model and these existing theories and practices gives us hope that we are not reinventing the wheel, but rather iterating and evolving these frameworks to inform the work of inclusion and belonging in higher education.

The same human tendencies that lead us to prefer solutions over process are important to acknowledge and address when leveraging human-centered design as a strategy. Even when designers have the best intentions for inclusion in developing solutions that will impact others, there is still the potential for important voices to be excluded if we don't reflect on the ways exclusion is ingrained in our culture (Noel & Paiva, 2021). Who is impacted by the systems and practices we wish to change? What are the intended outcomes or impacts of those systems and practices, and do those align with the lived experiences of the intended beneficiaries? Who has been and is currently involved in their design and implementation? Who has the power and authority to make meaningful changes within those systems? And finally, how are students positioned within those systems, and what do they need to understand about the experiences of others in order to uncover possibilities for change?

Visioning, planning, and implementing change through an action project can be challenging work to accomplish in the span of a single semester, and the scope of some students' work can mean that seeing a project to completion is impossible. As an example, some student groups have focused their efforts on increasing the diversity of scholars hired into faculty positions in STEM at the college; this important issue is one that is unlikely to meaningfully shift across such a short time course. Instead, our goal for these HSTEM action projects is to help students cultivate habits of mind that are grounded in curiosity and humility, and to help empower them to continue to model and test their ideas for change with other stakeholders in the community beyond the course's end. Students develop these habits of mind by reaching out to potential campus partners as part of their project ideation process and inviting relevant campus partners to the HSTEM salon. The community's feedback on these proposals adds depth and complexity to the students' understanding of the challenge they are engaging and to how the issues are contextualized, and the public sharing of the proposals serves to invite others into thinking concretely and proactively about ways to address those challenges—with the students' framing of them in mind—in the months and years ahead. We have found it to be very important to approach action projects from this framework of partnership because the sustained implementation of this work generally falls more heavily on the shoulders of the staff and faculty, who remain full members of the campus community after students have graduated or shifted focus. The development of empathic engagement in students and campus collaborators seems to be a critical predictor for the success of these projects and, perhaps more importantly, their ability to partner (see chapter 4 for discussion on how empathy can be cultivated through the HSTEM process).

Testimonials to the Power of Partnership

We have been moved by the power of partnership with students to reveal important disconnects at our institution, to name and heal harms done, and to chart a way forward in the pursuit of inclusive STEM education. In this final section of this chapter, we share a number of reflections from students, faculty, and staff at Amherst College who have been involved in the HSTEM initiative, many since its inception. Time and again, these reflections demonstrate the personal and community-wide importance of being an agent and collaborator and the far-reaching effects of these experiences. The following selection of responses emphasize the specific ways in which partnership between students, faculty, and staff generates new insights and awareness about one's self and opens up possibilities for shared action.

All educators hope that the skills and ways of being that we support students to develop in our classrooms and lab spaces continue to serve them well in their continued studies and their personal and professional lives. HSTEM students' engagement with partnership through community action projects seems particularly impactful in shaping students' emergent ability to serve as "agents of change" in their communities, as one faculty cofacilitator noted. Another cofacilitator also reflected on the empowerment of students that occurs when students are invited into meaningful partnership, saying, "The strength of the course, as I see it, is that students are able to respond to their negative experiences with collective action, and the course structure gives them space to explore their experience and how it aligns with the experiences of others on campus and in STEM programs in general through background research for their projects." This same person goes on to note that some "students are already activists when they start the course, but the formalized structure helps provide a conduit to faculty and administration so their voices are amplified."

Many students also report continuing to seek out ways that they can build partnerships in their lives beyond their undergraduate experience. An alumna currently pursuing medical school shared, "I've adopted a mindset geared toward fruitful collaborations between diverse members of my communities in hopes of enacting change." As she reflected on how intentional partnership will be a key aspect of her approach to practicing equity-minded health care, she said, "Conducting needs assessments and highlighting the voices of those you'd like to assist in situations of inequality is paramount in the field of social justice work." Similarly, another student alumna also noted that being able to contribute to change "has reverberated through many aspects of my life since [HSTEM]. Now, I see and assess how I might be able to take partial ownership over a problem more than I think,

'Someone [else] should do something about this.'" A third individual wrote about how the insights they gained through partnership in HSTEM have helped them navigate their studies at a large, research-intensive medical school. This person said, "I just finished my first year at [medical school]," which is a "large research university where these problems we discussed [in HSTEM] are just pervasive throughout the society. It is a society in which, for my voice to be heard, I have to prove myself to others by first being 'successful' despite these problems (and really ignoring many of these problems), and *then* speak up. I had never felt more vulnerable in my identity as an Asian woman trying to pursue medicine and science. My experience in HSTEM, though, taught me that this is a fault in the system and made me more open to talking about these issues with other students."

In their own reflections, many faculty and staff cofacilitators share how partnering with students generates new insights and avenues for them to understand and advocate for themselves, their students, and their colleagues. One faculty member said this experience "has made me a better listener and more interested in learning about people I meet in a deeper than surface-level way. I think this has impacted the way I interact with everyone but especially for those who are different from me in some way or another." This same individual said that they now have the "confidence and background knowledge to stand up for my students and challenge harmful policies or approaches that my colleagues might be considering." Another faculty member shared that "it can be so easy to get bogged down with classes and research and committees and not carve out the time to interact with those who can really help us in making these changes." A third faculty member also notes how much change is needed and the time that is needed, in partnership with students, to help make those changes happen. They shared, "I have come to appreciate the enormity of the work that needs to be done, and also how wonderfully resourceful our students are. Given the necessary support, I can only imagine how much better they will contribute to make the study and practice of STEM disciplines a much greater success and an engine of both social and scientific change."

Finally, Sheila shared how partnering with students has provided hope that inclusive change in STEM is possible. She wrote, "With the course serving as a perpetual engine for authentic and informed conversation and for designing and piloting interventions, culture shifts toward a STEM community where all feel included and thrive just may truly be possible." We hope that as you reflect on how you already invite students into partnership at your institution, and avenues for additional points of collaboration around change, that you too see ways forward and find reasons to continue to be hopeful about the future of STEM education.

Conclusions

In the wake of the Amherst Uprising, our campus community needed to determine how we should respond. While wanting to be more equitable and to create an inclusive classroom, lab, department, or community is a good first step, it is not easy to even know what being inclusive is, let alone how to operationalize what the development of inclusive educational spaces should entail. Inclusion relies on the contributions of all involved, not simply those holding the most authority and power. What became clear was that partnership with students, with colleagues, and with other individuals on campus held promise for a positive way forward.

This chapter provides a model for engaging in partnership to build emotionally brave communities, expand our ways of knowing, and design collaborative and mutually beneficial campus partnerships. We hope that you are inspired to apply the processes of listening, validating, reflecting, and then partnering to create more equitable teaching and learning spaces at your institutions. In the next section of this book, we turn to a discussion of a range of strategies for building more inclusive classroom and research spaces, all of which have emerged, in partnership with our students, as important to their sense of community and belonging in STEM.

References

Cook-Sather, A. (2006). Sound, presence, and power: "Student voice" in educational research and reform. *Curriculum Inquiry, 36*(4), 359–390. https://doi.org/10.1111/j.1467-873X.2006.00363.x

Cook-Sather, A., Bahti, M., & Ntem, A. (2019). *Pedagogical partnerships: A how-to guide for faculty, students, and academic developers in higher education.* Elon University Center for Engaged Learning.

Cook-Sather, A., Bovill, C., & Felten, P. (2014). *Engaging students as partners in learning and teaching: A guide for faculty.* Jossey-Bass.

Deeley, S. J., & Bovill, C. (2017). Staff student partnership in assessment: Enhancing assessment literacy through democratic practices. *Assessment & Evaluation in Higher Education, 42*(3), 463–477. https://doi.org/10.1080/02602938.2015.1126551

Harding, S. (1992). Rethinking standpoint epistemology: What is "strong objectivity"? *The Centennial Review, 36*(3), 437–470. https://www.jstor.org/stable/23739232

IDEO (Ed.). (2015). *The field guide to human-centered design.* Design Kit.

King, A. (1993). From sage on the stage to guide on the side. *College Teaching, 41*(1), 30–35. https://www.jstor.org/stable/27558571

Longino, H. E. (1990). *Science as social knowledge: Values and objectivity in scientific inquiry.* Princeton University Press.

Meinking, K. A., & Hall, E. E. (2020). Co-creation in the classroom: Challenge, community, and collaboration. *College Teaching, 68*(4), 189–198. https://doi.org/10.1080/87567555.2020.1786349

Mercer-Mapstone, L., & Abbot, S. (Eds.). (2020). *Power of partnership: Students, staff, and faculty revolutionizing higher education.* Elon University Center for Engaged Learning.

Mercer-Mapstone, L., Dvorakova, S. L., Matthews, K. E., Abbot, S., Cheng, B., Felten, P., Knorr, K., Marquis, E., Shammas, R., & Swaim, K. (2017). A systematic literature review of students as partners in higher education. *International Journal for Students as Partners, 1*(1).

Mills, C. W. (1959). *The sociological imagination.* Oxford University Press.

Noel, L. A., & Paiva, M. (2021). Learning to recognize exclusion. *Journal of Usability Studies, 16*(2), 63–72.

Wiggins, G. P., & MacTighe, J. (2006). *Understanding by design* (expanded 2nd ed.). Pearson Prentice Hall International.

Zomorodi, M. (2020, September 4). *Jad Abumrad: How journalism taught me a new way to resolve conflict.* NPR. https://www.npr.org/transcripts/909198327

4
TEACHING WITH AND FOR EMPATHY

An ongoing challenge to building inclusive, welcoming classroom and laboratory spaces with diverse student populations is how to help students learn from each other in productive, open dialogue. This chapter proposes the concept of active empathy as a pathway for students, staff, and faculty to construct positive learning communities, so that the inclusive pedagogies we describe in previous chapters can be successful. Empathy requires active listening to the experience of others and the internalization of both the cognitive and affective experiences of the other person, without critique or evaluation. This empathic stance can be challenging both for members of majority groups, who may not relate to the experience of marginalized individuals or may feel threatened by their own potential contribution to this experience, as well as for members of minoritized groups, who may have difficulty engaging with the experience of the majority group. However, it is only when all perspectives are recognized and acknowledged as meaningful and valid that full community and belonging emerge. Thus, this chapter describes why empathy, coupled with agency and action, strengthens undergraduate classrooms and presents a set of practices for teaching students, staff, and faculty how to increase their own empathic responses.

Guiding Questions
- What is empathy, and why do you think that empathy may provide a helpful pathway forward toward more inclusive classroom and institutional dynamics?
- How might you teach to enhance empathy, and how might you teach from a position of empathy?

Defining Empathy

When we seek to emotionally connect with others in our lives, we often do so through shared experience. We may connect to others through a shared physical activity or interest, similar life experiences, or similar emotional reactions to something happening in our lives. For most people, identifying points of commonality is an automatic strategy for forming interpersonal bonds. Indeed, neurobiology points to the role of mirror neurons, which are neurons in the brain that are activated both when you experience a sensation yourself, and when you witness someone else experiencing that sensation, as evidence for this process as being innate or at least biologically adaptive (e.g., Oberman et al., 2007).

However, an assumption underlying our commonality-seeking interactions and perhaps encoded in our neural pathways is that we are able to accurately assess what emotions another person is feeling. This skill may in fact be more complicated than we recognize. Described as "cognitive empathy," the ability to engage in accurate perspective-taking is dependent upon our own theory-of-mind (ToM) abilities (e.g., Smith, 2016). ToM allows us to recognize our own emotional states and cognitions, the emotional states and knowledge held by others, and whether those affective states are congruent. This skill emerges quite early in neurotypical development and is a critical developmental milestone in children's growth into fully social agents. As adults, ToM continues to be an important building block for rewarding relationships, living in community, and indeed, for teaching and learning (Eisenberg & Strayer, 1987). That being said, our ToM assessments of the emotional states of others are often inaccurate (Apperly, 2012), as we tend to overestimate the overlap between our emotional states and those of others, specifically by assuming that they hold the same values, beliefs, and knowledge structures as ourselves. As we consider the context of our classrooms, these errors of cognitive empathy can serve to further alienate or silence students. Knupsky and Caballero (2020) discuss their approach to enhancing ToM abilities in the classroom, both for instructors and students, and later in this chapter, we will discuss additional strategies that you can employ to enhance your awareness of others' emotional experiences.

The second aspect of an empathic response moves us from identifying the emotional state of another to actually being in emotional congruence with that individual. This second empathic response, "affective empathy," differs from other common forms of emotional support we may offer, such as sympathy, in which we feel sorrow for another person without feeling the same sorrow ourselves. Affective empathy, which is sometimes described as emotional contagion, can motivate empathic concern and prosocial action (e.g., Batson et al., 1997). In other instances, however, very high levels of empathic distress can be demotivating to action, resulting instead in a sense of being emotionally overwhelmed and withdrawn (Klimecki & Singer, 2011). It can be challenging, as caring, engaged people, to strike a healthy balance of affective empathy without emotional overwhelm. As Sara Hodges and Robert Biswas-Diener (2007) describe in their work on empathic strategy management, "The empathic emotions, empathic concern and personal distress, are like other emotions in that they provide a signal that something needs to be attended to. Most emotions are like uninvited guests—sometimes good, often bad and only partially under our control" (p. 392). They go on to describe the kinds of resources that are consumed by empathic responses, such as physiological arousal, material costs, and decreased personal gains, to explain why empathic responses can lead to both meaningful support of others and, at times, emotional exhaustion.

As a person who is committed to improving students' learning and sense of community, you are likely already engaging in many practices that require emotional vulnerability and sacrifice. Adopting an empathic teaching stance requires that we step into new and uncomfortable affective spaces, with a true openness to the cognitive and affective positions of our students. The payoffs of empathy in the classroom, as described in Bryan Dewsbury's (2020) deep teaching model, include being able to develop refined, informed pedagogical approaches that are fine-tuned to the needs and abilities of your students, and improving the classroom climate as well as students' sense of community and belonging. This cycle of deep teaching both depends upon and supports further self-awareness by the instructor, such that they consider "the context of what they bring to the classroom. . . . The social positioning of the instructor is a function of their individual histories, and the ways in which those histories informed their development of a science identity" (p. 175). What Dewsbury's model of deep teaching points to, we believe, is the importance of self-reflection on one's own journey through STEM as laying the groundwork for empathy-driven pedagogy.

In addition to the benefits to the learning environment, teaching students the skills of balancing empathic interaction with self care better prepares them for their roles as team members, collaborators, and eventual managers as they progress in STEM and any career. Offering these activities in the context of STEM classes gives students the opportunity to immediately apply their learning and tools in interactions with lab partners, project members, and discussion groups. In the next section of this chapter, we turn to research on the teaching of empathy, and the challenges and opportunities this literature presents for our work in our STEM teaching and learning spaces.

Lessons on Empathy From the Medical Field

A large body of work indicates that empathy is associated with improved professional performance in a wide range of work contexts. One such context is medicine, a career to which many of our students in STEM aspire. In a medical setting, care providers with higher levels of empathy tend to have more satisfied patients who, in turn, are more likely to adhere to treatment recommendations and experience better clinical outcomes (Burns & Nolen-Hoeksema, 1992; Kim et al., 2004). There are many similarities, we argue, between high-quality medical practitioners and intentional, scholarly educators (see Table 4.1).

Helen Riess, MD, and her colleagues have been working to explore the impact of empathy training on physician practice. In a randomized clinical trial, 99 medical residents and fellows were assigned to receive standard graduate medical education with or without the inclusion of three 60-minute empathy training sessions (Riess et al., 2012). In the empathy training sessions, small cohorts were presented with information about how empathy (and lack thereof) is experienced by their patients, neurobiologically and

TABLE 4.1
Comparing the Roles of Educators and Medical Practitioners

Educators	*Medical Practitioners*
Develop curricula that actively engage and encourage students to take control of their own learning	Develop care plans that allow patients agency over their health care
Work to earn students' trust and build a sense of shared purpose and mutual respect	Work to establish patient trust and sense of shared purpose and respect
Listen closely to students to learn about who they are as whole people, and how those individual experiences contribute to their learning experience in the classroom	Listen closely to their patients to understand their holistic experiences and needs
Recognize how systemic inequalities can result in differential student outcomes	Recognize how systemic inequalities result in differential patient outcomes
Work within a hierarchical institutional system that fosters power differentials between themselves and their students, making bidirectional empathy more challenging (and needed)	Work within a hierarchical medical system that fosters power differentials between themselves and their patients, making bidirectional empathy more challenging (and needed)

physiologically; how to more accurately interpret their patients' emotional expressions; and how to respond with verbal and nonverbal empathic responses while concurrently increasing their own mindfulness. A particularly compelling component of this training involved the monitoring of physiological reactions (e.g., anxiety, hyperarousal, emotional distancing) of both the patient and physician during their interactions, with an emphasis on interactions in which the resident responded with arrogance or was dismissive of the patient. At those points in the interaction, physiological data diverged between patient and care provider, indicating a lack of affective empathy during that time. The data were shared with the physician to raise awareness of how their responses to the patient impacted the empathic dynamic. Residents who received empathy training over 1 to 2 months demonstrated significant improvements in their empathy, as rated by multiple patients who were blind to the condition, relative to those who did not receive the training.

There are many lessons from this work that align with our own work on building empathy with and for students in our classes. First, there is a need to recognize how our behaviors impact the emotional experience of others. Relatedly, we need to build mechanisms into our classes that allow for real-time feedback when we respond to others in ways that are not empathic. Finally, the work of Riess et al. recognizes that while emotional connection may be an inherent aspect to the human experience, we need help learning how to listen to and understand the emotional expressions of others, and we also need to be taught effective strategies to manage our emotions and respond in ways that are productive and compassionate.

Strategies for Teaching Empathy in the STEM Classroom

With all of the activities we share in this book, it is important to come back to the overarching goal of creating a learning community where all can show up as their full selves and feel included. We are, after all, humans pursuing STEM in a community with other humans. In this section, therefore, we present a series of activities and frameworks for building affective empathy in our classrooms and research spaces. We have employed these activities both within the HSTEM course and as a freestanding module in other introductory science courses. At their core, all of the following strategies focus on the first three components of the HSTEM cycle (listening–validating–reflecting). The goal of these exercises is to enhance a sense of connection and foster empathic concern. When we talk with faculty about incorporating empathy-building activities in their classrooms and lab groups, we often hear concerns about whether the process will be emotionally distressing for students, both for those who carry greater levels of stressors or risk in the conversation and those students who may not have developed high-level coping or emotion regulation skills. In response, we note two things.

First, it is critical to focus on the goals of the exercise and to make your goals for these activities transparent to students from the outset. As we note in chapter 6, "Telling Your HSTEM Story," the purpose of sharing our individual experiences in STEM is to both prompt personal reflection and to build a sense of community so that we can jointly work to bring about meaningful change toward a more inclusive climate in our STEM spaces. We encourage students, staff, and faculty to practice self-awareness as they reflect on and share their lived experiences in STEM, moderating their contributions and engagement where needed.

Second, in all of these practices, we encourage you and your students to remain focused on the emotional experience of others without attempting to relate it back to yourself or how you may have felt in similar circumstances. Take, for instance, the work of Dan Batson et al. (1997). In this study, they asked participants to listen to another's story of personal challenge and then to either imagine how that person was feeling during that event or imagine how they themselves would have felt or reacted in a similar circumstance. Results indicated that imagining how another person is feeling is associated with improved empathic concern on behalf of the listener. Trying to imagine how you yourself would or have reacted in a similar circumstance also elicits empathic concern, but also leads to increased levels of emotional distress. Intentionally attending to the experiences and emotions of another, without attempting to make the shared information self-relevant, provides a more productive avenue for empathy to emerge. Following a recent active listening exercise that Sarah facilitated in an introductory STEM course, one student said that they felt "more heard and more seen" during that class exercise than they had felt in friendships that they have had for years, and another student in the course said that learning how to listen would dramatically change how they talk with and listen to others going forward. That is the kind of shift we hope these activities bring to your teaching and to your classrooms.

Here are some additional pedagogical contexts in which foregrounding a course activity with an exercise to activate empathy and active listening skills may be particularly helpful:

- when asking students to serve as an active audience for class presentations
- when preparing to engage students in a potentially challenging or contentious discussion of a journal article

- when preparing students to work collaboratively with others in lab or in team-based learning environments
- when students are working on projects that involve community partnership or multiple stakeholders
- when students are engaging with peer review or instructor formative feedback on a complex work product

Practicing Active Listening Exercise

One of our biology colleagues, Sally Kim, first experienced this practice in a workshop on science communication. In partnership, Sarah and Sally have adapted this activity to the undergraduate classroom context, and it is now consistently employed in an introductory biology course at Amherst. Here's how it works:

Step 1

Place all class participants in pairs; these pairs will take turns serving as the speaker and the listener. The speaker is asked to respond, over 2 to 3 minutes, to the following prompt: "Tell me about a time that was challenging or frustrating for you [in STEM or in a broader setting]. How did you overcome that challenge, and what people, structures, or communities helped you overcome that challenge?" The listener is instructed to do just that—listen. They may not ask follow-up questions, expand upon the content that is shared with information about a similar life event, or comment on the perceived severity of the event. Instead, after the speaker has shared their experience, the listener may thank the speaker for sharing their experience, and then the roles reverse.

Step 2

Once both partners have shared their stories, bring the pairs into larger groups of four or six, depending upon class size. In this second setting, each listener will report on what they heard. However, instead of reporting on the content of the event that the speaker shared, they report on what they heard the individual speaker express that they most care about and value. This conversation continues until all participants in the larger group have a chance to share out.

Step 3

Following the larger group discussion, you can bring the whole class together to debrief that experience. What was the experience of active listening like for you? What was it like to be listened to in that way? How did this experience differ from other conversations that you typically have?

When Have You Felt Included? Exercise

In this exercise, participants coconstruct an understanding of inclusion using a welcoming, gallery walk structure. This exercise originated as part of an HSTEM Salon program collaboratively designed by the students of the spring 2019 HSTEM class. Students identified the goals of the gallery walk as twofold: to invite attendees to feel included in the event, and to support interactive and low-stakes learning about how members across different corners of our community experience inclusion and belonging. Since then, we have found that this exercise is a useful pedagogical tool to help students truly listen to and engage with the perspectives and values of others, a key aspect of an empathic response. It can be implemented at the start of the semester, to kick off the formulation of community norms, or as a framing activity prior to a particular class discussion. It works regardless of class size and requires only a physical space for displaying students' initial responses and the resulting group's visual products.

In the first part of the activity, provide all participants with a small set of sticky notes, writing utensils, and instructions to respond to the following prompt: "When have you felt included in an academic setting?" As the notes are completed, individuals randomly distribute their sticky notes (without putting their names on them) along a wall or other flat surface, and are encouraged to review the collective responses. This way, the experiences of everyone in the group are made visible, and participants are primed to engage with greater curiosity and empathy. In the second part of the activity, ask each person to take a note from the wall that was not their own contribution. Once everyone has collected a note, randomly put individuals into small groups (four to six participants per group works well). The group discusses the content on their collective sticky notes from the lens of the question, "What does inclusivity look like?" Each group will identify one person to serve as the visual notetaker or artist for the group, and this designated member of each group creates a visual representation of their group's shared insights and definition of *inclusion*. This visual representation can take many forms, including drawings, poems, or mind-maps, and all group members have the opportunity to augment the original draft. Finally, when the groups have finished, all participants are invited to conduct a gallery walk to visit each group's representation of inclusivity.

Meta-Reflections Exercise

When students complete reading reflections as preparatory work for their classes, the emphasis is rightly on their own perspectives, connections, and interpretations. They are asked to respond to various prompts: What resonates with you about the reading? How do you see the arguments being made by this author as connecting to other readings in the course? Which of the experiences described by the author are most consistent with your own experience? How do they differ? These individually focused reflective prompts play a critical role in helping students engage deeply with course materials, in refining their self-awareness, as well as ensuring that they arrive in class prepared to contribute meaningfully to the discussion. And yet, as we seek to build empathy and active listening skills, we want to encourage students to think about how their reflections and perspectives on the course materials may differ in important ways from their peers. The exercise we describe here, called "Meta-Reflections," is similar to the "When Have You Felt Included?" activity in that it also helps students to respond in a curious and open manner to the perspectives of others.

Megan originally developed the Meta-Reflections activity after several years of supporting HSTEM students in the development of their action project proposals. She realized that the students needed more scaffolding to make connections across the academic concepts they had learned, the varied perspectives of their peers, and their assessment of needs on campus. In the Meta-Reflections process, students individually review all of the class reflections for a given module. Groups of students then come together with others to discuss and summarize collective themes for their shared assigned module, which they then present to the class. In this way, the Meta-Reflections exercise provides an intentional cycle in which the collective experiences and perspectives of the class can inform the individual's learning, and vice versa.

Steps for This Activity
As students engage with course materials, ask them to write brief individual reflections about each source to help guide and focus the class discussions (See "Suggested Prompts for Students' Written Reflections on Readings" in chapter 2.). Importantly, these reflections should be shared with the instructor. After you have progressed through the readings related to a unit in the course or across several course units, create compilation documents of all of the students' reflections for each reading. You may choose to anonymize the contributions or include student-specific information; we encourage you to ask your students how they would like their self-authored reflections to be presented.

Assign small groups of two to three students to review the reflections for a single topic and identify three themes that they see as collectively emerging from their peers' contributions, both themes that resonate across reflections and those that are in tension with each other or the material.

Next, combine the small groups into larger groupings organized around complementary readings within a unit. For instance, in the HSTEM course, individuals who thematically read reflections on the nature of objectivity and standpoint feminism and those who read their peers' reflections related to the literature on Indigenous ways of knowing are merged into a larger group; this larger group explores commonalities across the emergent themes. Finally, bring the class together so that the larger groups can each report on their observations. What do they notice about the larger emergent themes? Are there new tensions or questions that emerge when we put our reflections into conversation with each other in this way? This assignment expands individually focused course reflection activities into the realm of empathy building by explicitly scaffolding students in their skills of identifying points of commonality and difference, by communicating the value of engaging with multiple perspectives, and by asking them to notice, rather than critique or evaluate, the patterns that emerge.

The Limits of Empathy

Many individuals have critiqued empathy, saying that the empathy is not a magic ingredient, and they are correct (Bloom, 2016; Waytz & Epley, 2012). For instance, Paul Bloom (2016) argues that "empathy is a spotlight focusing on certain people in the here and now. This makes us care more about them, but it leaves us insensitive to the long-term consequences of our acts and blind as well to the suffering of those we do not or cannot empathize with" (p. 9). Similarly, research by Waytz and Epley (2012) demonstrates the potential for selective empathy, such that we are more likely to empathize with people to whom connection is already established or more easily developed. Successful engagement with empathic reflection requires that we work to build bridges across these differences and do the hard work of engaging in perspective-taking that does not come easily or readily, but must rather be intentionally scaffolded and pursued. Finally, empathy is not the magic ingredient to functional relationships across differences, but rather one tool of many that we can refine and bring into conversation with other methods that seek to create more inclusive and collaborative learning and teaching spaces.

In our approach to HSTEM, we seek to develop what Lori Gruen (2015) describes as "entangled empathy," through an emphasis on relationships and partnerships within our STEM communities. In her book, Gruen points out that "we are not just in relationships as selves with others, but our very selves are constituted by these relations" (p. 64). She argues that it is through an emphasis on the entangled nature of all of our relationships and communities that we might partner and enact change in positive ways. Gruen writes,

> What if . . . we invited people to reflect on their own position within the tangle of relationships among people? Might they be better able to perceive that they are advantaged in some ways while simultaneously disadvantaged in others? Might they feel more moved to try to mitigate any injuries from which they have, however unwittingly, benefited? May they be better able to see how to do that? (p. 101)

Conclusions

Teaching with and for empathy in our STEM classrooms and laboratories requires a slowing down of our standard operating procedures, an appreciation that relationships with students are equally central to their learning as how we engage them through course content, and a willingness to actively listen to understand, even when it makes us uncomfortable. Again and again, we are struck by participants' responses to these active listening activities, which indicate that in the majority of our interactions with others, we are listening not with an intention to truly hear what the other is thinking and feeling, but rather we are listening for the opportunity to shift the conversation to our own self-relevance. When we do set an explicit intention to listen, without the expectation of response, the outcomes are more than worth it. We open avenues for more student-centered pedagogy, for more self-reflective learning and teaching, and for the opportunity to meaningfully and actively partner across our communities to improve the experience of all humans in our STEM learning and teaching spaces.

A final point about empathy that we wish to add here: Much has been written recently, by Loretta Ross and others, about the "calling out" culture and how we might better "call in" or invite individuals into equity-focused conversations (Bennett, 2020; Clark, 2020; Ross, 2019). By adopting a stance of empathy, we hope to create a more invitational, "call in" space in the academy, one in which we can acknowledge that we are all learning, in partnership with our students, from both our successes and our errors. We want to invite people into the work of creating a more inclusive STEM education, regardless of how new they are to these frameworks and the DEI discourse community. Our overarching goal is to expand the number of people who feel responsibility and engagement with the work within an institution; keeping this goal in mind allows us to adopt an empathic, inclusionary stance rather than one that serves a more gatekeeping function.

And this framework also allows us, as change leaders at our institutions, to remain open to seeing how people can contribute their own strengths to shaping and transforming teaching and learning STEM environments. In the next chapter, we describe a range of practices that HSTEM students have identified as helpful to fostering a sense of community and belonging in classrooms and labs. And in chapter 6, we turn to a signature practice in HSTEM, the "Being Human in STEM Story," which seeks to provide a mechanism for personal and collective reflection about our journeys in STEM, as students, staff, and faculty.

References

Apperly, I. A. (2012). What is "theory of mind"? Concepts, cognitive processes and individual differences. *Quarterly Journal of Experimental Psychology, 65*(5), 825–839. https://doi.org/10.1080/17470218.2012.676055

Batson, C. D., Early, S., & Salvarani, G. (1997). Perspective taking: Imagining how another feels versus imaging how you would feel. *Personality and Social Psychology Bulletin, 23*(7), 751–758. https://doi.org/10.1177/0146167297237008

Bennett, J. (2020, November 19). What if instead of calling people out, we called them in? *The New York Times.* https://www.nytimes.com/2020/11/19/style/loretta-ross-smith-college-cancel-culture.html

Bloom, P. (2016). *Against empathy: The case for rational compassion.* Ecco.

Burns, D. D., & Nolen-Hoeksema, S. (1992). Therapeutic empathy and recovery from depression in cognitive-behavioral therapy: A structural equation model. *Journal of Consulting and Clinical Psychology, 60*(3), 441–449. https://doi.org/10.1037/0022-006X.60.3.441

Clark, M. (2020). DRAG THEM: A brief etymology of so-called "cancel culture." *Communication and the Public, 5*(3–4), 88–92. https://doi.org/10.1177/2057047320961562

Dewsbury, B. M. (2020). Deep teaching in a college STEM classroom. *Cultural Studies of Science Education, 15*(1), 169–191. https://doi.org/10.1007/s11422-018-9891-z

Eisenberg, N., & Strayer, J. (Eds.). (1987). *Empathy and its development.* Cambridge University Press.

Gruen, L. (2015). *Entangled empathy: An alternative ethic for our relationships with animals.* Lantern Books.

Hodges, S. D., & Biswas-Diener, R. (2007). Balancing the empathy expense account: Strategies for regulating empathic response. In T. F. D. Farrow & P. W. R. Woodruff (Eds.), *Empathy in mental illness* (pp. 389–407). Cambridge University Press.

Kim, S. S., Kaplowitz, S., & Johnston, M. V. (2004). The effects of physician empathy on patient satisfaction and compliance. *Evaluation & the Health Professions, 27*(3), 237–251. https://doi.org/10.1177/0163278704267037

Klimecki, O., & Singer, T. (2011). Empathic distress fatigue rather than compassion fatigue? Integrating findings from empathy research in psychology and social neuroscience. In B. Oakley, A. Knafo, G. Madhavan, & D. S. Wilson (Eds.), *Pathological altruism* (pp. 368–383). Oxford University Press.

Knupsky, A., & Caballero, M. S. (2020). Do we know what they are thinking? Theory of mind and affect in the classroom. *Teaching & Learning Inquiry*, 8(1), 108–121. https://doi.org/10.20343/teachlearninqu.8.1.8

Oberman, L. M., Pineda, J. A., & Ramachandran, V. S. (2007). The human mirror neuron system: A link between action observation and social skills. *Social Cognitive and Affective Neuroscience*, 2(1), 62–66. https://doi.org/10.1093/scan/nsl022

Riess, H., Kelley, J. M., Bailey, R. W., Dunn, E. J., & Phillips, M. (2012). Empathy training for resident physicians: A randomized controlled trial of a neuroscience-informed curriculum. *Journal of General Internal Medicine*, 27(10), 1280–1286. https://doi.org/10.1007/s11606-012-2063-z

Ross, L. (2019, August 17). I'm a Black feminist. I think call-out culture is toxic. *The New York Times*.

Smith, E. J. (2016). Doing science while Black. *Science*, 353(6307), 1586–1586. https://doi.org/10.1126/science.353.6307.1586

Waytz, A., & Epley, N. (2012). Social connection enables dehumanization. *Journal of Experimental Social Psychology*, 48(1), 70–76. https://doi.org/10.1016/j.jesp.2011.07.012

5

PRACTICES FOR BUILDING COMMUNITY IN STEM CLASSROOMS AND LABS

This chapter describes a number of pedagogical practices that STEM practitioners have developed and adapted to increase inclusion and belonging for students across the curriculum. There are many more activities than can be featured here, and so we are highlighting the specific practices that our HSTEM students have identified as particularly key to their experience in their classrooms and labs: practices that foster a sense of community, practices that promote engagement and reflection, and practices that support productive and positive dynamics in group work. As you review this chapter, we encourage you to consider how the incorporation of each of these activities may align with your own goals for teaching, learning, and community.

We have also divided these practices into three categories, based on the pedagogical contexts in which you might commonly incorporate them. First-day class activities are designed to create a sense of welcome and set a positive tone in the class; these practices include introducing yourself to your students, name-learning practices, setting class expectations and community norms, and partnering with students to jointly define success in the course. Ongoing classroom activities are intended to sustain and deepen a sense of community, connect students' learning to their lived experiences and values, and enable students to set intentions and expectations for themselves and their colleagues. These ongoing practices include 1-minute papers and utility writing exercises, exam wrappers and other metacognitive activities, and midsemester formative feedback processes. Finally, lab-based practices emphasize the collaborative nature of science and develop transferable interpersonal skills, using activities that diversify partner groupings, build community through the sharing of extracurricular identities, and scaffold metacognitive reflection on group processes.

Guiding Questions

- Which inclusive practices cultivate an environment that models and practices shared responsibility for a learning community in ways that align with your values of equity and inclusion?
- Which inclusive practices support students in ways that you wish them to see themselves and diverse others as capable of succeeding in STEM?
- Which inclusive practices embody an individual practice of being human in STEM that models the centrality of inclusion and equity to your mission as an educator and scholar?

Throughout this chapter, we describe practical recommendations for implementing these activities into your teaching, and in the last section of this chapter, we share data we have collected that demonstrate the impact of certain practices on students' sense of belonging and motivation to succeed in STEM. From the early days of HSTEM, making evidence-based inclusive pedagogy more readily available to faculty and staff and, thus, more likely to be integrated into daily teaching and research practices across STEM, has been of central importance. The founding HSTEM students quickly realized two critical disconnects in STEM that were operating in their educational environment. First, students' experiences of alienation and exclusion in STEM stood in stark contrast to faculty and staff members' desires to help students learn and thrive to their highest potential. Instructor intention and student experience were clearly misaligned. Second, students recognized that many STEM faculty had not received training or focused support related to developing their pedagogy and inclusive practices. Indeed, at this point in the college's history, the Center for Teaching and Learning did not exist. Although STEM culture demands that faculty approach their research with a willingness to explore the literature and learn from others' expertise, applying that same approach to one's teaching is not always obvious. In some cases, attending to one's pedagogy is viewed as an ineffective use of one's time, a distraction from one's research. Thus, this second disconnect that students observed was faculty's desire to bolster student learning in the absence of pedagogical guidance that would inform and support those efforts.

The HSTEM founders recognized a potential mechanism for bridging these disconnects, by compiling a set of practices that these instructors could readily incorporate into their teaching and collaborative research with students. What resulted is the HSTEM (2017) curricular practices handbook.

This digital resource, which has continued to be refined and expanded by students, staff, and faculty over time, is provided to incoming STEM faculty and serves as a shared source for faculty looking to expand their inclusive teaching tool kit. Importantly, beyond lowering the barrier to pedagogical improvement and enhanced community in STEM teaching and learning spaces, the handbook clearly articulates that students, staff, and faculty share responsibility for shaping a STEM community where all can learn and thrive. Its public nature seeks to disrupt the traditional STEM experience of research scholarship being publicly shared while pedagogy is privately experienced (Shulman, 1993), and it anchors our community commitment to the goal of inclusion. Megan reflects:

> The evolution of the inclusive practices handbook is a great example of what's possible with HSTEM—the project started with students collecting stories from their peers about what makes them feel welcome in STEM spaces, and then . . . connect[ed] those stories with research on inclusive teaching practices. A small group of faculty and staff then built on that foundation, using their unique perspective as facilitators of learning to create guidelines for introducing these practices into classrooms and labs. The handbook was then shared with the community, with the understanding that it could be adapted and updated as we gained insight from its use. In keeping with the key elements of HSTEM, the project started with the students—both their lived experience and their idea for a possible solution.

This chapter picks up on and expands on what the founding HSTEM students began through the handbook project.

Facilitator Guides

To support you in integrating these activities into your STEM classrooms and labs, we provide detailed facilitator guides, available for download via hyperlinks and QR codes in the appendices, for each of the practices described in the following. While many of these practices are described on the Being Human in STEM website (beinghumaninstem.com), this chapter and the related facilitator guides expand on those resources to help you refine these practices so that they are explicitly aligned with your own approach to inclusive teaching. To support your reflection and implementation of these practices, each facilitator guide contains a triad of metacognitive scaffolding prompts related to principles of transparency, connection, and modeling.

To maximize the effectiveness of each of these inclusive practices in our classrooms and research spaces, we need to help students understand

- why this activity is beneficial to their learning and/or experience in the class (transparency)
- how the activity intersects with our teaching goals and with their own learning goals (connection)
- how they can comfortably and successfully engage with the activity (modeling)

In terms of transparency, each facilitator guide contains sample framing language that you can draw on in your conversation with students about the benefits of the activity and scholarly evidence regarding its impact on student learning. Sharing this information with students before you engage with a practice helps to establish the context and credibility of the activity as being grounded in the science of learning (e.g., Schinske et al., 2016). The prompts related to connection encourage you to consider how you will communicate to students about the value of the skills being enhanced by each of these practices and how those skills connect to who they are striving to become, as they hone their expertise as scientists, collaborators, and professionals. You may also wish to highlight how the skills being developed through a specific practice are beneficial to your own work and the work you do in collaboration with others. Finally, an important approach for increasing students' willingness to engage in these practices involves lowering the threshold to participation through modeling. Each facilitator guide identifies a range of possibilities for demonstrating the activity and/or demonstrating the variety of ways that students may choose to participate, or not, in the process.

A Note About Flexibility

Our own thinking has evolved about the relative value of making inclusive pedagogical practices easy and accessible, like recipes to be followed, compared to providing guiding principles that help instructors consider how to tailor an activity to best align with their teaching goals and the goals of their students. Providing a curated buffet of "plug and play" inclusive practices alongside step-by-step guides lowers the barrier for faculty who lack experience and confidence to experiment with inclusive practices. On the other hand, we do not wish to reinforce the attitude that it is possible to become an inclusive pedagogue by merely adding a few activities into one's teaching without engaging in sustained and intentional reflection about one's teaching goals and values. Absent such reflective practice, how can a faculty member develop their own guiding principles and intuition for making complex decisions about how they will center equity and inclusion to support the learning of their students? And if we, as instructors, are not able to articulate why we are allocating time and energy to community building, active listening, and other equity-minded practices in our classrooms and laboratory spaces, our students will be less likely to invest in, and thus benefit from, our efforts.

Therefore, our approach attempts to strike a balance between these two options. In our description of the implementation of each activity, we provide prompts for you to reflect on why you might elect to incorporate a specific practice and multiple ways that you might introduce and demonstrate your own value, or connection, for the skill that is being supported by this practice. Additionally, the far-right column of each downloadable facilitator guide provides space for "Your Plan." We encourage you to jot down notes about how you will adapt these ideas to best align with who you are as a teacher and human in the classroom, as well as your goals for student learning and inclusion. We hope that the prompts serve as a spark, rather than a prescription, as you consider how you will personalize each practice for you and your students. And finally, we encourage you to include student feedback in your evaluative process of the impact of these practices on learning and the classroom experience. You hold deep knowledge about your teaching context; coupled with students' perceptions of their own learning and affective experiences in the classroom, you will be better able to hone your approach to inclusive course design.

First-Day Class Activities: Building Community in STEM Pedagogical Spaces

The first days of the semester present us with an incredible opportunity to set the tone for how we wish to teach and learn together as a class, and how we hope to support students in feeling like welcomed and important members of our class community. We can take this time to begin to work on establishing the kinds of relationships and values that our class will strive to uphold. While some of our students may already enter educational spaces with a sense of agency and belonging, for others these self-conceptions may be more fragile. The pushing out of many students from STEM can occur regardless of whether departments intend their courses to serve a gatekeeping function or not (Montgomery, 2020), especially for marginalized or underrepresented students. While we cannot eradicate students' experiences of imposter syndrome and stereotype threat in the other educational spaces they navigate (e.g., Good et al., 2012; Jones et al., 2013; Steele, 2011), we can seek to foreground community and inclusion in our own courses and laboratories. In the following section are several strategies we recommend for establishing those dynamics in your classroom in the early days of the semester.

Humanize the Professor

The psychological distance between students and yourself, the all-knowing expert scientist, can feel vast, particularly for students who do not have a history of positive, close relationships with STEM instructors. How can you convey that you welcome and recognize that your students are complex, full people and also share some aspects of yourself with students? Either in the preclass materials that you distribute prior to the start of class or in the first class meeting, we recommend the Humanize the Professor exercise, which incorporates many of the same student-focused prompts we describe in the Being Human in STEM Story activity in chapter 6. In this case, however, you as the instructor are singularly sharing your own path through STEM with your students. You might choose to address some or all of the following in your narrative: What or who sparked your initial interest in STEM? What challenges have you experienced along your journey to becoming a scientist, and how have you worked to overcome these challenges? What do you love about the research process or your research focus? What mistakes or unanticipated events served as prompts for you to recalibrate or adjust your STEM journey? What events have brought you to this current moment in your STEM path? The facilitator guide is available for download in Appendix B.

As an example, here is Sheila's visual narrative of her pathway through STEM, which she shares with her students on the first day of class (following the images in Figure 5.1 in a semicircle from top left to top right):

> My father is from Bham, Punjab, located in northern India. He was the first from his village to go to the United States. My Caucasian mom is from Nebraska, and I was raised in Nebraska, alongside my three brothers, by my academic parents and frequently cared for by a beloved babysitter who also happened to be a female physicist. I went to Mills College and majored in biochemistry and German and rowed crew. I then pursued doctoral work at UC-San Francisco, where I fell in love with the question that still fascinates me: How does the amino acid sequence of a protein encode not only folding to the functional active structure, but

also its stability and dynamics? An important turning point for me as a scientist was when I failed my oral qualifying exam. I had not felt prepared to discuss the underlying thermodynamics of my protein folding experiments, and indeed, a line of questioning from committee member Ken Dill, a member of the National Academy of Sciences, confirmed my weakness. This was my worst nightmare: "Failing." And yet, this experience also confirmed that I needed to trust myself. I had known I wasn't ready, and that I had more to learn. I signed up for Ken's class using statistical mechanics to understand thermodynamics that next semester, and I attended every office hour he offered. Ken challenged me to grow in an area of weakness and I am so proud that the first paper I published when I started my own lab at Amherst College resulted from a collaboration with Ken. At Amherst I love mentoring students in my lab and teaching students, but it all comes back to family, the core of my life, my wife and my children.

Why This Works
The Humanize the Professor activity highlights the multiple dimensions and passions of an individual instructor, which may span teaching, research, and nonacademic domains. In the discussion of your STEM journey, you may offer points of identification and accessibility for students to more readily see themselves as scientists. We have found that students particularly benefit from hearing that their instructor's path in STEM, and in life more broadly, has been nonlinear. Our journeys include mistakes that have stung but enabled learning, and unplanned detours that facilitated other aspects of ourselves and our goals to emerge. Many students report surprise and relief to learn that their professors have also experienced points of struggle, as it allows them to normalize challenge and frustration as necessary and common features of learning, rather than markers of not belonging.

The Airplane Game

HSTEM instructors use a number of strategies to get to know their students' names, interests, and goals for their learning in class. One such approach is the Airplane Game, a commonly used icebreaker activity (see Appendix C to download the facilitator guide overviewing our approach to this practice, and see Alsagoff, 2015, for another version of this activity). In our adaptation of this activity, we first ask individuals to write their name on a blank piece of paper as well as three questions they would like to ask of another student in the class in order to get to know them better. We then talk through folding our papers up into airplanes together. A 2-minute timer is

Figure 5.1. Brief history of a human in STEM.

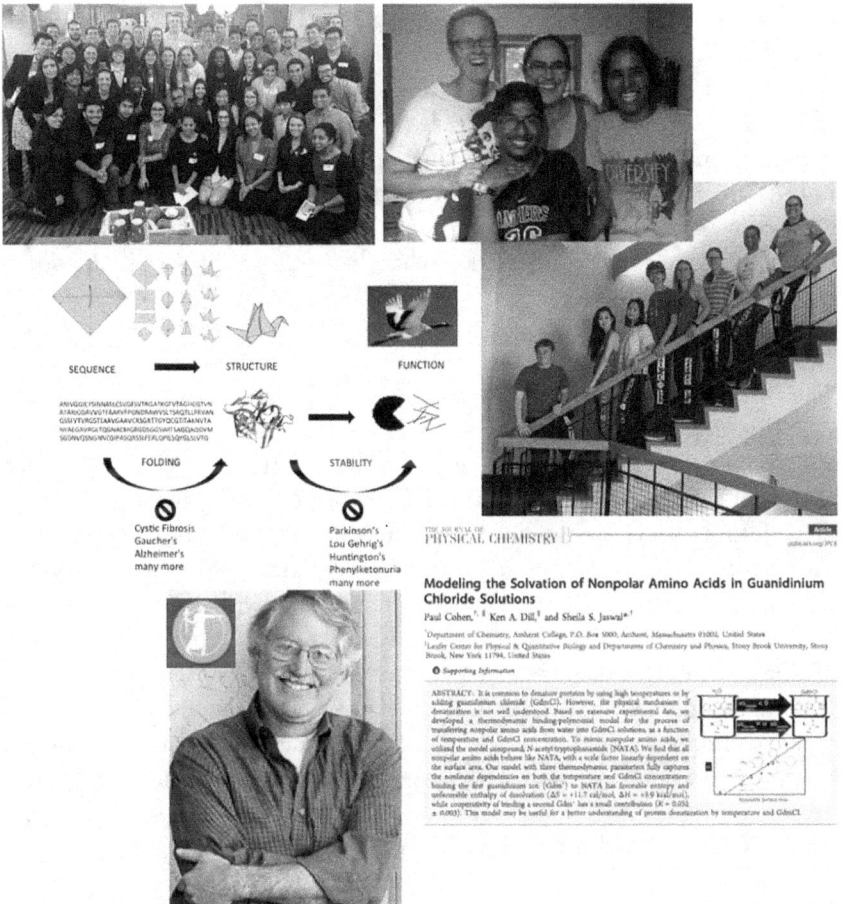

Note. © Sheila Jaswal, 2019.

set, and students are challenged to fly as many airplanes as possible. At the end of that time, each student picks up the airplane that has landed closest to them, locates the original owner of the airplane, and answers two of the three questions on the airplane. Each student meets and has two rounds of conversation with other students: one with the owner of the airplane they found and another with the finder of the airplane they authored. Once all of these conversations have been completed, each student introduces the finder of their airplane to the class, sharing what they learned about that individual from the activity.

Why This Works
The Airplane Game provides an explicit, early framework for students that who they are as people is important and valued in our classrooms. Folding an airplane is a low-stakes activity that some students have experience with and others do not, but no one is expected to be an expert in airplane folding. In fact, this allows the instructors to model not being experts themselves. The physical and often raucous nature of the task prompts all students to move around the room to interact with each other, which we have found disrupts what can otherwise be a somewhat awkward early dynamic, one in which students limit their interactions to people with whom they already have established relationships. Finally, allowing students to choose a subset of the peer-generated questions to answer provides them with an opportunity to select what, and how much, they share about themselves, so as not to feel overly vulnerable or uncomfortable in these early days of interactions.

This I Believe

As important as it is to build initial connections and community among the students in your class, it can be equally important for you to provide avenues for students to share information about their background, their concerns, and their hopes for the course with you. Incorporating student sharing via written submissions to the instructor signals to students that what they are bringing as individuals to the pedagogical space is valuable. One such practice employed by Bryan Dewsbury, one of our HSTEM partners, is a "This I Believe" essay assignment, adapted from National Public Radio's *This I Believe* essay series. Many of our HSTEM facilitators have adapted this approach to their courses; you can download the facilitator guide in Appendix D. In this activity, you invite students to complete a brief preclass essay, describing a core value that they hold and how that value relates to their interpersonal connections, their learning, and their daily lives. Reading each of these essays before the start of the semester provides the instructor(s) with a deeper sense of the students in the class and their goals and values.

Other lower effort approaches for getting to know your students include having students complete a preclass survey that prompts them to share goals and values, or allocating time during the first day of class for students to answer similar prompts by writing on an index card that gets turned in. Regardless of the specifics of your approach, we encourage you to take a few minutes to reflect back to students the common concerns, goals, and values that emerged from their reflections, in order to develop a sense of shared class identity and help to normalize common anxieties students may bring to the classroom.

Why This Works

As Bryan notes in a recent *Teaching in Higher Education* podcast (Stachowiak, 2018), engaging with students' experiences and identities through this assignment allows him to consider how to best build community and adapt his pedagogies to support the individual learners in his class. He states, "It's never the same class. When we're talking about teaching for liberation and teaching for inclusiveness, you are incorporating new voices, the actual voices of the students in how you design the curriculum." This practice allows the instructor to both get to know their students and flexibly shift their teaching approaches. Even when responses are submitted anonymously, this gives the instructor a better sense of the values and experiences that exist in the class community. Further, research shows that metacognitive benefits accrue to students when they take time for such reflection to explicitly connect their values to the class (Efklides, 2011; Harackiewicz et al., 2014; Trujillo & Tanner, 2014; Zimmerman, 2011). Throughout the semester, you can then continue to reflect with your students about how they are enacting their self-identified goals and values and celebrate with them as they progress toward those aspirations.

Discussing Class Expectations

When students first receive our syllabi, it is common for them to quickly flip to the information about deadlines, the format and number of assessments in the course, textbook requirements, and the grading scheme. While these structural aspects of the course design are important, we encourage you to help students engage with the syllabus with a focus on how the course has been designed to help them be successful. You have spent many months (or many years!) thinking about the design of this course, the points where students will likely get stuck and need more support, and the learning goals you have for your students. The Discussing Class Expectations activity (download the full facilitator guide in Appendix E) can help you to share that thinking and your intentions with your students. On the first day of class, you can use this time to be transparent with your students about the *why* of the course structure, requirements, and expectations. In addition to getting to know your students, and allowing them to get to know you, the first day of class also provides an important opportunity for you to convey your goal that in your classroom, all students should feel included and supportive. As the instructor, you set the tone for what happens in the classroom and you want to make transparent the intentions behind your course design.

Why This Works
When students engage in pedagogical partnership with instructors around the design of a course, they often report a newfound awareness of the complexities and complex decision-making that goes into course development (Cook-Sather et al., 2014). They articulate a sense of how "seeing behind the curtain" of course design provides them with a new appreciation for the intellectual work of teaching. Although we encourage many of you to consider student partnerships in your courses, you can extend some of the benefits of this awareness to all students by being transparent with them about your pedagogical priorities and decision-making processes (Fisher et al., 2016; Harrison et al., 2019; Mulnix, 2018).

Designing Success and How to Achieve It

In conjunction with the discussion of your learning and community-based goals for the course, consider incorporating the Designing Success and How to Achieve It activity. This activity prompts students to set intentions and goals for their own learning, recognizing that not all students will want or need the same things from this learning experience. This practice encourages students to consider these questions: At the end of the semester, what would make you feel that you have been successful, and what strategies will you employ to meet those goals? The introductory framing of this activity serves to emphasize students' agency in determining, and then working toward, their own goals for learning in your course (Elliot et al., 1999; Hofer et al., 1998). Throughout the activity, students work to identify and refine their goals as well as the measures by which they will determine that they have met these goals. As you can see in the facilitator guide for this activity (available for download in Appendix F), we recommend multiple points of iteration and refinement, as thinking about one's own goals for learning, rather than merely striving to meet the preordained learning goals that have been set by the instructor, is a new process for many students. At the end of this activity, we encourage you to gather and review the goals that each student has set for themselves, and to bring these goals into conversations with students throughout the semester. Check to see if the goals that they set for themselves are still those that are important to them, if they feel they are making adequate progress toward those goals, and what additional support they need to accomplish these goals by the end of the term.

Why This Works
The Designing Success and How to Achieve It activity asks students to identify their own goals for their learning and their strategies for achieving those goals; this sets an early tone for your classroom as a space that cares about students' values and agency in their learning. It also allows you to gain new insights into who your students are and their motivations for learning in your classroom. Finally, by talking with peers about their goals, students develop an increased awareness and appreciation for the wide range of learners and individuals in the space. One point to note for this practice: Reading through students' reflections about their goals for their learning, and then building in structures throughout the semester for returning to these goals, can be time-intensive, depending upon how many students are enrolled in your class. An approach that many faculty have adopted asks students to review their day 1 goals at two points later in the semester (midsemester and end of semester) before writing a self-assessment of how well they have met their goals and what they may need to modify in their learning practices in order to meet those goals for themselves going forward. In this way, students benefit from the reflective exercise in a manner that is less time-intensive for the instructor.

Community Agreements

It is encouraging to see an increasing number of instructors including practices that allow for the class coconstruction of a Community Agreements activity (see Boyes-Watson & Pranis, 2020, for a range of community agreement strategies). This activity asks all members of the class to identify the interpersonal conditions that will allow them to engage with the course, collaborate with colleagues, and feel a sense of community in the learning space. Once a set of coconstructed agreements have been created (download the facilitator guide from Appendix G), everyone is asked to endorse them as the guiding principles for the class community. STEM course structures can include a number of scenarios in which community agreements can be helpful. For students who tend to dominate discussions or team-based work, being explicit about your community agreements can draw attention to the benefits of creating space for others' contributions. For students who feel less welcome into STEM spaces, a discussion of community agreements can help to identify the conditions that will contribute to a more inclusive space for them. And for instructors, the establishment of community agreements can provide you with a tool to draw on if classroom dynamics become challenging. You can remind the class of the community agreements that they all endorsed and facilitate a conversation about how they can better work to meet these shared goals for your community. You might also encourage students to think about the concrete behaviors and actions that support the agreements they have generated.

Some of the community agreements developed by students in recent HSTEM classes include the following:

- practice self-care
- trust the intent of others
- be patient with yourself and others
- be aware of the space you are taking
- listen actively
- disagree with love
- be accountable to each other
- bring and offer questions respectfully
- acknowledge and honor differences
- be okay with feeling vulnerable and taking risks
- be kind to yourself and others
- enjoy everyone's company

Why This Works
The Community Agreements activity highlights the interpersonal nature of learning in the classroom. The structure of the activity provides students with the opportunity to both reflect on their own responsibility to others in the classroom and their expectations for others toward them as a fellow learner and colleague. In addition, establishing a set of community agreements in your classroom allows you to more adeptly navigate interpersonal challenges as they arise throughout the semester. As the instructor, acknowledging that challenging dynamics are part and parcel of learning while emphasizing the importance of drawing on the community constructed norms in addressing challenges reminds students of their responsibilities to each other and themselves.

Circling back to the agreements at predetermined times in the semester allows students to have the agency to ask questions: What are we doing well? Where are we falling short of our intentions, and what can we do to support each other more fully and intentionally going forward? When conflict arises, anyone—instructor or student—can ask that the group revisit the agreements, and students can take the lead in asking questions of themselves and each other that help move the conversation forward. Making it clear that the community agreements are the guide reminds everyone that you as instructor are not solely responsible for ensuring the nature of class dynamics. Rather, everyone has participated in and agreed to be responsible for upholding the learning community.

Ongoing Classroom Practices for Maintaining Engagement and Enhancing Learning in STEM

While the first-day activities seek to build community, foster connection between faculty and students and students to each other, and engage students in early goal-setting practices, it's important to continue incorporating practices that promote metacognition and help students connect their human lives to the course material throughout the semester (McGuire & McGuire, 2015; Zimmerman, 2011). Many of our students arrive in our classrooms already fairly well versed in strategies that allow them to check their understanding, identify misconceptions, and connect their in-class learning to their lived experience. Other students, however, have not received instruction in these practices and are at a distinct disadvantage in our courses, which presuppose that students know how to monitor their own learning. Additionally, even when students have received guidance about how to reflect on and improve their learning in a particular course, they may experience challenges in translating these practices into an unfamiliar learning context. What we are aiming for is what Saundra McGuire (2021) describes as "metacognitive equity," such that all students in our classes have the metacognitive tool kit and mindsets to be successful (p. 70). In other words, a critical component of creating an inclusive classroom is to help students help themselves thrive by guiding them in how to use their own learning experience as data that can and should inform how they tune their habits of in-class engagement and out-of-class studying. In this way, we are hoping that students are applying the scientific scholarly method to their own efficacy as a student: inquiring about, gathering evidence upon, reflecting, and then modifying their approaches to learning. In this section, therefore, we highlight some commonly employed practices for building students' metacognitive skills and discuss how and why feedback can improve student learning and inclusion in undergraduate STEM courses.

Minute Paper

One simple practice to help students monitor their learning is the Minute Paper activity (Angelo & Cross, 1993; Stead, 2005), although others also refer to this activity as the "Muddiest Point" activity. For those of you not familiar with these classroom assessment techniques (Angelo & Cross, 1993), these are brief writing activities that students complete at the end of class to prompt them to make connections and reflect on their level of understanding of the course material from that day. The facilitator guide, available for download from Appendix H, outlines this activity. Depending upon the nature of the class, you may wish to ask students to identify points of confusion (e.g., What was the muddiest point from today's class?), moments of curiosity (e.g., What are you wondering about after today's class?), contexts of application (e.g., What is a real-life example of what we talked about in class today?), or the specific course activities that supported their learning (e.g., What explanation/example or activity was most helpful from today's class?). Gathering and reading through these responses after class ends allows you to "take the temperature" of the whole class, rather than just those students who ask questions. In the next class, you can draw on these responses to address any common misconceptions or points of confusion and share examples of the kinds of connections and applications that other students in the class generated in response to the class material.

Why This Works

The Minute Paper exercise teaches students the importance of self-assessment as well as the benefits of elaborating on one's knowledge by making connections across topics and between course material and personal experience. It also allows the instructor to quickly correct or reteach areas that need further scaffolding or explanation. You may be surprised to see which concepts were confusing and which concepts were most engaging for your students. And, perhaps most importantly, it continues a sense of community between students and the instructor; students feel that they are being heard and that their contributions are valued and taken into account in the teaching process.

Utility Value Writing

A slightly longer metacognitive writing activity, which prompts students to connect key course concepts to their own lives, is the Utility Value Writing activity (facilitator guide available for download from Appendix I). This practice has been shown to improve motivation and retention in STEM, particularly for students from underrepresented backgrounds and those who are the first in their family to attend college (Harackiewicz et al., 2014).

In this activity, students are asked to summarize a key skill or concept from the course unit which they found particularly interesting and relevant to their lives and their larger learning goals. Drawing on their notes and readings, they then write a one- to two-page essay explaining the concept, its importance to the larger discipline, and how the concept relates to their own life or will help them to meet a goal that is important to them. By asking students to complete this activity at multiple points in the semester, you are helping to demonstrate to students the utility of what is learned as extending beyond the course itself.

Why This Works
The Utility Value Writing activity, similar to the Minute Paper, reinforces for students the importance of building connections across, and elaborating on, what they are learning. Beyond that, this activity helps to maintain students' motivation for learning, as it highlights the self-relevance of the course material. Finally, the Utility Value Writing prompt focuses students' attention on their larger goals and values. As you read through these essays, it can be helpful to refer back to the student's initial goals for their learning from the Designing Success and How to Achieve It activity. What links do you see between what the student selected as holding utility for them and their self-identified goals for their learning and success? These links may not be immediately obvious to students, and you may be able to help them evidence some important self-relevant insights into their learning and their values.

Exam Wrappers
A final metacognitive exercise that encourages students to reflect on the efficacy of their study techniques and practices is the Exam Wrappers activity (Lovett, 2013), also sometimes referred to as "cognitive wrappers." Marsha Lovett and colleagues at Carnegie Mellon University developed this technique following the observation that the study strategies that many students were taught in high school did not transfer well to the kind of learning that students were being asked to do at the college level. For instance, the strategy of using flashcards for memorizing terminology can be effective, but using that same strategy when preparing for an application-focused, rather than memorization-focused, assessment is ineffectual. Exam wrappers help raise students' awareness of the need to develop new or refined strategies in the face of new learning demands.

This activity, whose implementation is described in the facilitator guide (available for download from Appendix J), should be timed so that students have recently completed a substantial exam or other assessment in the class.

The exam wrapper process asks students to reflect on the strategies that they have been employing in preparation for assessments in your course, and the amount of time or effort that these strategies require of them. It also asks students to identify the level of understanding (e.g., explanation, application, prediction) that they were asked to demonstrate on the assessment, and the areas within the assessment that were most challenging or surprising to them. Pulling those two threads together, then, allows students to see when their studying was appropriately aligned with the nature of learning that was expected of them, and where there are points of misalignment. Reminding students of their reflections and insights as they prepare for the next assessment in your course can help them to be more intentional in their studying and strategy selection.

Why This Works
An exam wrapper highlights for students that while exams provide you with an evaluation of your current understanding in the course, they also provide you with the opportunity to learn about yourself as a learner and refine your study strategies. Further, incorporating exam wrappers into your courses gives you, the instructor, information on how students are approaching learning in your course and where you can be more transparent about the kinds of understanding you value and will evaluate. Finally, reviewing students' responses to these prompts creates a bridge that can help you connect with a student who is struggling but may be reluctant to come to office hours or reach out. As a former HSTEM student reminded us, "If a student doesn't do well on an exam, don't assume that they aren't coming to you for help or advice because they don't care. It makes a *huge* difference to have a professor care enough to reach out when you are struggling." Initiating a conversation with a student who has struggled on previous assessments, guided by their exam wrapper reflection, can help you to actively demonstrate your commitment to them as a learner and provide concrete mechanisms by which you can support them in developing additional learning and studying strategies.

Midsemester Feedback

In addition to establishing avenues for students to self-assess their learning approaches, we also encourage you to provide students with a structure for giving you feedback about their experiences as a learner in the class. The timing of the Midsemester Feedback activity allows students to have experienced a substantial portion of the class content, have developed familiarity with common course activities, and have navigated group or collaborative dynamics with their peers; they are now in an informed position to provide you with information about their sense of belonging and success in the class. Further, at this point in the semester, there is commonly enough time left in the semester for you to respond to and meaningfully incorporate student feedback. Whether you use the prompts provided in the instructor guide for this activity (see the facilitator guide for download from Appendix K) or draw from other midsemester feedback processes (Hurney et al., 2014; Hurney et al., 2021), we encourage you to ask students about what they are doing to support their learning, how the course and course instruction is supporting their learning, and the concrete recommendations that they may have for improving learning in the class.

As you review the feedback, explore any patterns that emerge. Are there particular assignments that are confusing or less clear to students than they would like? Are students reporting particular strategies for their learning (e.g., small study groups or accessing secondary study materials) that you might be able to facilitate for all students in the class? If modifications have been suggested, consider how they align with your own learning and community-focused goals for the class. If they are consistent, identify which changes are feasible now, and in what ways, and which changes will need to be incorporated into future versions of the course. Thank students for their feedback and share your plan for implementation with them. If students have generated recommendations that are inconsistent with the goals for the class (e.g., a number of students indicating that they would prefer individual work, even though a primary learning goal of the course focuses on collaboration), you can take this moment to remind students of the themes you shared in the Discussing Class Expectations activity (Appendix E) earlier in the semester.

In some cases, student responses may be divided, with half of the class viewing an aspect of the course positively, while the other half of the class reflects negatively on that same aspect of the course. What should you do in that case? Rather than throwing up your hands in frustration, we recommend that you share this pattern of feedback with your students to prompt a collaborative discussion. Is there more information about their experience of that particular course component that students could provide to help unpack the disparate responses? Inviting students to process the feedback with you can demonstrate that you are both invested in their learning and in partnering with them to shape the course.

Why This Works

Asking students to reflect on their own learning strategies, and to be open to receiving feedback from you about how to improve their learning, can place them in a vulnerable position in the class. Extending the same opportunity for them to reflect on how the class and your teaching is supporting their learning, and what modifications may enhance their learning, demonstrates that you are also open to feedback and have areas of growth. Sharing your HSTEM story early in the class demonstrates to students that you are a complex human who has learned from life's challenges and frustrations; inviting students to provide feedback about the course and inviting them to be in conversation with you about how to incorporate this feedback into the rest of the semester continues to strengthen your commitment to supporting and being in relationship with your students.

Lab-Based Practices for Creating Inclusive and Collaborative Research Spaces

Many aspects of our work as scientists involve working in close collaboration with others, often in the pursuit of answers to questions that cannot, either because of the scope of the question or the wide range of disciplinary expertise required, be addressed alone. That being said, while we often work on collaborative endeavors, most of us were not explicitly taught how to collaborate successfully. Further, while the research demonstrates multiple benefits of diverse learning and working communities (Ahmed, 2012), effectively navigating communication styles, power dynamics, and social norms that may differ from your own requires practice and intentionality. In this final section, therefore, we focus on activities designed to transparently teach the skills of collaboration and communication, as well as provide a summary of some of the assessment work we've done to explore the impact of these practices on students' sense of belonging and persistence in STEM. These practices can also be readily transferred to research groups, another space where scaffolding a strong sense of community and shared purpose can be beneficial.

Lab Partner Formation

As the English proverb says, "Birds of a feather flock together," in the lab as well as other areas of life. It is natural for students to seek out friends with whom to work in the lab, as these friends provide a sense of security and predictability about how the nature of collaboration will go. Our friends also tend to be similar to ourselves across multiple demographic dimensions, including race, class, ability, gender identity, and extracurricular interests (e.g., Liberman & Shaw, 2019; Selfhout et al., 2009). Given the learning opportunities of diverse working groups, however, we seek to disrupt this pattern on a frequent basis. One approach pairs students in the Scientist Trading Cards activity (see the facilitator guide for download in Appendix L); on one side of the card is printed an image of one of the many diverse scientists in the field, and the other side provides a profile of that scientist and their contributions to the field. Alternatively, you may be able to collaborate with students in making cards that profile the faculty and staff in your department or science division, use elements (and fun facts) from the periodic table, or even use standard playing cards. Providing two copies of each trading card and distributing one card to each student in the course allows students to identify the holder of their matching card, the person who will become their new lab partner. For each successive lab activity, new lab partners are drawn in the same fashion.

Why This Works
Using a random structure to pairing lab partners decreases the social stress that many students feel about whether and by whom they will be chosen as a partner. Further, this structure, and the rotating of lab partner pairings throughout the semester, helps to build a more cohesive community across the lab while also helping students learn how to collaborate with individuals they might not otherwise have sought out. Finally, cards that feature diverse scientists in the field highlight and provide representation of the amazing range of scholars in our disciplines and emphasize to our students that they too can make great contributions to science.

Community Announcements

In lab classes associated with large lecture classes, our students often report feeling disconnected from their colleagues, and this experience can be even more pronounced for students who hold underrepresented identities in our classes. As previously noted, students often form connections and friendships around shared interests and identities; the Community Announcements activity can promote the discovery of new opportunities for exploring shared interests, learning more about each other, and celebrating exciting moments in the lives of our colleagues (download the facilitator guide from Appendix M). At the beginning of each lab class, students, staff, and faculty are encouraged to share any announcements they have about recent or upcoming events in the non-STEM aspects of their lives. For instance, one student may share about an upcoming play or musical performance, while another may describe an upcoming athletic competition or a recent success on the field. This can also be a great chance for students to learn about active affinity groups and clubs across campus about which they may not have been aware. And, building on the Humanize the Professor activity, we encourage faculty and staff participants to share about activities or upcoming events that are occurring in their own non-STEM lives or in their community.

Why This Works
The Community Announcements activity emphasizes that we are all whole people with lives and interests outside of the class. Many of us who supervise introductory labs enjoy the opportunity to interact with a small subset of the large lecture attendees in an interactive setting. Conversations that range broadly across academic and nonacademic topics often arise organically during incubation steps and natural breaks allow us to get to know these students as whole people. Integrating a community announcement time enables *all* students to benefit from learning more about each other and forging connections. Often, a community announcement event prompts connections between students outside of the lab and uncovers shared interests. For students experiencing moments of academic challenge or frustration, this activity can be an important and affirming reminder of their many strengths and values. Finally, the provision of personal announcements by faculty and staff in the lab can also decrease student levels of intimidation in reaching out for help or support. Indeed, a faculty-shared community announcement may provide an entry point for students to attend your office hours for the first time.

Group Work Reflections

As students work with a range of lab partners across the semester, we encourage them to reflect on the nature of that work and what they are learning about themselves through the process. Additionally, rather than assuming that students can intuit each other's expectations for collaboration and preferred styles of working, we teach students to be explicit in their expectations for working together and the roles they will play. To that end, students complete a Group Work Reflections activity at the start and end of each lab. After pairing students using the scientist trading cards and before students begin the lab work of the day, we ask them to introduce themselves and to have a brief conversation about how they intend to work together and support each other in that process. They are also prompted to review the tasks that are required of the lab and how they will allocate and approach these tasks together. After the completion of the lab, students write a brief reflection about the nature of their group work in the lab that week, both what worked well and how they could improve their approach to collaboration in next week's lab (see the link in Appendix N to download the full facilitator guide, which includes a complete list of reflective prompts).

These reflections are submitted as part of students' work in the lab, which allows the instructor to look for patterns across the group dynamics. What strategies are high-functioning lab groups employing? What are common stumbling blocks or interpersonal challenges? At the start of the following week, before the start of the lab, we encourage you to share the strategies that students highlighted as helping them succeed in the lab as well as make note of any particular areas that students wanted to attend to in their group dynamics this week. For instance, you may see that several students noted that their lab partner seemed to understand the process more quickly than they did, resulting in these students feeling behind and rushed as their partners progressed independently through the lab. In this case, you can share this observation with students and invite them to strategize with you. You may say, "We will all have moments in the lab that come more easily to us than others, and vice versa. When we are the ones who need more time, it can feel frustrating. How can we stay aware and make sure that we're not leaving each other behind?"

Why This Works
Prompting students to slow down and explicitly communicate with each other about how they want to work together, and the roles that each of them will play, can remove the individual pressure students may otherwise feel to navigate, or merely tolerate, these complex social situations (e.g., Leopold & Smith, 2020; Scager et al., 2016). Setting clear expectations for behaviors, roles, and communication decreases the likelihood of implicit biases intruding into ad hoc decision-making processes. Further, engaging in repeated metacognitive reflection on students' own practices in the lab, as well as their partners', can allow students to set future intentions for how they wish to collaborate and communicate with each other. Relatedly, proactively identifying a plan for completing lab tasks requires students to review the protocol together before jumping in. Orienting oneself to the entirety of a procedure prior to beginning an experiment not only benefits the nature of collaboration, it also builds a good research practice, one that often gets skipped when lab partners rush to get the lab started and completed as quickly as possible. Finally, including group work reflection prompts in the lab write-up assignment demonstrates to

students that learning to work together is a valued and important aspect of their work as scientists, while also providing instructors with a structure for both affirming what is working and talking openly and productively about aspects of collaboration that could be improved.

Assessment of Impact of Lab-Based Practices

To explore the effect of these lab-based practices on students' sense of belonging and motivation to continue in STEM, we conducted an inquiry project comparing student outcomes resulting from an introductory lab course that employed HSTEM-informed practices and one that employed a more traditional lab instructional format (see Bunnell et al., 2021). The traditional lab class placed a heavy emphasis on research skills and safety without an additional emphasis on collaborative work and community building. Students were enrolled in one of these two types of lab sections, and all lab sections completed the same laboratory experiments across the semester.

At the beginning and end of the semester, students were asked about their likelihood of taking another STEM class after the current semester was completed; students who were enrolled in the lab sections that incorporated the HSTEM lab practices demonstrated a substantial increase in their likelihood of taking another STEM class. This pattern was true of students in the class regardless of their high school mathematics preparation level, a key determinant of STEM retention (e.g., Wyatt et al., 2012). Conversely, students enrolled in the traditional lab sections with lower levels of math preparation demonstrated no change in their ratings, while students with higher math preparation who were enrolled in the traditional lab sections rated themselves as less likely to take another STEM class than they had been at the start of the semester.

Why might that be? It appears that the HSTEM-based practices for lab group formation, community announcements, and group work reflections jointly enhance the sense of community and connection across our students, and student reflections support that interpretation. Students commonly share how much they enjoy getting to know new individuals and working collaboratively with them, as well as feeling valued as a member of the STEM community. As evidence of that fostered sense of belonging, one student who experienced these inclusive lab practices shared that at the end of the semester, they now "feel proud to be a woman in STEM and love to see how many other girls are doing so well in my lab section." We take that as a sign that setting intentional goals of community, scaffolding reflection, and prioritizing collaboration are helping to move our lab communities in a positive, more inclusive direction.

Conclusions

In this chapter, we have provided a wide range of activities that we and our colleagues have adapted into our STEM classes and labs. The practices we highlight are not an all-inclusive set, and many have been used by others for a very long time in their teaching. We share them with you because they are all practices that current and past HSTEM students have identified as being important to their sense of self and community in STEM. We encourage you to consider how these practices may allow you to create a welcoming first-day classroom experience that invites all aspects of ourselves into the classroom to create ongoing goal-setting and reflective practices to help students connect to their learning and engage strategies in your labs that explicitly teach and lead to reflection on how students can work collaboratively, productively, and inclusively. More important than strict implementation of these specific practices, we invite you to use them as the foundation for strengthening your own practice of welcoming students into an explicit partnership, to jointly shoulder the responsibilities and reap the benefits of building an inclusive learning community.

We noted that we are navigating a tension between creating easily accessible guides for high-impact inclusive practices while not wishing to convey a sense that the incorporation of these practices, absent critical reflection on one's identities and goals for building equitable teaching and learning spaces, will dramatically transform students' experience in the class. We hope that our discussion of these practices, coupled with the related facilitator guides, will provide low-barrier entry points to experimenting with a radically different approach to STEM education compared to the STEM educational context that many of us experienced. At the same time, we hope that you are inspired to adopt a scholarly, scientific approach to your inclusive teaching tool kit: Select a practice or set of practices that align with your goals for teaching and learning, reflect on the evidence of how these practices are impacting your classroom climate, and then engage with the scholarly community and other practitioners as you make sense of what you are learning about what works in your context and how you will continue to iterate on these practices over time. The more that each of us take responsibility for creating inclusive and equitable spaces in STEM, the more we can establish a trusting relationship with our students and the more that students will invest in a course design that incorporates these and other inclusive practices.

Finally, because the roots of inequity and exclusion in science and academia are deep and embedded in complex and implicit structures, the pedagogical efforts each of us make are necessary but not sufficient. We must also reflect on our own biases, blind spots, and assumptions when faced with the day-to-day realities of the disparities in STEM. Embodying our commitment to helping all students achieve their highest potential in STEM means also continuing to do this reflective work ourselves. As you expand your inclusive teaching toolbox, we hope that these practices enable you to create more equitable STEM classroom and laboratory spaces.

References

Ahmed, S. (2012). *On being included: Racism and diversity in institutional life*. Duke University Press.

Alsagoff, Z. (2015, August 31). *Ultimate ice breaker? Making & flying paper planes!* Edutopia. https://www.edutopia.org/discussion/ultimate-ice-breaker-making-flying-paper-planes

Angelo, T. A., & Cross, K. P. (1993). *Classroom assessment techniques: A handbook for college teachers* (2nd ed.). Jossey-Bass.

Boyes-Watson, C., & Pranis, K. (2020). *Circle forward: Building a restorative school community*. Living Justice Press.

Bunnell, S., Lyster, M., Greenland, K., Mayer, G., Gardner, K., Leise, T., Kristensen, T., Ryan, E. D., Ampiah-Bonney, R., & Jaswal, S. S. (2021). From protest to progress through partnership with students: Being human in STEM (HSTEM). *International Journal for Students as Partners, 5*(1), 26–56. https://doi.org/10.15173/ijsap.v5i1.4243

Cook-Sather, A., Bovill, C., & Felten, P. (2014). *Engaging students as partners in learning and teaching: A guide for faculty*. Jossey-Bass.

Efklides, A. (2011). Interactions of metacognition with motivation and affect in self-regulated learning: The MASRL model. *Educational Psychologist, 46*(1), 6–25. https://doi.org/10.1080/00461520.2011.538645

Elliot, A. J., McGregor, H. A., & Gable, S. (1999). Achievement goals, study strategies, and exam performance: A mediational analysis. *Journal of Educational Psychology, 91*(3), 549–563. https://doi.org/10.1037/0022-0663.91.3.549

Fisher, K., Kouyoumdjian, C., Roy, B., Talavera-Bustillos, V., & Willard, M. (2016). Building a culture of transparency. *Peer Review, 18*(1/2).

Good, C., Rattan, A., & Dweck, C. S. (2012). Why do women opt out? Sense of belonging and women's representation in mathematics. *Journal of Personality and Social Psychology, 102*(4), 700–717. https://doi.org/10.1037/a0026659

Harackiewicz, J. M., Tibbetts, Y., Canning, E., & Hyde, J. S. (2014). Harnessing values to promote motivation in education. In S. A. Karabenick & T. C. Urdan (Eds.), *Advances in motivation and achievement* (Vol. 18, pp. 71–105). Emerald Group. https://doi.org/10.1108/S0749-742320140000018002

Harrison, C. D., Nguyen, T. A., Seidel, S. B., Escobedo, A. M., Hartman, C., Lam, K., Liang, K. S., Martens, M., Acker, G. N., Akana, S. F., Balukjian, B., Benton, H. P., Blair, J. R., Boaz, S. M., Boyer, K. E., Bram, J. B., Burrus, L. W., Byrd, D. T., Caporale, N., . . . & Tanner, K. D. (2019). Investigating instructor talk in novel contexts: Widespread use, unexpected categories, and an emergent sampling strategy. *CBE—Life Sciences Education, 18*(3), Article 47. https://doi.org/10.1187/cbe.18-10-0215

Hofer, B. K., Yu, S. L., & Pintrich, P. R. (1998). Teaching college students to be self-regulated learners. In D. H. Schunk & B. J. Zimmerman (Eds.), *Self-regulated learning: From teaching to self-reflective practice* (pp. 57–85). Guilford.

HSTEM. (2017). *Inclusive curricular resources.* www.beinghumaninstem.com/inclusive-curricular-resources.html

Hurney, C. A., Harris, N. L., Prins, S. C. B., & Kruck, S. E. (2014). The impact of a learner-centered, mid-semester course evaluation on students. *Journal of Faculty Development, 28*(3), 55–61.

Hurney, C. A., Rener, C. M., & Troisi, J. D. (2021). *Midcourse correction for the college classroom: Putting small group instructional diagnosis to work.* Stylus.

Jones, B. D., Ruff, C., & Paretti, M. C. (2013). The impact of engineering identification and stereotypes on undergraduate women's achievement and persistence in engineering. *Social Psychology of Education, 16*(3), 471–493. https://doi.org/10.1007/s11218-013-9222-x

Leopold, H., & Smith, A. (2020). Implementing reflective group work activities in a large chemistry lab to support collaborative learning. *Education Sciences, 10*(1), 7.

Liberman, Z., & Shaw, A. (2019). Children use similarity, propinquity, and loyalty to predict which people are friends. *Journal of Experimental Child Psychology, 184*, 1–17. https://doi.org/10.1016/j.jecp.2019.03.002

Lovett, M. C. (2013). Make exams worth more than grades: Using exam wrappers to promote metacognition. In M. Kaplan, N. Silver, D. Lavaque-Manty, & D. Meizlish (Eds.), *Using reflection and metacognition to improve student learning* (pp. 18–52). Stylus.

McGuire, S. Y. (2021). Close the metacognitive equity gap: Teach all students how to learn. *Journal of College Academic Support Programs, 4*(1). https://digital.library.txstate.edu/handle/10877/14189

McGuire, S. Y., & McGuire, S. (2015). *Teach students how to learn: Strategies you can incorporate into any course to improve student metacognition, study skills, and motivation.* Stylus.

Montgomery, B. L. (2020). Planting equity: Using what we know to cultivate growth as a plant biology community. *The Plant Cell, 32*(11), 3372–3375. https://doi.org/10.1105/tpc.20.00589

Mulnix, A. (2018, November 12). *The power of transparency in your teaching.* Faculty Focus. https://www.facultyfocus.com/articles/course-design-ideas/power-transparency-teaching/

Scager, K., Boonstra, J., Peeters, T., Vulperhorst, J., & Wiegant, F. (2016). Collaborative learning in higher education: Evoking positive interdependence. *CBE—Life Sciences Education, 15*(4), Article 69. https://doi.org/10.1187/cbe.16-07-0219

Schinske, J. N., Perkins, H., Snyder, A., & Wyer, M. (2016). Scientist spotlight homework assignments shift students' stereotypes of scientists and enhance science identity in a diverse introductory science class. *CBE—Life Sciences Education, 15*(3), Article 47. https://doi.org/10.1187/cbe.16-01-0002

Selfhout, M., Denissen, J., Branje, S., & Meeus, W. (2009). In the eye of the beholder: Perceived, actual, and peer-rated similarity in personality, communication, and friendship intensity during the acquaintanceship process. *Journal of Personality and Social Psychology, 96*(6), 1152–1165. https://doi.org/10.1037/a0014468

Shulman, L. (1993). Teaching as community property: Putting an end to pedagogical solitude. *Change, 25*(6), 1–3.

Stachowiak, B. (2018, July 26). *Teaching as an act of social justice and equity* [Audio podcast]. Teaching in Higher Ed. https://teachinginhighered.com/podcast/teaching-as-an-act-of-social-justice-and-equity/

Stead, D. R. (2005). A review of the one-minute paper. *Active Learning in Higher Education, 6*(2), 118–131. https://doi.org/10.1177/1469787405054237

Steele, C. (2011). *Whistling Vivaldi: And other clues to how stereotypes affect us and what we can do*. Norton.

Trujillo, G., & Tanner, K. D. (2014). Considering the role of affect in learning: Monitoring students' self-efficacy, sense of belonging, and science identity. *CBE—Life Sciences Education, 13*(1), 6–15. https://doi.org/10.1187/cbe.13-12-0241

Wyatt, J., Remigio, M., & Camara, W. (2012). *SAT subject area readiness indicators: Reading, writing, and STEM*. College Board.

Zimmerman, B. J. (2011). Motivational sources and outcomes of self-regulated learning and performance. In D. H. Schunk & J. A. Greene (Eds.), *Handbook of self-regulation of learning and performance* (pp. 49–64). Routledge.

6

TELLING YOUR HSTEM STORY

In chapter 5, we described a wide range of inclusive practices that you can employ in your classrooms and laboratories. Here, we turn to a signature HSTEM practice, the HSTEM Story activity. We have found that this activity can fast-track the building of an inclusive classroom community, because it foregrounds and fosters reflection on the human experience in STEM. The HSTEM Story activity invites participants to reflect on their early experiences in science and mathematics, their successes and setbacks, and who and/or what contributed to their continued engagement with STEM despite challenges. In Cy's HSTEM story (Figure 6.1), they describe being uninspired by STEM in middle school despite earning strong grades, feeling discouraged in their high school STEM classes, and then struggling to graduate from high school. In community college, Cy shifted their focus to sociology, discovered an interest in demography at University of California, Berkeley, and has now merged their interest in sociology with quantitative methods at Amherst College. Regardless of their current excitement about their classes and research, however, they ask whether their future self will again doubt their interest and motivation to pursue STEM.

In their HSTEM story, Cy demonstrates how they have reflected on the internal motivational factors and external opportunities that have contributed to their pathway in STEM so far. When this activity is incorporated into the STEM classroom, we ask faculty and staff cofacilitators to share their own HSTEM story before asking students to do the same; this both democratizes the classroom by increasing instructor vulnerability and communicates to students the important message that setbacks and nonlinear development are typical, even for those who have become successful STEM academics. In this chapter, therefore, we discuss the role of personal narrative in STEM, describe how to structure an HSTEM Story activity in your own

Figure 6.1. Cy's HSTEM story.

courses, and share stories from instructors about how including HSTEM stories in their pedagogies has impacted their classroom climate.

Guiding Questions

- What are the stories you tell about who does science in your discipline? Who is missing?
- Where do you see opportunities for bringing your own story in STEM into the classroom? How might sharing your HSTEM story alter the dynamics of your teaching and learning spaces?
- How can you invite students to share their own stories in STEM, with you and with each other? What might that sharing do in altering the nature of inclusive learning in your classroom?

Bringing Authentic Narratives of Science Into STEM Spaces

What are the stories that you have heard about important scientists in the field? Whose narratives do you know? For most of us, we think of Western scientists who have made great discoveries and contributed to grand theoretical shifts in our understanding of scientific processes and phenomena—Albert Einstein, Charles Darwin, James Watson and Francis Crick, Ivan Pavlov, John Dalton, Antoine Lavoisier, Marie Curie, and many others. What do you notice about these individuals? First, the vast majority of scientific narratives we know about are those of men, mostly white, and mostly dead. The lived experiences and identities of scientists who are highlighted in our textbooks and online spaces are not representative of the wide range of people doing science today—individuals with a range of racial, ethnic, gender, sexual, physical ability, and other identities. In presenting science in this way, focused primarily on white male experiences and accomplishments in STEM, we communicate to our students who hold nonwhite, nonmale identities that science is not a field made for them or one in which they will be successful. And this message seems to be one that minoritized students are paying attention to. In fact, students from underrepresented minorities in STEM report that they would be more motivated to pursue scientific degrees and careers if professional scientists who held their same gender and ethnicity identities were better represented in the field (e.g., Kricorian et al., 2020; Stout et al., 2011). For instance, work by Jane Stout et al. (2011) finds that even when women outperform men in their coursework, representation plays a powerful role in retaining them in STEM:

> The disproportionate "leakage" of women from the STEM educational pipeline may not be due to their actual performance. . . . Rather, women may be leaving STEM because, regardless of their accomplishments, the virtual absence of same-sex others in expert roles (in STEM classes, labs, textbooks, etc.) makes them feel like imposters. (p. 269)

Amplifying the stories of underrepresented scientists in your departments and disciplines helps students from a wider range of backgrounds and identities disrupt feelings of imposter syndrome and instead envision themselves as future scientists and members of the scientific community. Indeed, research by Jeff Schinske et al. (2016) demonstrates that assignments that enable students to see scientists like themselves enhance students' science identities and strengthen their resistance to stereotype threat.

Secondly, the stories we learn in our STEM training generally tell of grand accomplishments, successes, and discoveries. But for many of us as scientists, we wonder: Where are the failures, the missteps, the ideas we write on the backs of napkins that prove to be completely, unambiguously wrong? And what about the unanticipated opportunities and collaborations that take us, and our science, in directions we did not plan and at the time, we did not know how they would turn out? Solely describing scientific discoveries as emerging from a series of organized, sequential progressions leading to inevitable, grand achievements does our students a serious disservice. Why? When we present scientific history in this way, we communicate to students that the only way to contribute to science is through dramatic, field-transforming work (which, honestly, most of us will never do) and through flawless, error-free progress in our scientific journeys toward expertise (which almost none of us experiences). When students do inevitably experience hardships in their course-based learning or lab-based research, such as a research study that does not work as planned or an exam that was harder than expected, these students are likely to interpret these struggles as indicative that they do not belong in science, and even more so, that they truly were never "cut out for science"; this moment of failure is a powerful message they are likely to interpret as telling them to choose a different area of focus for their lives (Henry et al., 2021).

For students who were the top academic performers in high school, the interpretation of failure or struggle as a marker of nonbelonging in college can be even harder to disrupt. Many of these students arrive on our campuses with a long history of having been praised for their successes in school—their performance on spelling tests, their early reading abilities, their advanced scientific coursework—and this praise has often been coupled with messages of self-worth and identity: "You are so smart. I'm so proud of you! I love you so much." Being "good at school" is a core feature of their identities. Some of us even brag about our children's academic prowess on car bumper stickers. In many cases, college or university is the first place in which students experience substantial moments of failure in meeting their academic goals or expectations. And when challenge or failure finally comes, these high-performing students don't only have to reckon with how they should respond to this new experience, they often also struggle with a loss of identity and the worthiness they were told they had because they were "smart."

Lest we inaccurately convey that the challenge to self-worth in the face of academic failure is solely felt by students, many career academics and scientists face this same internal battle. Like our students, we too have internalized our academic expertise as a key feature of our identities and thus feel a sense of destabilization when we are not performing as experts. And like our students, we often feel like we are not accomplishing enough, regardless of our actual level of productivity and contributions, when we compare ourselves to others in the field. Others in our departments or disciplines may appear to be navigating their science effortlessly while we slog along, mired in challenges and failures. Of course, our peers' scientific journeys likely hold many experiences of challenge, struggle, and false starts too, of which we are not aware. Sharing only our stories of success, and hearing only stories of our colleagues' successes, presents a false narrative of the lived reality that most of us are navigating, one in which we are doing our best, and failing more often than not, in the scientific enterprise.

When we highlight the diverse range of scientists who have traversed success and challenges in science, we also have the opportunity to help students recognize the benefits of diverse scientific teams. Research demonstrates that the diversity of members in a group, and the range of problem-solving solutions that this diversity provides, serves to improve the science that is done and the innovations that are possible (e.g., Ahmed, 2012; Ford & Malaney, 2012; Gibbs, 2014). Individuals with a range of experiences in and outside of STEM bring with them new interpretations and creative solutions that a less diverse group may not have considered. As philosopher Helen Longino (1990) writes in *Science as Social Knowledge,* "The molding of what counts as scientific knowledge is an activity requiring many participants" (p. 74), and this collective molding is best achieved when a diversity of experiences, assumptions, and frameworks are present in critical discourse around a publicly available scientific observation. She continues,

Only if the products of inquiry are understood to be formed by the kind of critical discussion that is possible among a plurality of individuals about a commonly accessible phenomenon, can we see how they count as knowledge rather than opinion. (p. 74)

Nevertheless, not all students enter our classrooms and laboratories convinced that increased diversity in our pool of scientific talent leads to better science (Gibbs, 2014). Perhaps this skepticism about the benefits of learning from peers holding identities that are underrepresented in the sciences connects to the fact that the narratives of diverse scientists have not been made available to our students thus far in their training. Regardless, sharing stories of diverse scientists and varied pathways through STEM can help dismantle this skepticism and help our students learn with and from all members of the classroom community.

A final note about the value of sharing our individual STEM stories with our students and our colleagues, before we transition into a discussion of how you can write your own HSTEM story and encourage students to do the same. The process of constructing one's autobiographical narrative in STEM does not merely capture a static, fully formed understanding of oneself; instead, the process of reflecting on one's experience prompts on-the-spot meaning-making to occur (Greenhoot et al., 2013). We consider and refine our self-knowledge about who we are and how we have navigated STEM differently than others who hold identities, values, and sociological contexts that diverge from our own. What are some of the different pathways, advantages, privileges, and challenges that have led us to this shared moment as scientists? Many of us have not engaged in this level of intentional reflection about our journeys through STEM before. Crafting and sharing our HSTEM stories can make transparent the advantages and privileges that have lowered barriers for some of us and allow us to better grasp some of the challenges that others have experienced to reach the same point in their career in science.

The HSTEM Story Assignment, in Three Parts

In previous versions of this exercise in the HSTEM course, students, staff, and faculty wrote their HSTEM story once, at a single point in the first half of the semester. These stories were shared with the class for reflection and connection. In more recent offerings, the Being Human in STEM Story is written, and rewritten, across three points of the class. We call these stories the HSTEM Story (Past), HSTEM Story (Present), and HSTEM Story (Future). In each of the three writing moments, individuals are encouraged to reflect on their early experiences with STEM, both in formal STEM spaces (e.g., classrooms, research experiences) and informal STEM environments. The specific prompts are described in the next section of this chapter and detailed in the full facilitator guide for this activity, available for download in Appendix O. Across all three assignments, we encourage individuals to reflect on the following: In all of your encounters with STEM throughout your life, when have you felt welcomed, encouraged, and supported and what contributed to that? Conversely, what has contributed to feeling discouraged, disillusioned, or excluded?

The format of the HSTEM story is very open-ended, and we encourage students to think about the representational nature of their story that best captures their thoughts and feelings. Many students choose a written essay format for their HSTEM stories, although more and more students are opting for visual and audio representations, such as a visual timescale, a concept map, or a slide deck with photographs chosen to represent different stages of one's STEM experience. By encouraging students to select the genre for their HSTEM story that most resonates with them, we are hoping to model how one's interdisciplinary and humanist identities can be an asset to who they are as scientists. Each student's story is graded for completion only, which is a very intentional pedagogical choice. We as facilitators do not want to impose our own assumptions or expectations of what should be included in a student's narrative into their HSTEM story, nor do we wish to suggest that the quality of their personal narrative should be open to critical evaluation by us.

Building this kind of reflective activity into your teaching practice matters to students. In fact, after engaging in this activity in the HSTEM context, one student (E.M.) proposed that *all* students, not just those in the HSTEM setting, would benefit from reflecting upon their educational journey. E.M. argued, "It is important for students to understand their own identity and even acknowledge the differences among their peers." In her HSTEM action project proposal, E.M. suggested that the three-part HSTEM Story assignment could be adapted into a reflective exercise that students complete across their college experience. Specifically, E.M. proposed that first-year students would construct their HSTEM Story (Past) as they oriented to the college. In their second year, students would update their HSTEM stories as they developed a greater understanding of themselves and their peers in the context of their college education. Finally, in students' third and fourth years, they would work on writing their future story, reflecting on how they will build on the insights, values, and community they have established during their college years and carry those lessons into their postgraduation lives. Like E.M., we hope that you too find ways to adapt this practice to your teaching context!

The HSTEM Story (Past)

The HSTEM Story (Past) assignment is completed during the first week of class, in order to capture student, faculty, and staff incoming views of themselves and their experiences in STEM. Individuals are asked to reflect on the role that STEM has played in their lives so far and the experiences, both positive and negative, that stick out in their memory. The prompts remind us that everyone, whether they currently identify as a scientist or not, has engaged with STEM and has been touched by STEM methods, knowledge, technologies, and culture, through personal connections as well as social, cultural, and environmental systems and phenomena. Providing a limited amount of time during class to complete this assignment encourages participants to embrace the idea of developing a rough model to communicate their ideas versus focusing on perfection, and to help ensure that individuals across the course commit an equal amount of time to this activity.

The HSTEM Story (Present)

The HSTEM Story (Present) is completed at the midpoint of the course; this assignment asks individuals to connect themes from the readings and discussions to their HSTEM story, and to expand or revise their story of their HSTEM journey using these new understandings and frameworks. In so doing, this aspect of the HSTEM story assignment, in which personal insights are placed into conversation with the broader foundational academic material, reinforces this core HSTEM principle. Further, participants are asked to think about aspects of STEM that they find most engaging, most enjoyable, and view as most important for their future.

The HSTEM Story (Future)

One of the final activities of the course asks individuals to envision their future STEM selves and how they wish to further shape and support the STEM community. This last installment calls upon participants to set 5-year goals for their ideal HSTEM future selves and to think about how they will work to cultivate more welcoming and inclusive STEM communities for others. In conceptualizing that future, we ask, "How might you continue to incorporate what you have learned about yourself as well as both challenges and opportunities for inclusion in STEM? And how will you establish processes to hold yourself accountable to these goals and to your aspirational future self in STEM?"

HSTEM Story Evolution: The Story of S.J.

In this next section, we provide an example of the HSTEM story (Past, Present, and Future) of a recent HSTEM student, S.J., who provided their consent for their HSTEM story to be shared with others.

Part 1: HSTEM Story (Past)

S.J. began the first version of her HSTEM story by describing her family context as well as her first-generation, low-income status as contributing factors to her desire to pursue medicine. In childhood, S.J. writes, "My older sister was born with profound hearing loss, so growing up I was immediately exposed to the impact STEM and medicine can have on people's lives. It exposed me immediately to the field I eventually decided to pursue and made me curious about the human body and how it works." At the same time, S.J. also says, "Growing up as a FLI [first generation, low-income student], I was immediately exposed to disparity—not only with resources, but in particular with medicine and my education. I didn't understand why this was the case, but I very quickly became aware of its impact." In middle and high school, S.J. "managed to get into a lottery-based high school that taught the IB [International Baccalaureate] curriculum, and was taught by incredibly supportive teachers." Now as a student at Amherst, S.J. shared, "Being a FLI student contextualizes my experiences both as a STEM student and an Amherst student. I think the struggles and successes I've had are tied to the upbringing I've had, and I can note clear differences between my journey and those of some of my classmates. While I'm incredibly proud of my progress in spite of the various difficulties I've experienced, I also wish things were different—particularly because a lot of my FLI peers experienced near-debilitating imposter syndrome. I wish we'd been more aware of our worth! I really hope to do something about that in some way."

Part II (Present)

In the second draft of her HSTEM story, S.J. reflects on other aspects of her identity that she did not name in her first HSTEM story, especially her ethnic and cultural identities. She also discusses the additional layers of understanding she has gained about herself and other first generation, low income students. About her racial and ethnic identities, she writes,

"I view myself as a non-aligner.... I don't fit the normal Asian category because of my socioeconomic status, but I don't fit the Black/Latinx category because of my race.... The most recent readings on Indigenous science struck a chord with me and my own perspective on my cultural upbringing. It was weird because when I was reading and discussing the works, I didn't connect this to my own life until another student did—for some reason, I still didn't register the similarities! I do now though, and am even wondering the impact that my decisions have had on my mother and my extended family.... In an attempt to assimilate and not stand out from the crowd, I turned away from food, from holidays, from religion, and from traditional Indian science—and looking at myself now, it's not surprising that I feel disconnected from the stereotypical 'Indian' experience. Perhaps this is just a wake-up call." Finally, in terms of her first-generation, low-income status, she connects her experiences to Tony Jack's (2019) book on privileged poor students in elite academic spaces and describes a new sense of empowerment. S.J. says, "With both the Tony Jack readings and our classroom discussion, I've felt more in awe of what I and other FLI students have accomplished despite our disadvantages. My imposter syndrome is still just as real, but also my awareness of how much we've had to overcome to 'match' the others at this school—so, so proud! However, even though I was part of [a program at the college that aims to orient low-income and first-generation students to the college experience], I still felt like there were some areas where I felt like I had no idea what to do as a student and an individual; maybe there's something we can do here."

Part III (Future)

In her final version of her HSTEM story, S.J. describes a series of future goals that connect her interests in medicine, expanding her cultural awareness and supporting other first-generation and low-income students. S.J. says, "I like to imagine that I'll be in medical school or at least involved with the medical field in 5 years.... I dream of becoming a psychiatrist and serving people from underserved backgrounds, particularly those who have experienced trauma." To support her in this work, she writes, "I think I definitely want to continue exposing myself to similar literature, particularly written by people of color. I've never actively done this, but I feel like in [not] doing so, I've hindered my own academic development." Finally, in terms of working to support other first-generation and low-income students, she reflects on her desire to help other FLI students discover the same agency that she has realized. "Honestly, I don't know what it'd look like, but I guess I just want to ensure that FLI students feel more confidence in themselves and don't prematurely remove themselves from STEM because they think they aren't worthy or capable."

Reflecting on S.J.'s HSTEM Story

What stands out to us in these three iterations of S.J.'s HSTEM story are the ways in which she first emphasizes her individual identities and lived experiences, such as her sister's hearing loss and the quality of her high school preparation. As she revisits her story later in the semester, she places her individual identity into a larger context related to her ethnic and racial identities, her peer network, and her shared sense of community with other first-generation and low-income students. Finally, in her HSTEM future, she evidences a sense of commitment to both expanding her own knowledge base and giving back to others who have less privilege than she does, such as those in underserved medical spaces and FLI students who have not yet found their place in institutions of higher learning. What a journey she takes across the length of a single course!

Guiding Principles for Approaching the HSTEM Story Activity

While we have outlined a potential structure for engaging in this reflective narrative process, and engaging each other in community around these narratives, we want to stress that, should you wish to incorporate a "Being Human in STEM Story" activity in your courses, you should do so in a way that aligns with your individual teaching goals and pedagogies. There are no one-size-fits-all approaches to inclusive teaching. As an ever-increasing number of STEM educators invite their students to construct and share their HSTEM stories, we see a wide range of approaches that are successful. That being said, some shared recommendations, or guiding principles, have also emerged. We share those three recommendations in the following section.

All or None

Student narrative was a powerful element of the Amherst Uprising, but it came at a high emotional cost for students who shared their stories. In designing this activity, we kept the emotional labor and risk of microaggressions toward marginalized students in the class at the forefront of our minds. As highlighted by Derald Wing Sue et al. (2009),

> Professors who look to students of color to be the racial or ethnic experts [are] often viewed as unhelpful because (a) students of color are placed in

an educational role at the expense of their own growth, and (b) it often reflect[s] the lack of awareness, knowledge, and understanding of the instructor on racial matters. (p. 188)

In the HSTEM Story activity, therefore, we stress that the goal is to move away from marginalized students being forced to share their pain in order to educate others about their experience and wrongdoings. Rather, when all students, staff, and faculty construct their HSTEM story and these stories are then shared within the class community, we see that patterns emerge in the challenges and supports that have differentially impacted individuals and groups in STEM. And engaging in this shared activity highlights that we do not have a singular, shared experience, either in our individual pathways in STEM or in the level of vulnerability that sharing one's narrative with others requires of us in a classroom context. Finally, we emphasize that experiencing a dearth of challenges and barriers in an individual journey does not indicate the absence of structural racism and other forms of oppression.

Meaning-Making Occurs in Community

While the initial process of reflecting and capturing our stories in STEM is an individual act, these stories are intended to be shared with others in the class community. The sharing of HSTEM stories can occur in pairs, small groups, or across a larger class context; we find that what is important is for individuals to experience the act of being heard, without judgment. We recommend that faculty and staff cofacilitators share their stories first, as a model of openness and vulnerability, and then students share their stories with each other. It is important to keep in mind that as educators, many of us do not regularly share personal aspects of ourselves with our students. As such, regardless of whether the stories of faculty and staff members bring forward challenges they have personally experienced in STEM or not, the mere act of sharing one's personal narrative with students can be a humanizing act in the classroom.

Additionally, we recommend that you pair this activity with some preparatory community-building work, drawing from the practices described in chapter 5 or from your own repertoire of community-building activities. Asking students to share their personally lived narratives with their peers inherently places them in a position of vulnerability; this vulnerability is better navigated in communities where trust has already been built. As each story is shared, individuals are encouraged to practice active listening and individual reflection. There is individual value in engaging in meaning-making around one's lived experiences in STEM, and sharing the meaning that we have constructed from our lived experience with another. There is also the collective benefit of listening to and validating one another, to foster a sense of community and connection across members of our class. Beyond the positive community-building outcomes, this process also serves to highlight the inequities that exist across our local experiences. Although many students, staff, and faculty in the room may not have experienced targeted, marginalizing experiences or harassment in the discipline, for others in the room, those experiences have been frequently felt. By sharing our stories with others, across the full range of our individual experience, we are able to reflect on the ways in which we have navigated the academy, through points of relative ease and through moments of great challenge. Our collective stories and individual journeys demonstrate why this work of creating more inclusive STEM spaces is urgent, important, and relevant to us and to our institutions.

An Iterative Process

As we build our repository of knowledge about equity and inequity in STEM and we listen and learn from the stories of other individuals who have navigated their journeys in STEM, our understanding of ourselves in STEM evolves, and we revisit and expand our stories accordingly. This iterative, scaffolded approach offers a number of benefits. Throughout the semester, aspects of our identities become more self-obvious in the role they have played in our lives, as do the external factors, both privileges and barriers, that have opened or constrained opportunities for us. We are able to understand ourselves better or differently as we learn more about the contexts in which we have lived and by which we have been shaped. As we have previously noted, who we are as humans in STEM is not static; as such, iterating and redefining our STEM stories is an important ongoing process. By revisiting these narratives over time, we reinforce the dynamic nature of our lives in STEM.

Conclusions

STEM often prides itself on rigorous methods and objective evaluations of evidence. In that process of objective inquiry, however, the individual who is doing the science is often made invisible. We hope that this chapter has helped to highlight why that approach of separating the human from the science can be problematic in STEM educational spaces, especially as we seek to serve students who do not look like the historical figures often highlighted in STEM textbooks and awards, as well as students who internalize moments of struggle or failure as a marker of not belonging in the sphere of science.

The Being Human in STEM Story activity allows all of us, instructors and students alike, to incorporate narrative reflection into our STEM autobiography. Important to our inclusive efforts is the process of sharing one's story with others. In so doing, we can uncover aspects of our own journeys that we have not considered, and we are better able to see each other as full and complicated humans. Further, in encouraging the process of iteration on these stories, as well as the incorporation of empirical literature into one's meaning-making process, we model for students and our colleagues that self-knowledge and, indeed, self-compassion are skills that we continue to refine throughout our lifetimes. Finally, the writing and sharing of one's HSTEM story serves an important role in building the community that we are seeking to support.

References

Ahmed, S. (2012). *On being included: Racism and diversity in institutional life*. Duke University Press.

Ford, K. A., & Malaney, V. K. (2012). "I now harbor more pride in my race": The educational benefits of inter- and intraracial dialogues on the experiences of students of color and multiracial students. *Equity & Excellence in Education*, 45(1), 14–35.

Gibbs, K., Jr. (2014, September 10). Diversity in STEM: What it is and why it matters. *Scientific American*. https://blogs.scientificamerican.com/voices/diversity-in-stem-what-it-is-and-why-it-matters/

Greenhoot, A. F., Sun, S., Bunnell, S. L., & Lindboe, K. (2013). Making sense of traumatic memories: Memory qualities and psychological symptoms in emerging adults with and without abuse histories. *Memory*, 21(1), 125–142. https://doi.org/10.1080/09658211.2012.712975

Henry, M. A., Shorter, S., Charkoudian, L. K, Heemstra, J. M., Le, B., & Corwin, L. A. (2021). Quantifying fear of failure in STEM: Modifying and evaluating the Performance Failure Appraisal Inventory (PFAI) for use with STEM undergraduates. *International Journal of STEM Education*, 8, 43. https://doi.org/10.1186/s40594-021-00300-4

Jack, A. A. (2019). *The privileged poor: How elite colleges are failing disadvantaged students*. Harvard University Press.

Kricorian, K., Seu, M., Lopez, D., Ureta, E., & Equils, O. (2020). Factors influencing participation of underrepresented students in STEM fields: Matched mentors and mindsets. *International Journal of STEM Education, 7*(1), 16. https://doi.org/10.1186/s40594-020-00219-2

Longino, H. E. (1990). *Science as social knowledge: Values and objectivity in scientific inquiry.* Princeton University Press.

Schinske, J. N., Perkins, H., Snyder, A., & Wyer, M. (2016). Scientist spotlight homework assignments shift students' stereotypes of scientists and enhance science identity in a diverse introductory science class. *CBE—Life Sciences Education, 15*(3), Article 47. https://doi.org/10.1187/cbe.16-01-0002

Stout, J. G., Dasgupta, N., Hunsinger, M., & McManus, M. A. (2011). STEMing the tide: Using ingroup experts to inoculate women's self-concept in science, technology, engineering, and mathematics (STEM). *Journal of Personality and Social Psychology, 100*(2), 255–270. https://doi.org/10.1037/a0021385

Sue, D. W., Lin, A. I., Torino, G. C., Capodilupo, C. M., & Rivera, D. P. (2009). Racial microaggressions and difficult dialogues on race in the classroom. *Cultural Diversity and Ethnic Minority Psychology, 15*(2), 183–190. https://doi.org/10.1037/a0014191

7

BRINGING ABOUT CHANGE

How many of you have been in conversations with a departmental colleague who is bemoaning the fact that "we can't document the effect that our teaching has on our students. The real impact of our teaching on students won't be realized for years, if not decades, after students have been out in the 'real world.'" Frequently, it is the case that this individual has recently been tasked with writing the departmental annual assessment report and they are frustrated with the limited information they have at their disposal to inform their understanding of how practices and approaches have resulted in meaningful student growth and development over time. At the core of this expressed frustration is a recognition that change, indeed, takes time. And good, sustainable change often takes much longer. So how can we know when this kind of change is happening? How does it happen? And further, if you feel that you are in the minority of those on your campus or in your department who are working on inclusion-focused change, how can you bring more folks along to join you in your efforts?

In this chapter, we describe a number of ways that change can and does occur, and we offer recommendations for ways in which you might leverage mechanisms for change in your classrooms and research spaces, departments, and institutions. We also provide a number of individual and collective change case studies from our local institutional context that illustrate the ways that HSTEM has served as a lever for meaningful change to occur.

Guiding Questions

- How have you already seen the change process play out on your campus, at the individual and collective levels? What are the preexisting conditions and precipitating events that led to change?

- As you reflect on each of the change mechanisms described in the following, which of them feels most applicable to your own context? How can you chart a way forward that draws on some of these frameworks?
- Alternatively, where have attempts at inclusive institutional change been stymied, and why? What lessons can be learned from those moments of stagnation?

How We Wish Institutional Change Happened

As a student, I wanted changes fast and just pointed at the adults [as responsible] for the slow changes. As a [post baccalaureate HSTEM] fellow, I saw both the students' frustration as well as that of faculty and staff, and how slow change is not a problem within one person but because of the nature of these changes.

—M.K., Amherst College Class of 2017

As M.K. expresses, many of us are frustrated by slow change in the face of a great harm or problem. We expect that institutions of higher education, with all of the power, resources, and good thinkers that they contain, should be able to make rapid changes to their structures and processes when the need for change becomes apparent. Further, we often hold the expectation that increased awareness of a problem in the institution will naturally prompt changes in behaviors, values, or worldviews. It was only the lack of information that led to these behaviors in the first place, right? And so, we may believe, once clear information about the problem is provided, this new knowledge and wisdom will be employed to make immediate course corrections. As the great poet Maya Angelou said, "Do the best you can until you know better. Then when you know better, do better." We have worked with many HSTEM students who approach their action projects with this assumption, that change will happen quickly and logically once people are made aware of a challenge in need of address. Scientists, whose disciplinary approach to understanding phenomena is through the examination of empirical evidence, are even more likely to hold tightly to this expectation, that better knowledge will lead to "better" collective behavior. Objectively, we believe that we have identified the most logical and productive approach, and yet we find ourselves repeatedly surprised and frustrated when people don't immediately follow what we see as the obvious solution.

How Institutional Change More Commonly Occurs

There are cases we can point to where institutional change has happened quickly and logically. In most cases, however, system-level change happens slowly and follows a nonlinear progression. Why? These slower progressions can commonly be traced to the presence of at least one, if not more, of the following challenges: (a) A set of shared values have not been identified and embraced by the larger community; (b) all members of the community do not feel equally invested in seeing change happen, and in some cases, a subset of the community may actually benefit from preventing said change; and (c) the individual(s) tasked with leading the change efforts have not been granted the agency or resources to make that change happen (Borrego & Henderson, 2014; Holt et al., 2007). In this next section, we turn to strategies we have identified as potential approaches for recognizing when these change barriers exist and approaches that may help move change forward at our institutions.

Change Barrier 1: A Lack of Shared Value or Direction

Most of our institutions espouse, through mission statements and regular messaging, that supporting students is a core value. And we trust that members of our institutions seek to align that value with the actions of the institution—its practices and policies. Despite our assumption around this shared holistic value, however, we accept that our institutions differ in how they conceptualize what it means to support students or create inclusive spaces. And that makes sense, because our diverse institutional cultures, resources, and student demographics demand individualized approaches to inclusion. Further, students on our campuses may hold a different set of values or priorities than institutional leadership; helping students identify institutional values and develop action project plans that seek partnership with others on campus around a set of shared values and priorities is an important aspect of the HSTEM project process. Looking to the practices and policies that are core drivers at our institutions can be a helpful first step in uncovering how an institution's values are defined and then enacted.

What is an implicit set of shared values at your institution? One space in which values of inclusion may "show up" is in a college or university's policies of advancement, tenure, and promotion. For those of us with teaching positions, consider the criteria used to judge one's teaching efficacy. How are principles of inclusive teaching incorporated into the process of teaching evaluation? Student course evaluation questions may ask whether the instructor "treated students with respect" or "created a welcoming learning environment." Inherent in these metrics is the value of meaningful faculty–student relationships. Other sets of questions may ask students whether they felt "challenged by the material" or how much effort they had to exert in order to excel in the course. These questions evidence a shared value of holding high expectations for students' intellectual work, sometimes captured under the umbrella term of *rigor*. When you examine the course evaluation questions at your college or university, do they articulate a vision of inclusive teaching that resonates with you and your colleagues? If not, perhaps this observation may serve as a helpful prompt for an open conversation, with colleagues and students, about what *should* be contained in the question set, thus articulating a set of shared values that can motivate and inform institutional change and priorities.

Beyond course evaluations, a deep dive into institutional data can also prompt a conversation in which you are better able to articulate what those shared values may be, or where you notice gaps between institutional actions and institutional values. An ever growing number of colleges and universities are adopting learning analytics dashboards that allow instructors to explore student learning outcomes in their courses and departments according to student background preparation and demographics. Engaging with data that explores the outcomes of students in your courses, majors, and institutions can reveal inclusion blind spots. Time and again, departments report a sense of awakening when they see the data demonstrating differential rates of student success across student identity groups (e.g., Ndukwe & Daniel, 2020; Nunn et al., 2016). Exploring that data together with departmental or institutional colleagues, as well as in partnership with students, allows for a level of transparency and accountability that can bring about meaningful shifts. Conversations centered around student outcome data allow for a realization of where we are not in alignment between our mission, or values, and our actions, and can lead to an articulation of shared values aligned with action.

Change Barrier 2: A Lack of Shared Consensus About the Need for Change

The reason that shared values are so important for change is because our different lived experiences and identities mean that daily acts of exclusion and marginalization are not evenly distributed across all members of our community. Students, staff, and faculty holding minoritized identities carry the burden of psychological energies needed both to individually persist as scientists in a climate hostile to them while also being more likely to serve in supportive and mentoring roles for others in similar positions (e.g., Social Sciences Feminist Network Research Interest Group, 2019). When asked about their experiences at the college, through focus groups or as part of HSTEM action projects, students continue to bring our attention to the toll that navigating noninclusive spaces takes on them. As an example of this alienation, one student shared,

> I felt alienated from my classmates. Whenever I expressed these problems to close friends, they were unable to believe that it was really happening. I began to think it was something I was just perceiving wrongly. I became

unwilling to disclose that I had never had a lab class before college, that I had never worked in a lab, and that I truly was struggling to understand the material in the intro courses. This, of course, led to further alienation because it rendered me unable to find people like me who were struggling for a reason they could not understand.

Minoritized faculty and staff also speak about the additional challenges they experience navigating STEM spaces, and the ways that they work to support students and themselves within these environments. After the Uprising, Sheila reflected on her desire to be involved in change efforts, saying, "As a lesbian woman of color in STEM, students' feelings of alienation, invisibility, and doubt about belonging resonated with me. . . . [I want to] honor the courage of the students who spoke out even though talking about and improving inclusion in STEM is such a big, amorphous, and hopeless-seeming thing." One issue that we hear from inclusive STEM instructors who are working to empower students and bring about change at their institutions is that they often feel alone in their efforts. Sometimes these faculty and staff members will even report a sense that because they are working intentionally on issues of equity and inclusion in their courses, others in their departments seem to feel as though they do not need to attend to inclusion in their own classrooms or research spaces. That the checkbox for inclusive teaching has been checked, so to speak.

In a recent national convening of instructors and students who are leading HSTEM initiatives on their campuses, it was readily apparent that the majority of these individuals—students, staff, and faculty alike—were from historically excluded groups—female-identifying, people from minoritized racial and ethnic backgrounds, individuals who do not identify as heterosexual, folks with visible and invisible disabilities, people who identified as low-income or first-generation college students, and caregivers of minoritized individuals. Why is that the case? Why do we see individuals with a history of being marginalized in higher education spaces also leading the charge to change these spaces for others? In part, we believe, it is precisely because these individuals have a higher likelihood of experiencing exclusion that they are more likely to take on the work of inclusive change. As described by Amos Tversky and Daniel Kahneman (1973), the availability heuristic explains that we judge an event as having a high likelihood of occurring or reoccurring when that event is readily accessible or salient. For people with a history of marginalization, the likelihood that another act of harm or exclusion will occur again, against oneself or against another marginalized peer, is quite high. The awareness of the need for immediate and expansive institutional change is felt acutely.

A key question that we wrestle with in HSTEM is how we can bring more allies and accomplices along in this work, who perhaps have fewer personal experiences with exclusion and feel the need for inclusive change less urgently. We wonder if perhaps the availability heuristic may be leveraged in support of building a larger community of change agents. Reflect back to Sanyu Takarimbudde, Katyana Dandridge, and Lerato Teffaro sitting in the Amherst College library in the fall of 2015, discussing the publicized murders of people of color by police officers (described in chapter 1). In addition to the fact that the events were personally relevant to each of these three women, news coverage of the events was rampant. One could not avoid discussion of these violent acts and the protests and unrest that followed, and the pervasive nature of these events undoubtedly prompted more immediate and wide-ranging responses, at the local and national level, than would have been brought about by less publicized acts. We believe there is an important lesson to be learned from this: As we think about strategically bringing more individuals into this work, especially those individuals who have been insulated from some of the challenges faced by many at your college or university, making public the challenges as well as the positive efforts that have been made may work in your favor.

Often we hear frustration when the conversation turns to one that focuses on "all the good things that have happened" or "how much better it is now than when I started as a faculty member." It is true that compared to the state of higher education 20, 30, or 40 years ago, there have been *dramatic* increases in access, and tireless crusaders have worked to bring about these shifts in systems that seemed intractable (e.g., Tienda, 2013). At the same time, these celebrations of past gains can feel tone-deaf to the ongoing struggles of students, staff, and faculty at your institution. But they need not be in conflict. In fact, a concurrent approach of publicizing past gains while working toward ongoing change can make systemic change possible—and make it more likely to continue. In HSTEM, for instance, we encourage students to build on past students' action projects when possible. In addition to creating more sustainable work within the course of a single semester, the process of reflecting on what has already been accomplished, as well as the work that remains, helps students see that changes have indeed been made in response to student voice and partnership. And when more individuals believe that change is possible, then more change is, indeed, possible. As we help our colleagues and our students see that they are members of communities engaged in reflection and iterative change, we create conditions whereby iterative change is more possible.

Change Barrier 3: A Lack of Resources to Enact Change

When we talk with HSTEM instructors and inclusive change leaders, an issue that consistently arises is one of sustainability. Sustainability is not just about physical resources, but instead requires both structural and psychological support. You may find yourself asking: How long can I sustain this work, which is both energizing and emotionally demanding, on top of my full-time professional commitments? We turned this question to our HSTEM cofacilitators across the network, and here is a summary of the recommendations they provided for institutions working to support faculty, staff, and students in inclusive change efforts:

Structural Support

If increasing student agency, self-efficacy, inclusion, and institutional awareness of issues of diversity and equity are important to your institution, then this work should be structurally valued and recognized. When crafting institutional budgets, you will often hear the phrase, "Money is a statement of value." You invest in what you value, and you can discover what an institution values by exploring how they are investing their structural resources. What would placing a high value on DEI look like at your college or university? Likely, it would mean that instructors would receive credit for teaching or coteaching DEI courses, in the same fashion that they receive credit for teaching and coteaching their discipline-specific courses. In many institutions, this instructional work is performed as an "overload," as a course that is taught as another course on top of the full teaching load of an instructor. Not only is this a statement that the institution does not see equal merit in the student- or campus-related benefits of such courses, they are also choosing not to recognize the intellectual efforts and pedagogical expertise required to design and implement these courses. In a parallel fashion of crediting what is valued, students should also receive course credit for completing these courses, equivalent to credits earned in discipline-specific courses.

Speaking of students, they bring with them a wide range of expertise and insights about their experience on campus. We encourage you to invite student voices into the conversation to ensure that inclusive STEM education is something that we do *with* students, rather than a set of practices that we enact *upon* students. And when students share their expertise in the service of institutional change, we believe they should be compensated. In the same way that stipends are provided to outside speakers and external consultants are paid for their contributions to grant-funded research, student expertise should also be compensated. Too often, the students invested in changing campus climate are those who are most negatively impacted by its current state. We risk further devaluing of these students when we ask them to provide their expertise as an act of free, unrecognized labor. One of our recent HSTEM student fellows described this tension, in a conversation with faculty, staff, and administrators, as follows: "I have a double-edged sword here. You want to partner with students because they know what they want, but then the students who volunteer for the positions are the ones that are losing time from this issue anyway . . . responsibility is once again being put on the people who need help the most." This student, J.C. (who held a paid position as an HSTEM intern), went on to reflect on the longer-term implications of investing uncompensated time and energy into institutional change, saying, "Maybe if I didn't spend so much time thinking about DEI-related things, I would have better grades, or I would have more time to commit to 'hardcore STEM.' I made this decision, so I am very happy with it, but I know other students out there who feel burdened by the various antiracist work that they're doing for their departments. . . . Partnering with students is great, but we have a workload too."

Psychological Support
Partnering with students, staff, and faculty colleagues to highlight inequities and argue for change can be draining. Especially for individuals who are experiencing acts of marginalization and exclusion while concurrently fighting for more inclusive practices and policies for themselves and others, the risk of eventual "burnout" is real (Lent & Schwartz, 2012; Maslach et al., 1996; Viehl et al., 2017). *Burnout* is categorized as consisting of three phenomena: the experience of "(1) emotional exhaustion, (2) depersonalization, and (3) feelings of ineffectiveness or lack of personal accomplishment" (Viehl et al., 2017, p. 354).

How can we combat the processes that lead to burnout and argue for the psychological support needed for ourselves and others? First, we recommend emphasizing the building of community, by supporting the creation of networks of individuals working on shared enterprises at your institution and across campuses. Creating structures for weekly or biweekly check-in conversations, preferably with food or coffee provided, go a long way in helping people feel that they are not alone and that they have each other as sounding boards as they navigate institutional challenges and needs.

Second, consider how you can foster a collaborative network of DEI leaders and teachers, individuals who can share resources and share the load of teaching your equity-minded courses and mentoring students around issues of institutional change. In doing so, individuals can step into, and when needed, take time away from this work, to recharge and reenter without feeling that the work will stop without their ongoing presence and leadership. There is a danger in becoming the solo hub and leader of inclusion at your institution, especially when you haven't been provided with the recognition, resources, or partnership to enact and support those changes and yourself over time.

Finally, it's important to think about how you might use existing institutional review and recognition structures to acknowledge the work of your colleagues. DEI work does not fit nicely into our typical academic categories of teaching, research, and service, in large part because this work transcends multiple categories. We argue that due to this "bleed" across dimensions of our work lives, it is even more important to recognize this otherwise invisible labor. Adding inclusive teaching to teaching review criteria, calculating advising and service loads that acknowledge the time that particular individuals spend on DEI work, and highlighting individuals who are advancing inclusion at their institutions, are all ways to signal that this work is seen and valued.

Translational Support

A final category of support that individuals consistently identified as essential is that of helping them translate ideas into action and plans into implemented, sustained initiatives. Frequently, we leave a workshop or conference with great excitement and enthusiasm about the plans and ideas that we intend to implement and explore when we return to campus. Upon returning, however, we are quickly swept up in our daily to-do lists and urgent tasks, and our visioning rarely has the space and time to come to fruition. Similarly, students in HSTEM generate a wide range of action plans for how they will create more welcoming and inclusive campus experiences for others; they present these plans enthusiastically at the HSTEM Salon to their peers and to potential campus partners. And yet, as students navigate their other coursework and commitments, many of these action plans languish.

These observations point to a need for what we're calling "translational support," for taking these good ideas and giving them the time and resources to flourish. Perhaps this takes the form of student internships in which HSTEM alums or other students with ideas for institutional change partner with relevant campus offices to implement their action plan across a semester. For faculty and staff, perhaps there is a stipended learning community in which participants support each other in the implementation, assessment, and reflection upon the impact of equity-focused initiatives that they have designed as a result of a shared workshop or conference experience. We present these possibilities as a few of the ways in which an institution could support faculty, staff, and students in the follow-through, or translation, of their good thinking into concrete action.

Case Studies of HSTEM-Driven Change at Amherst

The HSTEM course has served as the engine for a number of levels of change at our institution. In most cases, these changes were propelled, and continue to be driven, by student voices, projects, and partnerships. These individuals experienced substantial personal change as they developed new understandings of themselves and others and new tools for being change agents on campus. Further, they contributed to larger institutional change, by articulating a shared sense of values around inclusive education, demonstrating the urgent need for change, and activating campus resources around equity-seeking work. We focus this section on some of the voices of students as well as teaching staff who have experienced individual change and contributed to larger collective changes on campus as a result of their participation in HSTEM.

Case Study 1: Student Individual Growth Through Engaging With the Course Materials

In this first case, S.T. speaks about her experience as an HSTEM student, and how her thinking about herself and her identities grew as a result of taking HSTEM. She says, "My experiences with HSTEM have led to immense academic and personal growth. I've learned how to advocate not only for myself but on behalf of those that come from all types of marginalized backgrounds. Before HSTEM, I saw science as an objective field of study where you leave your background and identity at the door when you enter that lecture room." She specifically mentions the benefits of engaging with the larger literature on diversity and marginalization in science, saying, "I know now that the intersectionality of my background, my trials and tribulations, [and] my struggles, bring fresh [and] innovative ideas to the table and in STEM fields. That's what we need if we want to collaborate as academics in answering the questions we pose as scientists in understanding the world around us. So post-HSTEM, in interviews and applications, I am happy to talk about why my identity as a Black woman is a strength and not a weakness. And I'm so sad that as a freshman I thought [what I did about myself] in my intro courses." In the previous quote, S.T. is able to extend compassion to her past self and reflect on her identities and experiences as assets that she brings to STEM. Finally, S.T. describes her hopes for the impact of HSTEM: "I hope with the work that we've all done collaboratively through this initiative, now on several colleges across the country, no freshman that arrives on campus excited about pursuing academic coursework in STEM is led to believe that they are not good enough to be the next great scientist." S.T. now understands herself to be someone who is contributing to an initiative that has the capacity to change the experience of future emerging scientists.

Case Study 2: Student Individual Growth Through the Action Project Process

In this second case study, S.A. first describes his own experiences in STEM and articulates how the Amherst Uprising allowed him to recognize that he was not alone in his feelings of marginalization. During the 2019 Amherst College Black Alumni Weekend, he shared, "I had a pretty rough first semester coming from the South and being a low-income student and just being in a completely different environment with a different demographic. I feel like transitioning was pretty hard. My first year, I was pretty close to transferring. . . . With the Uprising, something I saw is that I wasn't the only one that had these kinds of feelings, as if you didn't exactly belong on campus or that there wasn't a space for you. . . . Seeing that people from all over campus were feeling that way brought some new perspective for me."

In the HSTEM course, S.A. partnered with three other students to develop an HSTEM action project; this project took the form of designing a condensed HSTEM summer course for students who were pursuing summer STEM research. The goal of the project was to enhance community and belonging for other students interested in scientific research. In his description of their work on the project, S.A. emphasizes the important role of partnership and assessing the needs of your collaborators: "A lot of what we did is work together as a group and talk to [the faculty] and a group coordinating the summer students, to see what would work best *for them*."

When asked what he learned from this experience, and the changes he saw in himself as a result of HSTEM, S.A. focused on changes in interpersonal awareness and empathy. He said, "I feel like it's very obvious to think, 'Oh, I can recognize certain barriers that some people may have,' but actually going through the literature, seeing actual numbers, and seeing how people can fall off the STEM pipeline . . . just actually seeing that helps you understand better. . . . What is the best way to interact to bring in a positive STEM experience for somebody else? There's just been so much that I think people who have been a part of the class have been able to get out of it, in terms of not only just for STEM but just interacting with people in general."

Case Study 3: Student-Led Curricular Change

In this third case, D.S. describes the meaningful connections that he built with colleagues in the HSTEM class and the continued role that this community played in his future ability to partner to enact curricular changes in STEM. He says, "I think that one of the best downstream impacts of the class is the creation of a community, specifically a community full of students, faculty, staff, and alumni focused on improving the institution. . . . Even after the semester ended, many of us came together to help direct our respective departments as they responded to the murder of George Floyd (May 25, 2020). During this time, my classmates helped [STEM] departments lead workshops and they wrote letters to departments guiding them to adopt concrete, transparent action plans to address systemic racial racism and inequities in education."

It is interesting to note the importance of letter writing in this case; students wrote letters the STEM departments after the Uprising in 2015. Five years later, during the summer of 2020, D.S. led other alumni and students in writing a letter to their major department, saying, "I urge the department to make HSTEM a mandatory course for the major." Following departmental discussions, the Biology Department voted to include an equity and inclusion course as a requirement for students graduating from Amherst College with a degree in biology. Reflecting on this process, D.S. credits the HSTEM course and ongoing community with enabling him to bring about change. In his words, HSTEM "gives validation to students in STEM, builds empathy between students, and gives students the tools to become leaders in STEM and social justice work in STEM."

Case Study 4: Students Connecting Their Learning in HSTEM to the Broader National and Institutional Context

In this fourth and final student-focused case study, we present the case of N.C, a student alum of HSTEM who served as a peer facilitator for a later offering of the course. N.C. also explored the impact of HSTEM on students, faculty, and staff through her senior thesis research. In her reflections, N.C. describes how the course structure prepared her to engage with national events as well as larger campus-wide antiracism initiatives. Throughout her reflections, we note her sense of shared agency and responsibility for departmental-level inclusion efforts and change. She states:

> One of the goals of HSTEM is for participants to continue the practice of being human in STEM long after the course is over. So the activities and assignments in the course equip us in three critical ways for this kind of lifelong practice: (1) A grounding in the scholarly literature, (2) continuing reflection to bring the academic concepts and data into conversation with lived experiences, and (3) low-stakes practice with navigating difficult conversations and working together to affect changes on our campus. One key moment that really exemplifies this everyday practice occurred over this past summer, in early June (2020). After the high-profile lynchings of George Floyd, Brianna Taylor, and Tony McDade, we were ready to do more than go to rallies and treat this moment as another iteration of performative activism or just another forgotten headline in the news. Grounded in our HSTEM practices and tools, we were all ready to talk to our families and our friends and our peers in our communities not only about police brutality, but also ways in which structural racism surrounds us in our own academic and STEM communities. . . . We were also eager to implement our President's anti-racism call to action, while also holding the knowledge that the list of demands crafted 5 years ago from the Amherst Uprising was just a starting point.

N.C. and her colleagues leveraged their skills of partnership around several inclusion-focused initiatives at the college that year. One such initiative was the national "ShutdownSTEM" movement (Chen, 2020), a call for STEM academics to "pause their work . . . to support the ongoing Black Lives Matter movement and efforts against racism in the scientific community and society at large" (para. 1). These students worked quickly and collaboratively to seize the moment. N.C. says, "In under 48 hours, several HSTEM alums collaborated with [faculty] to assemble an hour-long workshop that would help us focus on confronting systemic racism in academia, particularly in STEM fields." N.C. also worked to partner with her major department, the Chemistry Department, to advance curricular changes and conversations across faculty, staff, and students.

Again, we note N.C.'s sense of belonging to a community that sees a need for change, as well as the impacts that she and her colleagues helped to bring about. She describes this work as follows: "We were particularly cognizant of the ways in which we needed to change as a Chemistry Department, and also as part of a larger STEM community with a history of oppression and bias. . . . We formed the Chemistry AntiRacism Advisory Committee, which is called CARAC. . . . Some of the major projects that we have established over the past year or so are (1) crafting a syllabus statement to be part of each faculty member syllabus . . . as a testament to the Department's commitment to inclusion, (2) using our weekly seminar slot to build community within the major and open up conversations about antiracism, and (3) currently in progress is our plan to implement a DEI requirement for the Chemistry major, as our fellow Biology Department has recently done." In reflecting on the changes that have been possible through HSTEM, N.C. shares, "HSTEM helps us understand that students, staff, and faculty have to partner authentically together and commit to doing the hard work, because real progress is really grounded in our lived experiences and literature and begins with listening to each other. And we can't forget that the work will never be over, because progress is rooted in communal commitment to changing our structures, and not just our behaviors."

Case Study 5: An Example of Faculty-Focused Change

In the previous case studies, we have highlighted the impact of HSTEM on students, as reflective individuals, as collaborative partners, and as change agents. We also have seen evidence of a number of faculty and staff cofacilitators and partners who have changed their pedagogical approaches and have become agents of change in their departments and at the institution. We present one such case in the following, of an instructional staff member, L.R., whose first interaction with HSTEM was through an end-of-course salon, an event to which she was invited by one of the HSTEM founders. This individual shared, "In the end, I ended up in this first annual community salon. I was already actively thinking and using inclusive practices with my teaching, but I wanted to know how the students were feeling about this because *they* are who I'm teaching, so I need to be able to think about them and what's going to best affect them and their learning."

In terms of the challenge of identifying which inclusive practices to prioritize in her teaching, L.R. said, "How can I do this in a way that is going to both benefit my students while also creating an environment where everyone feels as though they can do the work and they can feel included?" It was after that first inaugural salon that a strategic planning retreat occurred and the idea of the HSTEM inclusive handbook collectively emerged. L.R. was a key partner in crafting that resource based on the initial student action project. Pondering the benefits of the inclusive practices handbook, L.R. said, "Sometimes, honestly, the hardest part is just knowing where to start, and this document can help others have a jumping off point. . . . We drafted this handbook to ensure that the activities could be feasible in an actual classroom setting, so that you wouldn't feel overwhelmed by how much you had to do. This project was an early example of the emerging HSTEM ethos of shared responsibility for cultivating a thriving STEM community and the importance of doing the work in a partnership."

This instructor also reflected on how the HSTEM initiative helped to create a sense of community for her, as a scholar and teacher. L.R. said, "Before HSTEM, I often felt isolated in my trials for what I was trying to do to help the students in the learning process, or just how to bring them in. . . . It wasn't until HSTEM that it brought a like-minded group of people together across many disciplines, at my own institution, that were all going for the same goal. And I had no idea that so many other people felt this way because sometimes you just feel very isolated. Feeling that I wasn't alone was great and it opened up a whole new world of resources for me."

L.R. has continued to take these lessons into her work as a change agent in her department. Through an internal, departmental curricular redesign grant, she is joining with departmental colleagues to assess and identify avenues for change in the major. L.R. describes the goals of their grant-funded work: "The main actions that we were focusing on were being transparent about how our courses grow from one another, giving students resources to explore and solidify those connections, and integrating inclusive practices within these courses." Drawing on the principles of partnership, the department hired N.C. and another student to join them in their efforts to identify an even more inclusive approach to the curriculum. Finally, in terms of how this plays out in her daily teaching practice, L.R. says, "We incorporate these inclusive practices in active learning, and we're transparent about what we're trying to do. And then we allow everyone to be a human in that classroom, and so everybody feels a bit more welcome."

Conclusions

Inclusive institutional change requires transformation, in which the institution moves toward an increased level of alignment of programs, values, and missions across all departments and offices. It requires an articulation and investment in shared values and goals, a shared sense of the change as being good and needed, and the allocation of resources and agency to implement change for those tasked with doing so. For those of you who work in, or study, higher education, you know that systemic change is challenging and rare. More often than not, change happens at a smaller scale and in a less cohesive manner, through the addition of individual programs, offices, or initiatives. And when changes do occur, they typically occur over a slow institutional time course.

While we encourage you to meaningfully partner with students around institutional change, we also recognize that the time scale of an individual student's life at the college or university is quite short. Students can understandably be impatient and intolerant of this slow change. As one HSTEM instructor who has adapted and taught HSTEM on their own campus articulated, "One of the challenges is helping students to feel empowered while not giving them a false sense of agency. Many of our institutions are old and slow to change, even the ones that are labeled as 'progressive.' And that's very frustrating for students."

We walk a fine line with students in HSTEM around this issue, as we seek to help students deepen their understanding of how institutional change occurs while also working to help them make change happen more quickly, by supporting them in the development of projects that build on and extend the change work that has come before them. In this way, we can help students place their goals in a larger institutional frame, to see how their efforts align with the efforts of others, in order to sustain hope and understand challenges yet to be tackled. As you pursue your own equity-minded work, where can you also align your efforts with those that have come before? And how can we, at our own institutions, identify places to elevate student voices and enable them to be a part of driving change, in ways that enable them to serve as respected partners whose ideas are welcomed and whose labor is appropriately recognized?

This chapter has focused primarily on the processes of systemic and institutional change, but there is another level of change that we also want to draw forward: the process of becoming a more self-reflective, scholarly teacher. Undertaking this work, in partnership with students and colleagues, allows us to further our understanding of ourselves and our missions as educators. After teaching an HSTEM course, another cross-institutional partner said, "I feel like HSTEM has been really transformational for me. Doing the readings, having discussions with [students] has really opened my eyes to the range of student experiences at this institution. I think I come from a very privileged background. A lot of the assumptions I had about what my job was, how I should be doing my job, and how I should be recruiting majors and encouraging students in my classes. . . . I have really re-examined almost every part of the way I'm going about things, and it's been very meaningful to me. I've come around to a very different sense of what my role as a STEM educator is, that I'm here to help students achieve their goals and meet their dreams, rather than picking out the ones who are 'best suited for STEM.' So, I think that has been a major shift in the way I understand the work that I do." And now, expanding on the case studies and stories of change, we turn to frameworks for measuring changes, large and small, in chapter 8.

References

Borrego, M., & Henderson, C. (2014). Increasing the use of evidence-based teaching in STEM higher education: A comparison of eight change strategies: Increasing evidence-based teaching in STEM education. *Journal of Engineering Education, 103*(2), 220–252. https://doi.org/10.1002/jee.20040

Chen, S. (2020, June 9). *Researchers around the world prepare to #ShutDownSTEM and "Strike for Black Lives."* ScienceInsider. https://www.science.org/content/article/researchers-around-world-prepare-shutdownstem-and-strike-black-lives

Holt, D. T., Armenakis, A. A., Feild, H. S., & Harris, S. G. (2007). Readiness for organizational change: The systematic development of a scale. *The Journal of Applied Behavioral Science, 43*(2), 232–255. https://doi.org/10.1177/0021886306295295

Lent, J., & Schwartz, R. (2012). The impact of work setting, demographic characteristics, and personality factors related to burnout among professional counselors. *Journal of Mental Health Counseling, 34*(4), 355–372. https://doi.org/10.17744/mehc.34.4.e3k8u2k552515166

Maslach, C., Jackson, S. E., & Leiter, M. P. (1996). *Maslach burnout inventory manual* (3rd ed.). Consulting Psychologists Press.

Ndukwe, I. G., & Daniel, B. K. (2020). Teaching analytics, value and tools for teacher data literacy: A systematic and tripartite approach. *International Journal of Educational Technology in Higher Education, 17*(1), 22. https://doi.org/10.1186/s41239-020-00201-6

Nunn, S., Avella, J. T., Kanai, T., & Kebritchi, M. (2016). Learning analytics methods, benefits, and challenges in higher education: A systematic literature review. *Online Learning, 20*(2). https://doi.org/10.24059/olj.v20i2.790

Social Sciences Feminist Network Research Interest Group. (2019). The burden of invisible work in academia: Social inequalities and time use in five university departments. *Humboldt Journal of Social Relations, 39*, 228–245. http://www.jstor.org/stable/90007882

Tienda, M. (2013). Diversity ≠ inclusion: Promoting integration in higher education. *Educational Researcher, 42*(9), 467–475. https://doi.org/10.3102/0013189X13516164

Tversky, A., & Kahneman, D. (1973). Availability: A heuristic for judging frequency and probability. *Cognitive Psychology, 5*(2), 207–232. https://doi.org/10.1016/0010-0285(73)90033-9

Viehl, C., Dispenza, F., McCullough, R., & Guvensel, K. (2017). Burnout among sexual minority mental health practitioners: Investigating correlates and predictors. *Psychology of Sexual Orientation and Gender Diversity, 4*(3), 354–361. https://doi.org/10.1037/sgd0000236

8

MEASURING THE IMPACT OF INCLUSIVE EFFORTS

For many of us working in educational development and/or change in higher education, thinking about how to develop and implement assessment practices that meaningfully evaluate and inform inclusive initiatives is a key part of our practice. What is the evidence that we can draw on to demonstrate that our work is transformative for students, staff, and/or faculty partners, or for the institution of higher education more broadly? What are the secondary ripples that are emerging as a result of our efforts, and what are our aspirational goals for our scientific communities? What makes the assessment of inclusive teaching practices exciting, and also particularly challenging, is its messiness—the complexity of human behavior, the wide range of factors over which we have no control, and the varied timescales during which changes can and do occur.

As scientists, this kind of inquiry work can be a particular challenge to wrap one's head around: We cannot control all, or indeed most, of the variables acting in the system of our classrooms and labs—students' motivations, the previous experiences that students bring to our courses, the curricular and departmental demands that constrain our choices in the classroom or lab—just to name a few. But while we cannot control all of the variables within the system, we *can* be systematic in our assessment approach, asking how a change in one condition corresponds with a change in another. For instance, we might explore how the establishment of community agreements (or not) corresponds with differences in students' willingness to participate in class discussions. Or we may evaluate how metacognitive reflection as a required aspect of laboratory report assignments correlates with changes in students' collaborative work over time. If observed changes in students' learning and/or learning experience align with our visions for an inclusive STEM learning environment, then we move forward. If, however, the observed shifts demonstrate decreases in student engagement or learning, or we observe differential student experiences that suggest particular groups of students are less invited to the learning space, we can and, indeed, *should* adjust our practices.

Guiding Questions

- How do you define success? What does a more equitable, inclusive STEM community look like for you, and how will you know when it has been achieved?
- How can you tell if your institution is truly ready for, and open to, change?
- Although change processes are slow, where can you look for evidence that inclusive change is happening? How can you celebrate those markers of change, or enhanced change readiness, at your institution, to maintain momentum and energy?

Adopting an Ethic of Inquiry Into Inclusive Teaching

As Pat Hutchings writes in her introduction to a series of chapters by Carnegie scholars about their approaches to the scholarship of teaching and learning, scholarly teachers are motivated by an "ethic of inquiry"; their assessment work "is not only a practical and intellectual task but often a moral and ethical one as well" (Hutchings & Carnegie Foundation, 2000, pp. 2–3). We agree and see our moral responsibility to our students and colleagues in HSTEM and more broadly as one that requires us to take a stance of open curiosity about the impact of our practices and actions in the classroom and laboratory spaces we inhabit, to ask if these practices are meeting our intentions, and to iteratively respond to this information with improved actions and reflection. Indeed, as scientists, this approach is well aligned with how we approach our scholarly research, through the framework of the scientific method. Sarah and her colleague, Dan Bernstein, describe an inquiry-based approach to teaching in this way:

> [T]he teacher serves not only as a source of knowledge but also as an active pursuer of knowledge about how learning progresses in the course. Scholarly faculty members see the classroom as a laboratory, in which they design and reflect on assignments and activities that have the power to generate greater understanding in students and themselves. (Bunnell & Bernstein, 2012, p. 15)

Building on her argument that the assessment of teaching and learning is our ethical responsibility as educators, Hutchings provides a guiding taxonomy of assessment question types that one might ask about the impact of one's inclusive practices on teaching and learning outcomes (Hutchings & Carnegie Foundation, 2000). These questions, which also align with the steps of human-centered design (IDEO, 2015), are categorized by the type of question asked, as noted in the following section.

"What Is" Questions

These assessment questions focus on deep descriptions of the practices or conditions operating within a learning environment. It is not uncommon for a "what is" question to serve as a launching pad for future inquiries into the other question types. An example of a "what is" question in HSTEM: How are students working together in their small-group discussions of the readings, and what are the cognitive and affective strategies that they are employing in these collaborations?

"What Works" Questions

This kind of assessment question is the most common, focusing on how student outcomes shift following the implementation of a set of practices or programs. An example of a "what works" question in HSTEM: Does the use of metacognitive reflection exercises, such as exam wrappers, lead to improvements in students' learning across the course of the semester?

"Visions of the Possible" Questions

Hutchings describes these assessment questions as those that identify future potentials in teaching and learning—an identification of a desired change in the status quo of teaching approach or value. An example of a "visions of the possible" HSTEM question: What would it look like to build a fully inclusive STEM experience for students, and how would the meeting of this condition change how students learn and experience the process of learning at our institutions?

"New Conceptual Frameworks" Questions

Finally, these questions ask us to develop new ways of envisioning how teaching and learning occur, as well as whether frameworks from other disciplinary arenas may serve to inform our own thinking about teaching and learning in our local context. An example of a "new conceptual frameworks" HSTEM question: How can we take lessons learned from community organizing to improve our inclusive approach to partnering with students in our courses?

Self-Questions

In discussions of our work through Being Human in STEM, we are often asked how we evaluate the impact of this work. While it is most common to read in the literature about "what works" in DEI efforts, and we share some observations about "what works" in our own context in chapter 7, we believe that it is important to take the time to engage with the other assessment question types as well. The "what is" questions allow us to engage deeply with the process of learning, so that we can better understand the key mechanisms and variables that contribute to inclusive or less inclusive education. The "new conceptual frameworks" allow us to challenge our ingrained disciplinary assumptions and adapt the good work of others to our own teaching context without the need to fully reinvent the wheel. And finally, "visions of the possible" give us hope and excitement for what might be, in our institutions, our departments, and classroom spaces.

Student Perspectives on "What Works" and "Visions of the Possible" in HSTEM

To help prompt your thinking about how you might engage these forms of inquiry in your own inclusive teaching investigations, we present the following example. In June of 2021, we convened HSTEM partners from 12 institutions across the country, all of whom have implemented a Being Human in STEM course on their own campuses. Faculty, staff, and students from these institutions spent 2 days engaged in dialogue about their experiences teaching and learning in the HSTEM course, reflecting on successes, challenges, and opportunities for growing the HSTEM network. In chapter 9 of this text, you'll find an in-depth discussion of how each of these network partners have modified and adapted the HSTEM course to their own institutional context.

In one of the 2021 conference sessions, student participants and student cofacilitators reflected on the individual and institutional impacts that they have observed as a result of HSTEM.

What was clear from those reflections is that students were answering many "what works" questions about HSTEM. They identified the course as a place that allows them to think more critically about STEM, about others' experiences, and about how scientists make their work public. Students also recognized that the flexible nature of the course is a strength, because it is able to evolve its focus based on the current needs and events on a campus, as well as the students, staff, and faculty in the classroom. And they identified three "small things that have made a big difference" for them and their growth as individuals, including "hearing others' stories in a safe space," receiving "micro affirmations" about the value and importance of their contributions, and experiencing "accessibility of resources," including faculty, staff, campus offices, and peers, who were committed to supporting them in their efforts and action project proposals.

On the other hand, students also reflected on the challenges, or "what works" less well. Here they focused on a desire for more partnership across campus, to include a greater amount of perspectives and voices, a frustration with what they sense is a tendency toward institutional inertia, and a need for greater administrative support. And finally, they looked forward toward a "vision of the possible," one in which a course focused on inclusivity, awareness of one's own and others' identities, and partnerships is an institutional requirement for all students pursuing a higher education degree. These students felt that the skills and experiences fostered in the course were essential for all students, regardless of career trajectory.

Establishing Your Operational Definitions of Success

The first step in this process of assessment, therefore, is honing in on the questions that feel most important to you about the impact of your inclusive teaching practices. Following that process, the next step is to determine where you will look for information that will help you determine whether your teaching practices are having the desired effects. What we are talking about is setting an operational definition, which can prove to be more challenging than one may expect, especially if you are new to this kind of assessment. For those of us who conduct research in the natural sciences, setting operational definitions of the outcome variables in our disciplinary work can seem almost automatic. Let's look at Sheila's disciplinary research for an example: To explore whether a computer modeling algorithm is accurately capturing the protein folding and unfolding process, Sheila and her research team calculate a goodness-of-fit statistic for the data simulated by the model compared to the behavior of the actual experimental data; improvements in the alignment of the simulated data with the experimental data demonstrate improvements in the computer algorithm. In this case, it's clear that an improved alignment between the simulated and experimental data is her operational definition of success.

When we think about creating inclusive STEM communities or evaluating the impact of a particular HSTEM course module or practice, the operational definitions of what constitutes success can become more complex. How would I know that my teaching practices have significantly impacted a sense of community or belonging for students? What would I measure to demonstrate that students feel less marginalized in our research labs than they did prior to our efforts? How could I demonstrate that a departmental climate has become more inclusive for students, staff, and faculty? These questions first require defining what evidence would be compelling to us as markers of an increased sense of community, reduction in experiences of marginalization, or an enhanced departmental inclusive climate. Those are complex constructs, and the measures we employ to evaluate changes in these aspects of student experience and institutional climate should reflect that complexity.

In the next sections, we discuss several areas where you may focus your own operational definitions of success, along with their benefits and limitations. What you ultimately select as your operational definitions of success, however, will depend upon several contextual factors that will be specific to your work, including the nature of your inquiry question itself, the data that you can systematically collect or access, and the values and aspirations that you, your colleagues, and your institution hold.

Measuring Persistence and Retention

In many scholarly domains, metrics of retention and persistence serve as the operational definition of success for an inclusive teaching intervention. These measures may document the percentage of students who declare an undergraduate STEM major and then graduate with a STEM degree or, using a longer time horizon, the percentage of STEM undergraduates who continue on to graduate or professional degree attainment in a STEM field. Indeed, there is much evidence that speaks to the "what is" retention question in STEM. Referred to as the "leaky pipeline," students from marginalized identities are more likely to fall out of the STEM training pipeline than students from majority identities. In a North American context, that means that at the end of the pipe's route, a greater number of white and male students flow out of the preparatory pipeline into STEM careers than students of other identities. Further, when we examine the proportion of minoritized students (nonwhite or Asian, nonmale identifying) who begin their higher educational studies with an intention to major in STEM, the proportional decline of these students as STEM graduates and in STEM careers is greater than the decline in STEM persistence of their majority counterparts (Blackburn, 2017; Blickenstaff, 2005; Estrada, 2016).

While the succinct analogy of the leaky pipeline is compelling, it also ignores several features of STEM training phenomena (Gibbs, 2014). First, it assumes that all students travel down the same pipe. Instead, we know that nonwhite and nonmale students experience higher levels of alienation, stigmatization, and harassment in their training programs than do their male, white, and Asian counterparts (e.g., Clancy et al., 2014). The inside of the pipe is objectively a more hostile environment for these students. Secondly, the pipeline analogy positions students as passive agents who merely travel through the pipe over time, rather than agentic, conscious beings who make choices about whether they wish to remain in the pipeline and, if so, how they will act on the pipe to change the nature of the pipe itself. In a survey of 1,500 recent biomedical sciences PhD graduates, Gibbs et al. (2014) found that individuals from minoritized racial and ethnic backgrounds, and especially women from minoritized backgrounds, were significantly less likely than white, male PhDs to be interested in a faculty research career. These individuals were actively choosing less traditional STEM careers, such as public policy work, and often described the traditional STEM pipeline as a place that did not feel supportive, welcoming, or aligned with their goals for their own work. Indeed, after interviewing their study participants, the authors concluded that attempts to create more inclusive STEM pathways need to "consider the influences of the broader dynamics and reward structures operating at the institutional and systemic levels, and whether/how they might exert differential selective pressures across social identity" (Gibbs et al., 2014, p. 14).

Similarly, Beronda Montgomery, a science communicator and plant biologist, encourages us to consider a "new conceptual framework" question, one in which we apply the knowledge from how environmental processes contribute to individual plant processes to the work of inclusive institutional change. Montgomery (2020) writes,

> We would be better served, even if only as a starting point for engaging growth-based perspectives, to approach our assessments and support of colleagues through a stewardship-based transduction model that, in effect, mirrors what we know about plants. Such framing would allow us to transfer what we as plant biologists know about plant fitness and success being significantly influenced by environmental conditions, and the ability of plants to perceive and respond to dynamic conditions, to interpersonal relationships within our communities. (p. 3374)

Doing this work

> will require us to shift from "gatekeeping" practices, in which we carefully guard the gates and make subjective, and often biased, decisions about who "fits" and is worthy to enter, to actively using "groundskeeping"

practices, whereby we thoughtfully tend our environments to actively support access and progress, and recognize and remove barriers to individual success. (p. 3374)

Taken together, these arguments point to a problematic aspect of the leaky pipeline metaphor: When a pipe is leaking, we shouldn't keep putting more water through the pipe. Rather, we should excavate the pipe and build a stronger one in its place.

Pursuing a college degree requires extended effort, hardship, and perseverance from all students, and even more so when students feel unwelcome in their learning spaces. Measures of retention and persistence that do not account for institutional climate may actually be telling us more about students' own grit and determination to sustain their efforts in the face of adversity than they are about our own efforts to help them succeed in STEM. And so we ask: Where in our own institutions are we structurally unsound in our support of women and students of color in STEM? Only when we commit to the infrastructural revisions required to create a fully inclusive STEM educational pathway will measures of retention and persistence help us clearly address our questions of "what works."

Measuring Student Self-Efficacy and Belonging in STEM

As liberal arts educators, it is our goal to empower students with self-knowledge and transferable skills to make active and informed decisions about their future areas of study and how they will make impacts on their communities. For us (Sarah, Megan, and Sheila), retaining 100% of students who indicate initial interest in STEM within STEM majors or careers is not an aspiration. Rather, we hope that the practices we describe in this book, and the good work that so many others are doing, will provide students with the support and structures to allow them to feel as though they truly belong in the STEM community, while also facilitating their self-exploration into whether they desire to focus their careers in STEM fields or in other areas of study.

Bryan Dewsbury (2020) describes an inclusive classroom climate as one in which "all stakeholders feel a sense of belonging, and buy into the concept of the community," which allows the classroom to "become a place of trust." He argues further,

> Inclusion means creating an environment where exposures to diverse experiences are structured into the course, helping students strengthen themselves socially, emotionally and mentally. . . . For this space to occur, there needs to be an atmosphere of trust and community in the classroom that allows each individual to feel that everyone, including themselves, is fully invested in their success. (p. 186)

How do we know that we have cocreated such a space with our students? Gloriana Trujillo and Kimberly Tanner (2014) provide some helpful assessment frameworks for evaluating students' experience of the classroom climate, specifically focused on the areas of students' self-efficacy, belonging, and the amount to which they identify themselves as scientists. Measures of self-efficacy, or belief in one's ability to successfully complete a challenging task, include questions such as "How confident are you that after reading an article about [disciplinary topic], you could explain its main ideas to another person?" Changes in performance on this kind of assessment over time, especially when compared to baseline changes in self-efficacy across the semester in a course that did not place a heavy emphasis on fostering a positive classroom climate, would provide evidence that your interventions are making meaningful shifts in student experience.

When exploring if you are making headway on creating a stronger sense of belonging for all students in our courses, you may consider incorporating questions from the National Survey of Hispanic Students Sense of Belonging Scale developed by Sylvia Hurtado and Deborah Carter (1997). This scale explores students' general sense of belonging on campus (e.g., "I feel that I am a member of the campus community") as well as their level of disciplinary belonging (e.g., "When I am in a math setting, I feel respected"). Incorporating assessments of belonging are particularly helpful when coupled with the onset of specific campus climate efforts.

Finally, for most of us who have made careers in the sciences, one of the most powerful aspects of our identities is that of being a scientist. This strongly held sense of identity in science appears to be a powerful predictor of whether students, and especially minoritized students, persist in STEM (e.g., Seymour & Hunter, 2019). Assessments of science identity may ask students to reflect on the amount that they recognize themselves as being a particular kind of scientist as well as their evaluations of the quality of their science-specific skills (i.e., how you talk about and conduct science; Carlone & Johnson, 2007). Over the past several offerings of Being Human in STEM at Amherst, we have asked students at the beginning and the end of the course to rate, on a 1 ("do not identify at all") to 5 ("identify strongly") Likert scale, how much they view themselves as

- a STEM person who is thriving
- a STEM person who is surviving
- a non-STEM person who is thriving
- a non-STEM person who is surviving

An analysis of the change scores, examining students' ratings from the beginning to the end of the semester in a recently offered HSTEM course, indicates that students' perceptions of themselves as STEM people who are thriving significantly increased from the beginning to the end of the course. This is exciting, as it suggests that investing in the work of building inclusive STEM communities, through an emphasis on reflection, vulnerability, and humanity, changes how students view their own empowerment in our STEM classrooms and laboratories over the course of a single semester. As one student from this class wrote, "What I feel like has changed is what I think it means to be a 'STEM person.' I definitely recognize the humanity and social aspects of STEM a lot more and account [for] that in my definition of a STEM person."

When asked to explain why they rated themselves as they did, a student who identified themselves as a STEM student who is surviving, rather than thriving, said, "I have survived in all my classes due to personal resilience and grit, and supportive professors and friends. I have, however, not thrived in all my classes because of a gap in preparation level making some concepts really hard to grasp, dealing with imposter syndrome, and balancing my coursework." Another such student said, "As far as the surviving vs. thriving component, I feel that I have had very few courses in which I feel like I'm welcomed in the space. For one thing, I don't think I've been in a class that highlights the achievements of scientists that look like me, which from my perspective makes it easy for my classmates to view my participation as an anomaly. In general I'm not very comfortable talking to my peers because of a bit of general shyness coupled with a general experience of being belittled or ignored." This student completed their reflection by saying, "Most of my STEM classes feel like I'm just passing through so that I can achieve my greater goal of being a doctor instead of having a deeper appreciation for the various disciplines."

For students who rated themselves as thriving in STEM, they tended to emphasize the sense of community, belonging, and support they receive in their courses. A student who rated themselves as someone who is thriving in STEM wrote, "What I feel now is not that the barriers and systems of oppression that pervade STEM have changed, it's just that I have a wider, understanding and loving community to walk through and climb over those barriers together." Another thriving student mentioned the contribution of HSTEM to their thinking, saying, "I have thrived in that I have gotten through every STEM course with a good grade, I have not been discouraged from leaving STEM, and I have been able to get help when I needed it. . . . [My] view of the struggle has changed since taking this course because I realized that struggling with the material is normal." Gathering these reflections from students, and seeing the significant change in the number of students who see themselves as thriving in STEM after a semester in HSTEM, provides us with meaningful evidence that the course is having the kinds of changes on students that we value and seek to provide to others.

Institutional Readiness for Change

As the previous sections have demonstrated, there are several approaches we can draw on to evaluate student outcomes and students' experiences of our inclusive efforts. Looking more holistically, you may also wish to ask "what is" questions about the nature of your own institutional culture and landscape. What are current indicators that you can point to as signs that your institution is becoming one that is ready for change to occur? In the previous chapter, we presented a series of processes through which systemic, institutional change can occur, and we shared a number of case study examples of how students, staff, and faculty have brought about meaningful inclusive change on our campus. "Institutional readiness for change" might be operationally defined as an increase in breadth and depth of campus conversations that attend to inclusivity. As you consider your own institutional landscape, who are the individuals talking about issues of equity in their teaching, practices for inclusive mentoring of research students, or antiracist practices for supporting untenured faculty in their departments? Are these folks the same people who were in these conversations 5 years ago, or have you noticed an expansion in the number of people involved in these conversations, their positions at the institution, and/or the depth of the discourse? What institutional projects are current priorities, and do you notice an increase in the number of initiatives that are working to support DEI missions? And what is the nature of student-driven initiatives at your institution? Do you notice an increase in the number of student efforts that are attending to inclusive teaching, learning, and holistic student success?

All of these shifts in the on-the-ground climate of an institution indicate a priming for the community to make greater strides later. When you learn of these efforts (big or small) by your colleagues, we encourage you to document them and shout them from the rooftops. At our own institution, we utilize "hack sessions" to encourage faculty and staff to share the inclusive practices that they are using in their classes and laboratories, for just this reason. Not only do these sessions foster a sense of shared values, but we have witnessed the power of such sessions to spark larger initiative and enhanced partnerships in the future.

We make no secret of the fact that doing the work of enhancing the inclusivity of STEM can be exhausting and frustrating. But on days when this work feels draining or impossible, highlighting what *is* happening can serve as a much-needed source of sustenance. And even more than that, triangulating those efforts and looking for points of convergence will provide key insights into potential ways forward that will have shared momentum and respond to an institutional readiness for change. As Roxå et al. (2011) note in their network modeling approach to organizational change in higher education,

> The sheer complexity of culture construction and maintenance in academic organizations is likely to cause any single, isolated attempt for change to fail. Instead, we argue that a multitude of interrelated initiatives over a long period of time is likely to distinguish strategies that are successful in influencing academic teaching and learning cultures. (p. 99)

We agree, and we hope that this chapter has helped provide some ways forward in thinking about how to evaluate the impact of the multiple, interrelated inclusive initiatives on your own campuses.

Conclusions

As you think about your own inclusive efforts, in STEM or more broadly, we encourage you to reflect upon the kinds of questions you have and will continue to ask of this work ("what is," "what works," "what is possible," and "what emerging conceptual frameworks would inform your understanding") as well as your operational definitions of success. Existing institutional data on persistence and retention may well serve to address these questions, but partnering with students to explore these questions together may provide insights into student experiences at your institution, and opportunities for improved inclusion, that you would not have thought to address on your own. You cannot merely add an HSTEM-type course into the curriculum and expect institutional change to result. However, intentional partnering with others on campus, and the establishment of shared assessment practices and goals, driven by and informing the work of a community of engaged partners, can spark transformative, across-campus conversations and open avenues for change to occur.

References

Blackburn, H. (2017). The status of women in STEM in higher education: A review of the literature 2007–2017. *Science & Technology Libraries*, *36*(3), 235–273. https://doi.org/10.1080/0194262X.2017.1371658

Blickenstaff, J. (2005). Women and science careers: Leaky pipeline or gender filter? *Gender and Education*, *17*(4), 369–386. https://doi.org/10.1080/09540250500145072

Bunnell, S., & Bernstein, D. J. (2012). Overcoming some threshold concepts in scholarly teaching. *Journal of Faculty Development*, *26*(3), 14–18.

Carlone, H. B., & Johnson, A. (2007). Understanding the science experiences of successful women of color: Science identity as an analytic lens. *Journal of Research in Science Teaching*, *44*(8), 1187–1218. https://doi.org/10.1002/tea.20237

Clancy, K. B. H., Nelson, R. G., Rutherford, J. N., & Hinde, K. (2014). Survey of academic field experiences (SAFE): Trainees report harassment and assault. *PLoS ONE*, *9*(7), e102172. https://doi.org/10.1371/journal.pone.0102172

Dewsbury, B. M. (2020). Deep teaching in a college STEM classroom. *Cultural Studies of Science Education*, *15*(1), 169–191. https://doi.org/10.1007/s11422-018-9891-z

Estrada, M. (2016). Improving underrepresented minority student persistence in STEM. *CBE Life Science Education*, *15*(5). https://doi.org/10.1187/cbe.16-01-0038

Gibbs, K. (2014). Beyond "the pipeline": Reframing science's diversity challenge. *Scientific American*. https://blogs.scientificamerican.com/voices/beyond-the-pipeline-reframing-science-s-diversity-challenge/

Gibbs, K. D., McGready, J., Bennett, J. C., & Griffin, K. (2014). Biomedical science Ph.D. career interest patterns by race/ethnicity and gender. *PLoS ONE*, *9*(12), e114736. https://doi.org/10.1371/journal.pone.0114736

Hurtado, S., & Carter, D. F. (1997). Effects of college transition and perceptions of the campus racial climate on Latino college students' sense of belonging. *Sociology of Education*, *70*(4), 324. https://doi.org/10.2307/2673270

Hutchings, P., & Carnegie Foundation for the Advancement of Teaching (Eds.). (2000). *Opening lines: Approaches to the scholarship of teaching and learning.* Carnegie Foundation for the Advancement of Teaching.

IDEO (Ed.). (2015). *The field guide to human-centered design.* Design Kit.

Montgomery, B. L. (2020). Planting equity: Using what we know to cultivate growth as a plant biology community. *The Plant Cell*, *32*(11), 3372–3375. https://doi.org/10.1105/tpc.20.00589

Roxå, T., Mårtensson, K., & Alveteg, M. (2011). Understanding and influencing teaching and learning cultures at university: A network approach. *Higher Education*, *62*(1), 99–111. https://doi.org/10.1007/s10734-010-9368-9

Seymour, E., & Hunter, A.-B. (2019). *Talking about leaving revisited: Persistence, relocation, and loss in undergraduate STEM education.* Springer. https://doi.org/10.1007/978-3-030-25304-2

Trujillo, G., & Tanner, K. D. (2014). Considering the role of affect in learning: Monitoring students' self-efficacy, sense of belonging, and science identity. *CBE—Life Sciences Education*, *13*(1), 6–15. https://doi.org/10.1187/cbe.13-12-0241

9

GROWING THE HSTEM NETWORK

Adapting the HSTEM Course Across Institutions

We are energized by the number of institutions who, after learning about the HSTEM initiative, express interest in adapting the HSTEM course and ethos to their local context and departments. In this chapter, we feature 10 institutions who were early adopters of HSTEM; in profiling these campus leaders and courses, we hope to provide inspiration and encouragement for others to do the same (see Table 9.1). These founding facilitators learned about the Amherst HSTEM course through word of mouth and personal connections in the early days of the initiative, and many have since offered multiple iterations of their adapted HSTEM course and shared their work with others.

In constructing this chapter, we drew from the content and reflections these institutional partners presented at the HSTEM National Conference in June 2021, a convening that was funded by the National Science Foundation. At this virtual gathering, individuals from these founding institutions shared their experiences as cofacilitators and/or students in HSTEM and reflected on the impact of this course for themselves and their communities. Their reflections revealed flexibility as a strength of the HSTEM course model; the HSTEM course is designed not as a static structure but rather as a flexible framework, able to evolve and be iteratively shaped by facilitators, students, and institutional dynamics. Indeed, the HSTEM network continues to expand each year, to more diverse and varied institutions, and institutional adopters then continue to share resources and engage colleagues in conversations about HSTEM, as the ripples continue to spread. We as authors therefore are not aware of the full breadth of how the HSTEM model has been adapted and modified; this chapter presents a slice of only some of the myriad ways that this process has occurred.

TABLE 9.1
Early Adopters of HSTEM: Institutional Profiles

Name of Institution	Type of Institution	Student Demographic Profile[†]
Amherst College	Private liberal arts college	1,745 undergraduate students 52% female, 48% male 47% students of color 13% international students 25% Pell Grant–eligible students 17% first-generation students (class of 2025) 21% students registered with office of disability
Davidson College	Private liberal arts college	1,983 undergraduate students 52% female, 48% male 24% students of color 9% international students 15% Pell Grant–eligible students 12.1% first-generation students 11% students registered with office of disability
DePauw University	Private liberal arts university	1,752 undergraduate students 52% female, 48% male 20% students of color 19% international students 22% Pell Grant–eligible students 20% first-generation students 3% or fewer students registered with office of disability
Macalester College	Private liberal arts college	2,049 undergraduate students 59% female, 41% male 33% students of color 12% international students 19% Pell Grant–eligible students 17% first-generation students 21% students registered with office of disability

Name of Institution	Type of Institution	Student Demographic Profile†
Mount Holyoke College	Private liberal arts college	2,040 undergraduate students 100% female 26% students of color 19% international students 21% Pell Grant–eligible students 18% first-generation students 17% students registered with office of disability
Skidmore College	Private liberal arts college	2,582 undergraduate students 60% female, 40% male 26% students of color 11% international students 16% Pell Grant–eligible students 15% first-generation students 16% students registered with office of disability
Soka University of America	Private liberal arts university	403 undergraduate students 66% female, 34% male 36% students of color 53% international students 21% Pell Grant–eligible students 3% or fewer students registered with office of disability
University of Rhode Island	Public land-grant university	14,908 undergraduate students 57% female, 43% male 22% students of color 1% international students 19% Pell Grant–eligible students 33% first-generation students 11% students registered with office of disability
University of Utah	Public state university	24,643 undergraduate students 48% female, 52% male 27% students of color 4% international students 24% Pell Grant eligible students 25% first-generation students 5% students registered with office of disability

(*Continues*)

Table 9.1 (*Continued*)

Name of Institution	Type of Institution	Student Demographic Profile[†]
Williams College	Private liberal arts college	1,987 undergraduate students 50% female, 50% male 40% students of color 8% international students 22% Pell Grant–eligible students 17% first-generation students 9% students registered with office of disability
Yale University	Private research university	4,703 undergraduate students 50% female, 50% male 54% students of color 11% international students 24% Pell Grant–eligible students 19% first-generation students (class of 2024) 22% students registered with office of disability

[†] All data, other than the percentage of first-generation students at each institution, were retrieved from National Center for Education Statistics for the 2020–2021 academic year (https://nces.ed.gov/collegenavigator). The information about the percentage of first-generation students was provided by the HSTEM partners at each institution. Additionally, we wish to acknowledge that given the limits of demographic information collected by higher education institutions, the data do not fully represent the range of student identities, including gender, sex, and race, held by students on each campus.

Guiding Questions

- What are the ongoing and emergent initiatives at your institution that you may leverage in support of starting an HSTEM course in your home department?
- Which inter- and intradepartmental colleagues may be excited to partner with you in this work?
- What are the pressing issues around inclusion for students at your campus right now? How might you incorporate those themes into your course design? How might you start to build bridges with campus offices that could support students in their change efforts?

Early Adopters of HSTEM: Institutional Profiles

An overview of the timeline for when the 10 institutions described in the following offered HSTEM courses on their campuses is included in Figure 9.1. Each circle indicates an individual course offering. Taken together, this figure demonstrates how HSTEM continues to grow.

Figure 9.1. Timeline of HSTEM course offerings.

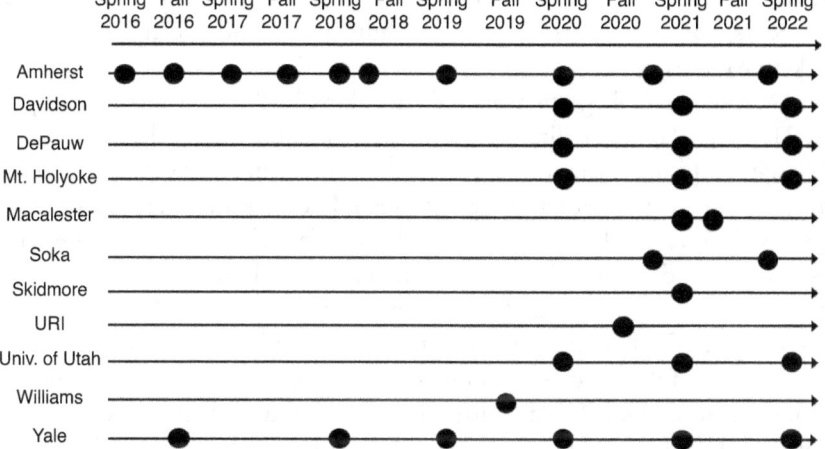

Davidson College first connected with the HSTEM network when Barbara Lom, the founding faculty member, attended a Liberal Arts Collaborative for Digital Innovation conference at Amherst College in April of 2019. Lom was already working with students and faculty members at Davidson who were pushing for more consideration of equity and inclusion in STEM; she recognized that the HSTEM course was an opportunity to formalize and institutionalize that mission. The course aligns with Davidson's work under their Howard Hughes Medical Institute (HHMI) Inclusive Excellence grant, and it also fulfills their justice, equality, and community graduation requirement for all students. The HSTEM course has been offered annually through the Biology Department since 2020, with Lom as the single faculty facilitator. The class enrolls predominantly STEM majors and has no prerequisites. This full-credit course meets for 75 minutes twice a week, and the faculty facilitator receives full teaching credit as well.

DePauw University received an HHMI Inclusive Excellence grant in 2018 to engage in work around issues of equity in STEM. Facilitators at DePauw first learned of the HSTEM initiative when their provost connected with Sheila after her presentation about HSTEM at an American Association of Colleges and Universities conference and invited her to campus in 2018. They launched their HSTEM course in the spring of 2020 following a student protest that was responding to both campus and national events. The DePauw HSTEM course has been cofacilitated by two faculty members, Dana Dudle in biology and Selma Poturovic in chemistry and biochemistry. The course is taught as a half-credit course that counts as an elective for students who are completing majors in either department.

Each faculty cofacilitator receives half credit for teaching the course. The class meets for 110 minutes once a week. While it primarily enrolls STEM students, some students majoring in humanities and social sciences also take the course.

Macalester College first offered their HSTEM course in the spring of 2021, taught by cofacilitators Devavani Chatterjea, a faculty member in biology, and Louisa Bradtmiller, a faculty member in environmental studies. In the wake of the murder of George Floyd, Chatterjea was approached by a group of students who had started a collective to improve equity in the classroom and student experience; these students were looking for mechanisms to engage faculty in these efforts. Chatterjea and Bradtmiller had learned about the HSTEM initiative through other individuals in their disciplinary networks, and they decided to offer a pilot version of the HSTEM course as a one-credit seminar. The class met virtually for 1 and a half hours each week for 7 weeks. The faculty cofacilitators did not receive teaching credit for this pilot offering of the course.

An open letter to the institution written by students in the pilot course, and others, prompted concrete commitments from STEM faculty members and departments toward a continued commitment to developing more inclusive STEM learning spaces at Macalester. Leveraging that momentum, Chatterjea offered a full-credit HSTEM course during the 2021 summer session. Unlike the previous offering that enrolled mostly third- and fourth-year students from the sciences, this version of the course was populated by STEM and non-STEM students in all stages of their academic studies. The equity-minded action project proposals that students generated in this version of the HSTEM course included interventions that suggested revising course registration processes, improving access across the college for disabled students, and providing academic credit for students who engage in STEM outreach efforts in the surrounding community.

Mount Holyoke College is the first women's college to offer an HSTEM course. The HSTEM course facilitator, Michelle Markley, first learned about HSTEM when she attended the HSTEM summit at Yale in 2018. At that time, student activists in STEM at Mount Holyoke were voicing concerns about access and inclusion in the classroom as well as challenges navigating pathways to graduate school, summer research opportunities, and other experiences critical to student success. As a result, there was a growing awareness on campus of the need to start working more directly for change. The Mount Holyoke HSTEM course was first offered in spring 2020. Markley is the lone faculty facilitator, although faculty colleagues assist with syllabus development. Additionally, a student cofacilitator serves as the community-based learning mentor; in this role, they provide training sessions focused on the principles of community engagement and qualitative research skills. The course is a full-credit, 200-level course, and the faculty facilitator receives full teaching credit. The course is taught under a cross-disciplinary course designation, has no prerequisites (with the exception of not accepting first-year students), and does not fulfill a specific distribution requirement.

Skidmore College launched their HSTEM course at a moment of synergy. At the same time that Kelly Sheppard was named chair of both the Chemistry Department and the college's committee overseeing the general education curriculum in 2016, there was a concurrent institutional push for courses to better engage issues of equity, inclusion, and justice at the college. Skidmore had just introduced a general education curriculum emphasizing social justice and reflection, including a "Bridge Experience" requirement that encourages students to integrate theory and application as they engage topics related to power, justice, and societal inequities. Skidmore was also a recent recipient of an HHMI Inclusive Excellence grant. When a group of students approached Sheppard about strategies for inclusion in the Chemistry Department, he reached out to Becky Wai-Ling Packard, a colleague in psychology and education at Mount Holyoke College, and she suggested that he explore the HSTEM model. He attended the HSTEM Summit at Yale in 2018 with some of his students, the college approved the HSTEM course in 2020, and the course was taught for the first time in spring 2021.

Skidmore's interdisciplinary HSTEM course counts as three credit hours for both student participants and faculty facilitators. As a Bridge Experience course, it is capped at 20 students and requires that students complete a written reflection about what they have learned in the course and how it has informed their understanding of their educational experiences and future perspectives. The class meets for 55 minutes 3 days per week. Sheppard has been the sole faculty facilitator, although other STEM faculty members have expressed interest in teaching the course in future semesters.

Soka University of America (SUA) launched their HSTEM course when M. Nidanie Henderson-Stull joined their faculty as an assistant professor of biochemistry and a faculty fellow in Soka's newly established Center for Race, Ethnicity, and Human Rights (REHR). The REHR Center was founded to encourage inquiry, research, and constructive dialogue related to race, ethnicity, human rights, and their intersections. As a fellow in this new center, Henderson-Stull had the opportunity to develop a new course engaging these themes. Having previously been a faculty member at Amherst College, she brought the HSTEM model and enthusiasm for partnering with students along with her. Henderson-Stull partnered with five students to develop an HSTEM course in the wake of Soka's own uprising, prompted by a non-Black SUA student sharing a post with the n-word on social media (for more information about this event, see Huỳnh et al., 2021). Their HSTEM course was further motivated by the killing of George Floyd by police in Henderson-Stull's own neighborhood and the blatant disparities in the impact of the COVID-19 pandemic on people of color. She and her students leveraged Soka University's learning cluster model, 3-and-a-half-week immersive courses codesigned by faculty members and students to explore a problem of interest, to launch their HSTEM course in January of 2021.

The University of Rhode Island invited faculty to develop one-credit, tuition-free courses, to be offered in the fall of 2020, focused on interesting topics that would motivate students to continue their studies during the COVID-19 pandemic. Cofacilitators Victoria C. Chávez, then computer science lecturer at URI, and Bryan Dewsbury, then associate professor of biology also at URI, each came to the course with a previous background in HSTEM. Chávez completed a course very similar in focus and origin to HSTEM while they were an undergraduate student at Brown University. Dewsbury learned about the course from an HSTEM student at Yale University who attended a lecture he was giving at the institution (he further connected with Sarah to learn more about the initiative and was asked to join the HSTEM advisory board). The HSTEM course at URI was offered through the Computer Science Department, and the facilitators note that the departmental affiliation had an impact on enrollment; it limited the population of students who would explore it as an option, but it also allowed the facilitators to emphasize the role that identity plays in technology fields. Both Dewsbury and Chávez have since changed their institutional affiliations, but they are appreciative of the opportunity to share the HSTEM model with the URI community when a unique opportunity to do so presented itself.

The University of Utah was the first large, public state university to offer an HSTEM course. The HSTEM course was launched in spring 2020 by Claudia De Grandi, who first served as a cofacilitator of the course when she was a postdoctoral fellow at Yale. The course satisfies the university general education diversity requirement for students and is one of the few such courses that do so from a STEM perspective; the course also grants credit for students enrolled in the Honors College and is designated as a community engaged learning course by the university. De Grandi serves as the primary facilitator, coteaching the course every year with a team of three to four STEM colleagues who volunteer to serve as course cofacilitators. The course meets twice a week for almost 2 hours each session. The course enrollment is capped at 20 students per semester in order to promote opportunities for all-class discussion. While students receive credit for taking the course, the instructors do not receive teaching credit, although there are ongoing efforts to provide support for the instructors and a few departments at the university do consider this course as part of the instructor's teaching load.

Williams College first offered their HSTEM course in the fall of 2019, cofacilitated by geoscience professor Phoebe Cohen and visiting professor of physics Savan Kharel. Kharel brought previous HSTEM experience to the course, having cofacilitated the course while at Yale. Their pilot offering of the course enrolled 13 students and was taught once a week, meeting for 3 hours each class session. The class fulfilled the college's difference, power, and equity course requirement, and was open to all students. Facilitators did not receive teaching credit for teaching the course, so Cohen is working to build a cohort of instructors who can rotate facilitation responsibilities for future versions of the course.

Yale University was the first institution to adapt Amherst's HSTEM model to their campus. In the fall of 2015, in response to a campus controversy about appropriative Halloween costumes, faculty members and students in STEM had been engaged in extended conversations about equity and inclusion. In these conversations, students shared that they felt alienated by the lack of discussion about this controversy and its impact on their ability to navigate their STEM coursework. The next semester, in spring 2016, Sheila and students from the first Amherst HSTEM course were invited by Andrew Miranker, professor of molecular biophysics and biochemistry and former postdoctoral mentor of Sheila's, to speak at a STEM inclusion event at Yale, which prompted Simon Mochrie, professor of physics, and Miranker to propose their own version of HSTEM. The course proposal was quickly approved in response to the demonstrated need on campus. A team of five faculty members and one teaching assistant cofacilitates the course. The structure of Yale's HSTEM course is such that two faculty members and a teaching assistant serve as primary course cofacilitators; these individuals receive teaching credit, while the other three faculty members who are not currently cofacilitating the course operate as volunteer course supports. The course is offered as a single credit seminar course through the Physics Department (cross-listed with molecular biophysics and biochemistry [MBB] as well as Education Studies), although all interested students can enroll regardless of their major. It fulfills students' social science graduation requirement, is an elective course within the education studies major, and fulfills a science and society credit for MBB majors. The course meets for 2 hours once a week, with students expected to complete an additional 2 hours of work outside of class time on their collaborative action projects.

Adapting the Core Pillars of HSTEM

Across the almost 40 offerings of HSTEM that have taken place at these 10 institutions since the spring of 2016, students, staff members, and faculty members have collaborated to adapt the HSTEM course model to suit their institutional context, facilitator and student constellation, and larger societal events (e.g., the COVID-19 worldwide pandemic). And yet the key features of the original course have remained at its core, albeit a molten, flexible core. This core structure includes intentional community building, practices that value identity and self-interrogation, engaging with the academic literature, and student collaboration to use their emergent understanding to develop an inclusive action project in their local STEM environment.

Community Building

In the first offering of the course at an institution, partners across the network report that the process of designing and teaching this type of course inherently creates a sense of community among participants. Students, faculty members, and staff members are partners on a journey, taking on a new challenge and working together to envision how HSTEM can best support their goals for their students, their departments, and their institutional priorities. And, regardless of the number of times an HSTEM course has been taught at an institution, facilitators and students across the network consistently describe the HSTEM classroom as unique in fostering levels of trust and vulnerability. HSTEM invites participants to consider their non-STEM identities, and the ways in which those identities influence their experience of navigating STEM; in so doing, it creates an avenue for meaningful and honest conversations around topics that may not have been discussed among STEM colleagues before. At the same time, the HSTEM pedagogy also invites cofacilitators to position themselves as nonexpert colearners. Cofacilitators model vulnerability by asking questions that expose their knowledge gaps and reflect openly on their own identity and lived experience; through this approach, HSTEM facilitators seek to actively democratize the classroom. Together with the HSTEM course content, creating a classroom context in which everyone identifies as a colearner serves to counteract the traditional social and psychological dynamics that can inhibit a sense of belonging in the classroom.

On top of the community-building structures inherent to the course premise and curricular design, there are also a number of mechanisms that institutions have pursued to refine how a sense of community is fostered in the course. Many HSTEM facilitators across the network have integrated variations on the practices described in chapter 5 (e.g., Humanizing the Professor, Community Agreements, Scientist Trading Cards, Community

Announcements). Further, the virtual teaching environment necessitated by the COVID-19 pandemic served to make even more apparent the need to emphasize community in our teaching and learning spaces; as a result, many of the practices commonly used in HSTEM have now been adapted to the digital sphere by instructors across the HSTEM network. For example, Dudle and Poturovic at DePauw University sought to help students feel more connected in the virtual setting before the semester started, by asking all incoming students to share a picture and information about themselves with their classmates. At the University of Utah, De Grandi's HSTEM class typically incorporates a cookie break; in the virtual class setting, the cookie break was maintained via breakout rooms. Each breakout room was named after a different type of cookie or snack item, often inspired by students' or class guests' preferences. A third example of community building comes from Davidson College, in which students took turns serving as the cohosts for daily "warm-up" exercises at the start of class. Across all of these examples, we see a shared appreciation of the critical role that community building plays in fostering a learning community in HSTEM.

Self-Interrogation

In addition to fostering meaningful community, another core pillar of the HSTEM course is the process of reflecting on one's own experience in STEM, with a particular attention to positionality and identities. Across the network, the HSTEM courses have been taught primarily using a seminar, discussion-based approach, with a balance of whole-class discussions and small-group conversations. Like many classes that focus discussions on issues of race, identity, and structural inequities, the nature of the course material lends itself to students' ongoing connection of the course content to themselves, their identities, and their experiences, as well as to the experiences of the other members of the class community. All HSTEM courses ask students to complete some form of ongoing reflection, although the amount to which these reflections are shared with others in the class or kept confidential varies across courses and assignments within a course. See the following for an end-of-semester reflection assignment from Yale University's HSTEM course.

Reflection Assignment From Yale's HSTEM Course

At the end of the semester, students complete a "3-2-1 Reflection Assignment":

> What are three core ideas you will take away?
>
> What are two ways you will apply what you've learned?
>
> What is one question that you still have?

For several HSTEM courses, including those taught at Davidson College, DePauw University, Soka University, University of Utah, and Macalester College, the Amherst HSTEM story assignment has been adapted and employed as a reflective course assignment. In some cases, students complete the HSTEM story as a singular activity, whereas other course models ask students to iterate and revise their HSTEM story across the semester, to incorporate new learnings about one's self that are uncovered over time. Regardless of the number of times that students revisit their stories across the semester, the HSTEM Story activity enables all members of the class to listen to each other's journey narratives in STEM and consider what can be learned about oneself, our colleagues, and the STEM community from that process. Students and facilitators consistently report how powerful this self-reflective activity has been for them. As one student from Macalester shared, "One of my favorite parts of the course was hearing other people's stories and learning that I was not alone in feeling invisible and suffering during my time in introductory STEM courses. Narratives are powerful, and I often forget how desensitized we can be to heavy topics. It's important to listen to these narratives and allow ourselves to feel."

Connecting Lived Experiences With the Academic Literature

Across the HSTEM courses that have been offered so far, the syllabi have primarily focused on peer-reviewed academic literature, with additional content drawn from popular media sources such as opinion pieces, blogs, podcasts, and films or documentaries. These sources speak to common challenges that individuals face in STEM (e.g., microaggressions, racism, imposter phenomenon, stereotype threat), highlight specific stories of individuals holding marginalized identities in STEM, and engage theoretical frameworks that seek to complicate the understanding of science as purely an objective, empirical field of study (e.g., feminist science, Indigenous ways of knowing). For many students, these frameworks and areas of study are novel, and the readings can be challenging. To help students at the University of Rhode Island engage the readings, the HSTEM cofacilitators created recordings of conversational lectures about the course material for students to review. The recordings are publicly available at YouTube (www.youtube.com/playlist?list=PLzn-iGwKeXiaY4F0Haa-AX1n0lxR4cOKy).

There are a number of readings that are commonly used across HSTEM courses (see Appendix A for selections and student reflections from the Amherst HSTEM curriculum). These readings have consistently resonated with students and served as critical sources for helping them make sense of their own experiences in STEM and the experiences of others. For example,

The Privileged Poor: How Elite Institutions Are Failing Their Most Disadvantaged Students, written by Amherst alumnus Tony Jack (2019), vividly captures the lived experiences of low-income students of color at an institution he refers to as "Renowned University." As we discussed earlier in chapter 2, Jack makes a distinction between "privileged poor" and "doubly disadvantaged" students: "Privileged poor" students are those who, while being from low-income families, attended primarily white boarding schools. Attending these schools enabled "privileged poor" students to learn to navigate elite academic and social culture. Conversely, "doubly disadvantaged" students are those who come from low-income families and have not had the opportunity to develop the same cultural or academic capital. Many HSTEM students say that they identify as being members of one of the two categories of students that Jack articulates. They appreciate how the readings provide them with greater self-understanding of their lived experiences on campus.

Further, students across institutional offerings of HSTEM also praise the impact of reading *Braiding Sweetgrass* by botanist and Indigenous scholar Robin Wall Kimmerer, which they say provides them with a novel way of understanding their relationship to the natural world and inspires them in their efforts to create more inclusive communities. Kimmerer (2013) writes,

> We need acts of restoration, not only for polluted waters and degraded lands, but also for our relationships to the world. We need to restore honor to the way we live, so that when we walk through the world we don't have to avert our eyes with shame, so that we can hold our heads up high and receive the respectful acknowledgment of the rest of the earth's beings. (p. 195)

Students feel inspired by this call for action as they think about the steps they may take at their institutions to restore their "relationships to the world."

In addition to the commonly employed suite of readings, many instructors have adapted and expanded their individual HSTEM course syllabus to directly respond to their institutional context. For instance, the student population at University of Utah consists of a large majority of students who commute to the university and students who work full or part time while concurrently pursuing a college degree. In response to students' limited ability to identify shared time outside of scheduled class times, the University of Utah HSTEM class schedule includes an additional weekly class meeting so that students can work collaboratively on their projects during class time. Additionally, given the dominant LDS Church (Church of Jesus Christ of Latter-Day Saints) population in the state of Utah and among the university student population, the HSTEM course includes a portion of the course which focuses on understanding religious identities from a scientific lens as well as how LGBTQ+ identities are viewed by the LDS community. Another example of such institution-specific modifications comes from the HSTEM course taught at Mount Holyoke College: As a gender-diverse women's college, the syllabus was modified to feature female-identifying authors and to attend to the ways in which individuals with a range of gender identities have navigated their journeys in STEM.

Another lens through which the HSTEM syllabus may be modified relates to the disciplinary expertise of the cofacilitators and students in the course. At the University of Rhode Island, for instance, the course was offered through the Computer Science Department and cofacilitated by Victoria Chávez, an instructor in that department. That course included readings related to technology and discussions often explored issues of inclusion and inequity in computer science, exploring topics such as the role of bias in algorithms and programming. Indeed, the HSTEM course structure readily adapts itself to a discipline-specific exploration: "Being Human in [*fill in the blank*]". One of our Amherst colleagues in philosophy has proposed a future offering of an "HPHIL" course for students in her department, exploring the literature and lived experiences of individuals across identities in philosophy.

In some sense, the exact readings are not the point or the power behind the HSTEM course model. Rather, it is the structure of engaging the literature, reflecting specifically on how the material relates to oneself and to lived experiences beyond one's own. Students at Soka University reported that this process "challenged us to think about inclusivity in STEM as a human rights issue rather than an economical or representation issue," while a student at the University of Rhode Island reflected, "I wish I would have taken this [course] earlier, as a first year, to have the ability to talk about these topics and relate them to how they affect me or don't affect me." Across campuses, we hear from students about the transformative nature of the course readings and discussions for their understanding of themselves and their communities.

Envisioning Change in One's Community

HSTEM culminating assignments enable students to leverage their reflections on literature and lived experience to propose equity-focused interventions, in partnerships with others in their community. These assignments offer a concrete means for students to synthesize the course material and practice applying their knowledge in relevant real-world contexts. The action project pillar of HSTEM allows students to test their own ideas with other members of their STEM community and reflect on the experience of engaging with diverse stakeholders. And yet, there are multiple ways that HSTEM instructors have approached this process; we review some of those modifications here.

Strategies for Selecting Action Project Topics
Course facilitators across the HSTEM network tend to take one of two approaches to working with students to select project topics. The first, and more common, approach is to scaffold students in the identification of their original project ideas. For example, HSTEM students at Soka University conducted interviews with peers about their experiences in STEM, both before matriculation and as current Soka students, with a particular emphasis on the ways in which these students' own identities shaped their past and current STEM experiences. In analyzing the content of these interviews, the HSTEM students at Soka were able to identify themes of behaviors and structures that enhanced and/or diminished a sense of inclusion in STEM, and then focused their project proposals around those emergent themes. An alternative approach is one in which facilitators present a range of preselected projects and allow students to choose the project that they will pursue that semester. At Yale, for example, course facilitators present a list of potential projects to students in the second week of the course; students then select the project option that most appeals to their interests. Some project ideas are generated by campus partners, while others are identified by course facilitators or previous HSTEM students. Many project topics are flexible and adaptable, and students are also free to pitch their own project ideas.

Each of these approaches (student-driven topics versus selection from a suite of topical options) has its benefits. For instance, allowing students to identify their own project focus ensures that students are pursuing projects that feel personally relevant and intrinsically motivating. On the other hand, Rona Ramos, one of the HSTEM course facilitators at Yale, reports that providing a set of curated choice options for student projects enables students to pursue more readily manageable and actionable projects within the scope of the course. She shared that "the general feeling [among facilitators] was that it was hard to get the students to narrow into something that was doable for them in the semester without this kind of starting point for them."

Grounding Projects in the Current Institutional Landscape
Many HSTEM courses include an assignment that asks students to collect qualitative or quantitative data about the lived experiences of campus community members in STEM. These data can become the basis of a project, inform the selection of project topics, and/or shape the methodologies that

students employ. For example, at the University of Utah, HSTEM students collected survey data from STEM students across campus and asked them about their positive and negative experiences with respect to inclusivity and diversity. Students then discussed the results of the survey with former university president Ruth Watkins (2020) as part of her *U Rising* podcast in April 2020.

In one of the most ambitious examples of HSTEM campus data collection, Yale University's first HSTEM cohort conducted a campus-wide climate survey that generated over 800 responses from undergraduate students about their experiences in STEM at Yale, exploring the experiences of students in STEM versus non-STEM fields at the university and how they differed based on student identities. The HSTEM students then held a workshop with faculty in which they presented the survey results, shared personal narratives from students who completed the survey, and proposed small changes that faculty members could make to address issues identified through the data. Ramos observed that "the data brought [faculty members] in, but what was really impactful were the narratives." Thanks to some follow-up work of students in the class the survey data were carefully analyzed and then later published (De Grandi et al., 2019). And at Skidmore, HSTEM students conducted a focused survey of STEM faculty members regarding their perceptions of learning disabilities and their impact on students' experiences in the classroom, then used the results of the survey to develop materials that addressed common questions and misconceptions.

Encouraging Partnership With Other Campus Entities
HSTEM action projects present facilitators and participants with the opportunity to partner with others on campus to envision or enact change. Some of these projects have focused on the partnering relationship that occurs through peer mentoring. For example, students at DePauw University conducted research into their peers' interest in and need for mentorship. These students were then able to use the data to develop a proposal for a mentorship program connecting alumni of color who had gained degrees in STEM disciplines with current students. In response to this proposal, the director of alumni engagement at DePauw, who is a STEM alumna of color herself, worked with this group of HSTEM students to reach out to alumni and enrolled students about their interest in such a program; a DePauw STEM alumni mentorship program was then piloted in 2021/22 by former HSTEM students and a program mentor in chemistry, Jackie Roberts. In another example, students at Skidmore developed a proposal to revise the peer-led team learning model in the Chemistry Department. Their proposal incorporated elements of social emotional learning, increased training

in peer-to-peer leadership, and the establishment of intentional avenues of collaboration between the peer-led learning teams in Chemistry with other departments at the college, such as the Departments of Gender Studies and Black Studies.

Other projects are designed to facilitate partnership with faculty members at one's institution. In one such project, students at Mount Holyoke College developed course modules for introductory STEM courses; they targeted these courses because they observed that these courses frequently serve as a critical pivot point for learners to either get excited about pursuing STEM or become discouraged from continuing in the field. One module, designed for large introductory courses, includes readings and videos with prompts for short discussions designed to help students learn about how to talk to each other about race, while another module focuses on recognizing and addressing racial microaggressions. In a similar vein, a group of HSTEM students at DePauw worked with the library's instructional staff to develop an online guide (a "lib guide") for STEM faculty members focused on readings about DEI in specific STEM fields.

Finally, other projects pursue partnerships by "calling in" campus stakeholders through the sharing of clearly articulated findings and/or recommendations. A powerful example of this type of project comes from Macalester College, where HSTEM students partnered with student organizers to write an open letter to STEM faculty members requesting increased accessibility, support for student success and inclusion in the departments, and increased faculty diversity. An article detailing the contents of this letter was published in the campus newspaper (Pinkert, 2021). The letter got the attention of Macalester STEM faculty; some departments wrote a collective response to students, and they have committed to future trainings on antiracism and inclusion.

Sharing Student Projects With the Campus Community
The first HSTEM cohort at Amherst College established the important practice of engaging the campus community with their findings and recommendations through a salon event at the end of the semester (see chapter 2 for a more detailed description of the salon). This tradition of inviting the campus into conversation has been carried forward by many network partners, through events on their own campuses and participation in gatherings of multiple institutions to celebrate HSTEM student work. At Mount Holyoke College, students were invited to present their action projects as part of the institution's BOOM! event (BOOM! = "Building on our Momentum!"), an annual DEI learning symposium featuring the voices and experiences of students, faculty, staff, and alumnae. Markley noted

that this was "a neat opportunity for students to share their skills, wisdom, and research in a way that some STEM students aren't used to being able to do until they are seniors."

Looking Forward: Lessons Learned From Network Partners About the HSTEM Action Projects

Most network partners point to action projects as a transformative and impactful component of the HSTEM experience for students. At the same time, instructors note that there are challenges to engaging students in the process of envisioning and implementing interventions in a short period of time. One such challenge was described by Dudle and Poturovic at DePauw, who observed that while their students' project development was strong, and the students did a good job (often "pulling rabbits out of hats at the last minute"), the course structure would benefit from more explicit processes of ensuring individual accountability, so that all group members are equally contributing their voices and ideas. When faced with a similar challenge at Yale, Ramos and her cofacilitators provided students with templates for a group contract and a weekly work plan to support more intentional project planning. Another challenge relates to the larger question, Who is responsible for institutional change? On the one hand, individuals with more institutional power hold greater responsibility; on the other hand, students are sharing their student-specific expertise and insights, and we want to ensure that they maintain ownership of that intellectual and emotional labor. While there isn't a clear answer to this challenge, Henderson-Stull articulates the importance of attending to this tension, noting the importance of "neither overburdening or overtasking students with the job of institutional change, nor coopting their ideas."

Impacts of HSTEM Across the Network

As we have discussed previously, there are a variety of approaches that institutions have adopted to incorporate aspects of the HSTEM course and ethos into their home setting. The variability in approaches is notable, we believe, because it demonstrates how HSTEM can be adapted in ways that attend to institutional climate, account for structural limitations and opportunities, leverage and intersect with existing initiatives, and create multiple pathways for students to shape and engage with the course. Additionally, across these implementation examples, we are encouraged by the consistent patterns that emerge, in terms of the impacts that the HSTEM experience has on students, on faculty and staff cofacilitators, and on the institutions in which it operates. In this next section, therefore, we share reflections from some of our institutional partners across the HSTEM network of early adopters about the changes they have observed, in themselves and each other, as a result of engaging with HSTEM.

Across the HSTEM Network: Impacts on Students

One of the common themes that emerges from reflecting on the student experience in HSTEM is the experience of belonging and validation that students develop through the class. The intentional creation of community among all class members (students, staff, and faculty), with an emphasis on treating each other as whole and complex people, allows for deep learning as well as deep connections. As Michelle Markley reflected, "When I think about HSTEM, I think about how helpful it is to know that you're not alone—a lot of people are experiencing these same things, and a lot of people are experiencing different things from a lot of different angles." The course creates avenues for students to understand that what they are experiencing, or witnessing their peers experiencing, is not happening in isolation. Rather, students learn that moments of exclusion, as well as moments of privilege, commonly result from deeply seated structural inequities. For example, Barbara Lom said that developing a shared awareness of the factors that propagate inequity was particularly important for students at her institution. She shared, "What seems most powerful for students [about HSTEM]? Discussing really common feelings and experiences, such as imposter phenomenon and stereotype threat." Learning about how these psychological phenomena can exacerbate inequity in the classroom, Lom stated, allows students "to understand that what they are feeling is not unusual or uncommon and there is a basis for it." And, as Chatterjea noted, "The language was a wonderful tool to add to the tool kit of students with all kinds of experiences."

A student HSTEM alum from Amherst College also spoke about the importance of validation of their experiences in STEM, saying, "One of the first assignments [in HSTEM] asked me to think about why I am a scientist, and that was a surprisingly emotional question. . . . I am the product of two doctor-parents but I'm also someone who doesn't want to be a doctor but can't see a future without STEM. In that way, HSTEM really validated me by showing me that you don't have to go a certain path. You can just be a human who loves science and that is enough." Conversely, another student articulated that their experiences in HSTEM confirmed their future career plans, saying, "HSTEM actually cemented my path of going to med school." Reflecting on this choice, the student wondered how they can incorporate an HSTEM ethos into their work: "In these next couple of years . . . how can I implement the things that we've learned into my practice and into my research?"

In addition to an enhanced sense of community and validation of experience, students also commonly experience a greater sense of agency and ownership as a result of HSTEM participation. There are many ways that student ownership in the course is accomplished, through student–faculty codesigned syllabi, student-led discussions, and of course, through the student-designed action projects and action project proposals. Lom reflected, "Students feel like they own this class in a really important way. . . . As an instructor, it was one of my favorite parts of the class." Ramos further noted, "One of my students said choosing the readings and leading the discussion was her favorite part of the class." Looking at the action projects that students have developed across the national network, we see that students are using the course to amplify issues that are specific to the lived experiences of students at their institution. For example, a student-led discussion at Yale University focused on issues faced by undocumented students in higher education, while some of the students in the University of Utah HSTEM course have focused their projects on enhancing the voices and needs of students with disabilities in STEM. In so doing, students are able to work on bottom-up institutional change and shape the focus of institutional conversations about inclusion and student success.

Student reflections also spoke about how their experiences in HSTEM have allowed them to envision ways that better allow for the intersection of what are traditionally viewed as cocurricular interests with their academic identities. For example, an HSTEM student from DePauw University shared the following: "For a large chunk of my life, the science and academics that I do have felt very separated from everything else that I do outside of class, whether that's working with cultural organizations or being a person and an activist. That's very distinct from being in science. . . . The intersection in bringing all those things together really captured my interest and I think that is the way that we really should be thinking about science. It's not only a field that is based on reproducible data, it's being done by humans." A student from Macalester spoke about how participating in the HSTEM course helped them recognize that "it's time to fix our institutions and find ways that they can serve every student. . . . I want to continue pushing for expedited change because it can happen."

Across the HSTEM Network: Impacts on Faculty and Staff Members

In addition to the beneficial impacts that we see for HSTEM students, the faculty and staff cofacilitators also consistently report positive outcomes from teaching an HSTEM course. One such benefit relates to pedagogical skill development. Not only are instructors expanding their content knowledge and understanding of inequities in STEM, but facilitating the course also provides avenues for expanding one's pedagogical tool kit. The design of the class, which is intentionally structured in such a way to position all individuals in the class as colearners, creates a supportive environment for faculty and staff members to innovate in the classroom. Dana Dudle spoke to her improved facility in navigating difficult dialogues in the classroom. She said, "Our students taught us a great deal about how to facilitate discussions about race and identity. Our students were very gracious and kind and also challenging to us, and to other students in the room, as we discussed difficult topics. . . . We appreciated that a lot."

Other instructors also reflected on how the course allows them to practice engaging in difficult class discussions without activating their own defensiveness. Phoebe Cohen noted, "I often found myself in the position of defending the institution that we're all talking about trying to change, which was uncomfortable for me, but also a valuable experience for me to hear their justified anger." A similar experience was shared by Rona Ramos: "One thing that we try to do consciously as instructors is to suppress an impulse to defend ourselves. Students had a lot to say about faculty and STEM faculty, and we tried very hard to just listen, not focus on ourselves, and just listen to what problems they were having." Ramos pointed out that the HSTEM course also helps humanize the faculty in the eyes of the students by revealing some of the constraints and challenges experienced by faculty members. She noted that this mutual empathy can help students see faculty as "more approachable, and maybe we can turn our combined efforts on changing the system."

In addition to the enhancement in teaching strategies that many instructors spoke to, others reflected on the experience of greater empathy and understanding of the student experience at their institutions. For example, Victoria Chávez spoke about the experience of engaging with the students' reflections in response to the class readings and other materials. They said that "the students were so open and vulnerable in their reflections, and it was so powerful." Phoebe Cohen reported a similar experience, saying that as a result of the HSTEM course, "I became aware of the barriers that many of our students face in a way that I hadn't previously. Students really opened up in a way that they don't in a normal academic course."

Claudia De Grandi spoke about the importance of emotional empathy and connection in the course, saying, "The most important part of the class is the emotional human part. Building a space together to be vulnerable and heard is fundamental for the growth and learning process of everyone in the class, students and also instructors." Developing a greater understanding of the student experience at one's institution not only facilitates connection with one's students, but it also allows instructors to incorporate these understandings into additional course offerings. For instance, Nidanie Henderson-Stull reflected that after learning through an HSTEM student action project about the challenges that international students experience with processing complex scientific terminology, she has added additional scaffolds and vocabulary processing time into her STEM classes.

Finally, a third outcome for HSTEM faculty and staff cofacilitators is that the experience of facilitating the course consistently results in an enhanced understanding of one's beliefs about the goals and purposes of education. What is, or perhaps what should be, the function and mission of higher education? And what does this look like specifically in STEM classrooms and laboratories? The HSTEM course makes it clear to instructors and students alike that the diversification of an institution's study body does not inherently result in an education that is inclusive and equity seeking (e.g., Tienda, 2013). The course encourages students to construct a new "vision of the possible" (Hutchings & Carnegie Foundation, 2000, p. 5) for the journeys of diverse individuals in STEM, which in turn results in many instructors reenvisioning their own views of their purpose and mission in the classroom and laboratory. Bryan Dewsbury reflected on this reenvisioning experience, saying, "Actually teaching the course and reading the students reflections, there are things you see on the ground. No matter how well someone who has taught the course describes it to you, you have to see it for yourself. For me, it was watching the students interrogate themselves. That was the most powerful component of this experience." He observed students who were "clearly encountering these concepts for the first time, or thinking about them in this particular way for the first time, and [they are] not being defensive, not pushing back. . . . They are opening their eyes to a different way of seeing the world and allowing themselves to be vulnerable in expressing that newness."

The process of self-interrogation demonstrates, from Dewsbury's perspective, "the essence of what it means to be educated." He reflected, "We're in a higher education system that privileges the knowing of 'stuff' [but] that's not what education really is. It is about how you cultivate your mind in a way that is able to be respectful of the people around you, even if you may disagree. And that is the fundamental piece of HSTEM." Markley also spoke about the role that teaching HSTEM has played in her thinking about her role in the classroom. She said, "I have really reexamined almost every part of the way I'm doing things, and it's been really meaningful to me personally." As a result of this reenvisioning process, she says, "I think

I've come around to a very different sense of what my role as a STEM educator is."

Conclusion

As you have seen through these examples, the HSTEM course has served an expanding number of institutions in providing equity-seeking educational opportunities for students in STEM. Its flexible framework has helped many of us create learning and teaching spaces that foster community, support self-reflection, deepen our understanding of the academic literature on equity and inequity in STEM, and reach out with a goal of partnership to pursue a more inclusive STEM. Along the way, we are witnessing consistent benefits for students, many of whom report finding their place and their community in STEM for the first time through this experience. Further, faculty and staff cofacilitators share a sense of renewed purpose and mission when they teach an HSTEM course at the same time that they are gaining an enhanced suite of pedagogical skills and a deeper understanding of their students as whole and complex learners and scientists.

A final note of reflection: As we were reviewing the network of early HSTEM adopters, we couldn't help but be reminded that a large number of facilitators hold identities that are underrepresented in STEM. We also noticed that, while students always received credit for taking the course, instructors did not always receive credit for teaching the course. And we wonder: The benefits of teaching an HSTEM course, on students and cofacilitators alike, are multiple. Yet, as the HSTEM network continues to expand, how can we proceed in ways that do not place the burden of this important and emotional labor unequally on the shoulders that are under-powered in our institutions? The value of an HSTEM course to a campus community is widely recognized. The value of the work of teaching an HSTEM course should be recognized as well.

References

De Grandi, C., Smithline, Z. B., Reeves, P. M., Goetz, T. G., Barbour, N., Hairston, E., Guo, J., Muraina, F., Bervell, J. A., Chambers, L. M., Caines, H., Miranker, A. D., & Mochrie, S. G. J. (2019). STEM climate survey developed through student–faculty collaboration. *Teaching in Higher Education, 26*(1), 65–80. https://doi.org/10.1080/13562517.2019.1636219

Hutchings, P., & Carnegie Foundation for the Advancement of Teaching (Eds.). (2000). *Opening lines: Approaches to the scholarship of teaching and learning*. Carnegie Foundation for the Advancement of Teaching.

Huỳnh, V., Storms, K., Saito, J., X, P., & Rallin, A. (2021). Mobilizing BIPOC student power against liberalism at Soka University of America: A collection of voices. *Radical Teacher, 121*, 31–41. https://doi.org/10.5195/rt.2021.899

Jack, A. A. (2019). *The privileged poor: How elite colleges are failing disadvantaged students.* Harvard University Press.

Kimmerer, R. W. (2013). *Braiding sweetgrass: Indigenous wisdom, scientific knowledge, and the teachings of plants.* Milkweed Editions.

Pinkert, E. (2021, April 22). STEM students push for greater, equity, diversity. *The Mac Weekly.* https://themacweekly.com/79797/news/stem-students-push-for-greater-accessibility-diversity/

Tienda, M. (2013). Diversity ≠ inclusion: Promoting integration in higher education. *Educational Researcher, 42*(9), 467–475. https://doi.org/10.3102/0013189X13516164

Watkins, R. (2020, April 17). Being human in STEM. *URising.* https://president.utah.edu/u-rising-podcast/being-human-in-stem/

10

CONCLUSIONS

Many of you are currently working and teaching at institutions that are grappling with their historical and modern-day inequities. Student protest has become a recurring feature of campus life and can serve to draw our attention to the long-standing disparities that have existed at our institutions. Unfortunately, in some cases, protests result also in a further separation of campus factions—students versus administrators, administrators versus faculty and staff. In chapter 1, we shared the story of the Amherst Uprising as an example of how protest can instead strengthen a community. What was different about that moment? What features contributed to its transformative impact and unusually long-lasting legacy? One key difference we notice: The original motivation behind the event was that the three Black women organizers wanted to stand in solidarity with student protesters *on other campuses*. By drawing the college's attention to students protesting tuition hikes in South Africa, racial injustices at other higher education institutions across the United States, and the ongoing efforts of the Black Lives Matter movement, they sought to explicitly connect these seemingly external events to our community, and particularly to the lives of students of color at our institution. In doing so, they challenged the view of the academic community as being somehow separate from activities happening outside its walls. Students of color made the critical, organic move of sharing their own personal stories of marginalization at Amherst to highlight that racism and discrimination don't just exist in the outside world, but are alive in our own academic homes as well. Because Amherst advertised and celebrated that 45% of our student body were self-identified domestic students of color, it was all the more urgent for students of color to explicitly place their experiences of harm in our own community in the broader national context.

Further, the vulnerability displayed by the students, who publicly demanded that their experiences be centered, was transformative. It exploded any illusion of equal experience of students in our educational spaces. While all students can graduate from our institutions with the same degree, regardless of the identities they hold, they are not navigating the same experiences at our institutions in pursuit of those degrees. In collectively witnessing and experiencing our students' truth-telling, many faculty and staff members felt our hearts break, and in those few days of collective broken-heartedness, we experienced a sense of connection, trust, and open dialogue in a space that, for many, had not previously allowed that level of authenticity. The tantalizing promise of what a beloved community might feel like continues to inspire many of us to stay committed to the work and keep believing in the possibility of a truly inclusive educational space.

Lessons We've Learned From the HSTEM Experience

In this next section, we describe several lessons that we've taken away from the amazing work that we've been privileged to do, in partnership with students and colleagues, through HSTEM.

Institutional Change Requires Shared Values, Commitment, and Agency

Student voices and specific narratives about the lived experience of students can be powerful prompts for conversations about equity-focused teaching and institutional practices. As we listen to our students, we often become motivated by the urgent need to act, to make changes to our course designs, to our inclusive practices, and to the ways we mentor and support students. We encourage you to identify those spaces in which you can make changes now, to be more inclusive and equitable, and we provide a number of strategies throughout the book to inspire those actions. And yet larger institutional culture shifts require the identification of and commitment to common values, a shared sense of purpose in the work of change, and providing all individuals involved in the work with the agency and resources their efforts require. To make large-scale changes to how we teach and support students at our institutions, we must all be included and empowered as partners in this work.

The Role of Identity Matters, Even to Scientists

As scientists, thinking about how our own identities have created and lowered barriers to our educational and professional journeys may not come naturally. Indeed, many of us conduct research with target organisms or natural phenomena in which factors of identity are considered irrelevant (e.g., microbes, exoplanet formation, mathematical modeling). Nevertheless, the process of doing science and the experience of learning to do science is deeply influenced by our identities and how we are perceived by others. A critical aspect of the Being Human in STEM course involves creating, sharing, and continuously refining our understanding of how we have navigated our lives in STEM, and helping students to do the same. When did you feel included? When did you feel excluded? What challenges have you experienced and how have you overcome them, with support from others and/or from your own internal attributes? We argue that this continual process of reflection should continue beyond the HSTEM course and infuse all aspects of our scientific selves.

Empathy Needs to Be Cultivated

Fostering empathy, both in students and in ourselves as educators, is critical for making progress toward the creation of more inclusive communities in STEM. The vast majority of us readily engage empathy in our interpersonal relationships. We try to actively listen to what our friends and family are sharing, their fears and their joys, with an openness to supporting and validating their emotions. These same skills, of emotional validation and active listening, do not always get carried over into our academic spaces, making partnership and community building more challenging. Therefore, we explicitly emphasize the cultivation of empathy as an inclusive teaching practice in our classrooms and labs.

The Scientific Model Can Guide the Process of Designing Inclusive STEM Classrooms

The scientific approach, in which we coalesce our relative expertise to articulate questions of inquiry, specify our variables of interest, gather evidence, and reflect on our results, is one in which we already hold deep knowledge and expertise. This approach can and should be applied to the question of building inclusive STEM communities as well. Throughout this book, we provide examples of how to bring a scholarly approach to the question of inclusive teaching and institutional change, and we prompt you to consider how to frame your own, context-specific pedagogical inquiry questions.

The Arc of Individual and Collective Growth

In the first section of the book, going from protests to partnerships, we described how the Amherst Uprising created a key moment for us to build community and partner with students and others on campus. The Being

Human in STEM course served and continues to serve as an engine of partnership on campus, by revealing the vast range of experiences of students across campus, prompting them to reflect on their identities and lived experiences in STEM, and to collaboratively work to identify places where barriers to inclusion lie. In the next section, on inclusive practices, we described activities and strategies that can help us address those disconnects in our classrooms and laboratories. Finally, in the third section of the book, on making and measuring institutional change, we discussed processes for capturing evidence of the impact of these efforts and for extending the work of inclusion beyond the scope of our individual classrooms and research spaces in order to partner at the institutional level. Across these three sections, we have articulated what we see as a pathway for individual and collective growth driving inclusive change.

The Being Human in STEM course itself follows this arc. HSTEM began as a student-initiated course, but since its very inception it has integrated activities for sharing resources and building partnerships beyond the classroom walls. The goals of the HSTEM course continue to be twofold: (a) to facilitate learning about individual and collective experiences, as well as the context of structural inequities in STEM, and (b) to facilitate the collaboration of diverse individuals in STEM in reshaping their shared teaching, learning, and research environments to support humans of all identities. These goals are intertwined. Providing students with a scaffolded opportunity to understand their own path within the larger context of the STEM experience, and then to envision and take action to make equitable change in their communities, is a critical component of their education as leaders (in STEM or elsewhere) who can effectively move their future communities toward greater equity. Similarly, efforts to transform a culture need to involve the ideas and efforts of all of the stakeholders, working especially to listen to the experiences and perspectives of individuals who have been traditionally excluded from the community. The course structure provides participants with the experience of advancing toward both goals simultaneously, interweaving individual growth and self-knowledge with collective growth and shared agency for making change. Figure 10.1 provides a visual representation of how individual and collective growth manifests through HSTEM.

The diffusion of the HSTEM ethos beyond course participants is an intentional feature of the HSTEM course model. Feedback loops explicitly connect the inclusive work that happens in the classroom and the conversations occurring across campus. The project proposal design process incorporates outreach to relevant campus partners to inform the design and redesign of the proposal, and the salon invites faculty, staff,

Figure 10.1. Individual and collective change in the HSTEM course.

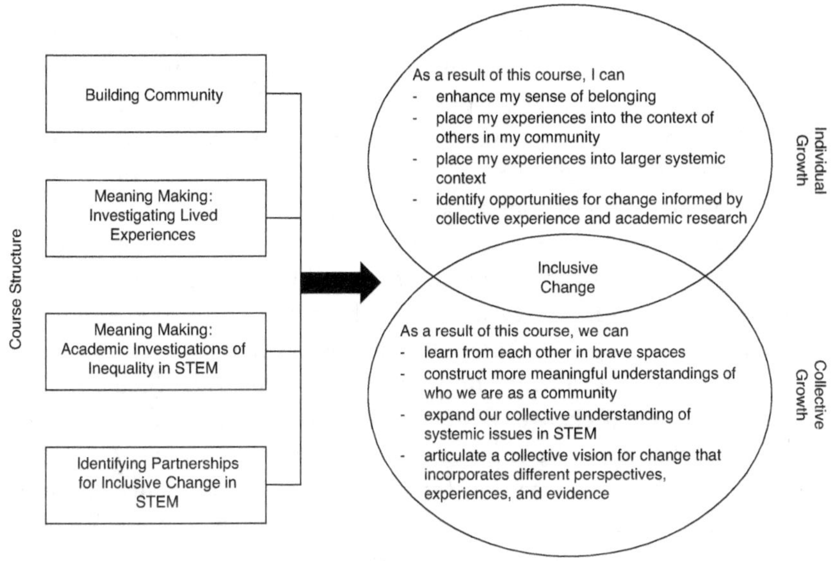

```
Course Structure:
- Building Community
- Meaning Making: Investigating Lived Experiences
- Meaning Making: Academic Investigations of Inequality in STEM
- Identifying Partnerships for Inclusive Change in STEM

→ Inclusive Change

Individual Growth — As a result of this course, I can
- enhance my sense of belonging
- place my experiences into the context of others in my community
- place my experiences into larger systemic context
- identify opportunities for change informed by collective experience and academic research

Collective Growth — As a result of this course, we can
- learn from each other in brave spaces
- construct more meaningful understandings of who we are as a community
- expand our collective understanding of systemic issues in STEM
- articulate a collective vision for change that incorporates different perspectives, experiences, and evidence
```

and students to learn from and help shape the work that students have identified as important. Further, this cycle of structured opportunities for engaging the campus community allows us to excite and inspire other educators across campus to adopt inclusive practices, partner with students around course design or action project work, or even to serve as future HSTEM facilitators.

Transformation of a community requires the coupling of individual learning and empowerment with collective growth and transformation. The skills of active listening and empathy facilitate this coupling process, by allowing us to be more open and welcoming to each other. We are a living, learning community. We appreciate the individual contributions and skills that each of us bring to our classroom and laboratory pedagogical spaces, and we recognize that all of us have more to learn—about ourselves, our students, and about the attributes of fully inclusive educational spaces. As scientists, we seek to identify our operational definitions of inclusion and equity, gather information that informs our understanding of the impact of our practices on those success metrics, and reflect on what that information tells us about areas for growth and about aspects of our practice that are working well. And then we share our findings and reflections with others so that the community can engage with, make meaning from, and learn from our efforts.

Returning to Our Guiding Questions

We hope that as you have navigated through this book, the guiding questions at the start of each chapter prompted you to pause and reflect upon how the concepts and practices presented may apply to, and perhaps even help to drive change within, your local context. The spaces where you teach, learn, and mentor students have distinct challenges and opportunities, and we recognize the deeply contextualized nature of inclusive teaching. The choices that you make about how you will teach and partner with students is uniquely informed by that context. As we conclude this text, therefore, we want to take a little time to revisit some of these reflective prompts with you.

A number of the guiding prompts encouraged you to reflect on your own assumptions and positionality in relationship to inclusion-focused teaching and institutional change. For instance, in our context of the uprising, described in chapter 1, we reflected on the disciplinary differences in how individuals respond to the nature of student protest as a mechanism for institutional change. What are your own views of the value of protest? What are your assumptions about how requests for change should be broached, in your department or at your institution? Are there places where being more open to listening for *what is* being requested, rather than *how* that request is being made, may help you forge inroads and productive dialogue? Throughout this reflective process, we encouraged you to consider how you might further activate your own empathy, and the empathy of your students and colleagues (see chapter 4), in the context of these discussions.

Another domain where the questioning of assumptions—one's own and those of others—contributes to how we design inclusive pedagogical spaces is in the operational definitions we hold about what inclusion looks like (discussed in chapter 8). Once we clearly articulate our shared values, we can then adapt our design of teaching and learning spaces to maximize those features and gather evidence to inform whether we have been successful or not. As scientists, we are well positioned to help lead our departments and institutions in these evidence-based conversations. Making sure that we first articulate our goals and values is a critical first step in shaping the dialogue. What are your goals for inclusive spaces? For your scientific communities? How do you know when you are making headway toward those goals?

Throughout the book, we also prompted you to make authentic decisions about which practices and frameworks you will incorporate into your teaching, based on how they align with your goals for inclusivity and the needs and desires of your students. Keep in mind that the activities we describe are not a panacea but rather a suite of possibilities that will be most impactful when they serve to reinforce the kind of learning community you are seeking to create and when they provide students with opportunities to play an active role in their learning, through reflection upon their own educational goals, values, and growth. For example, when we described the benefits of interdisciplinary coteaching as a form of partnership in chapter 3, we were not arguing that in order for you to be an inclusive teacher, you must coteach with someone outside of your discipline. Rather, we prompted you to consider how you might work within your institutional setting to partner with others in ways that will help to reveal blind spots, biases, and assumptions that you and your students may hold about STEM and the scientific way of knowing. Alternatively, if your inclusivity-focused teaching goals include creating more meaningful relationships with your students, you may wish to consider how you can infuse your HSTEM story (described in chapter 6), as well as the stories of a diverse range of other scientists, into the classroom or laboratory spaces.

Finally, we encouraged you to consider how inclusive institutional change can be brought about through partnership. Throughout the book, we prompted you to identify as yet untapped avenues for partnership—with students, with individual faculty and staff members, with departments and campus offices, and with administrators. In chapter 3, we also reflected on how you can serve as a partner for students in their bottom-up efforts to advocate for more equitable education. How can you help students align what they see as necessary changes with the past and ongoing efforts operating elsewhere on campus, about which they may not be aware or may need support in developing inroads for collaboration? And in chapter 8, we encouraged you to make public the good work that is being done, by students and others on campus, to both highlight opportunities and maintain institutional momentum.

At the same time, we know that many of you have likely participated in conversations in which students have expressed frustration with what they perceive as slow or absent change. In chapter 7, therefore, we provided some frameworks and mechanisms for promoting personal growth and institutional change. Sharing these frameworks with students may be beneficial as you mentor them in their process of acquiring skills of leadership and collaboration. What are the aspects of institutional change that are currently operating to support inclusive teaching and learning at your institution, and where are the barriers? Does your institution have a sense of shared values, collective investment, and structures that empower individuals with the resources and agency to make change happen? If your response to this prompt is "no" or "somewhat" or even "I really don't know," how might you work in partnership with students and others on your campus to explore these questions and make inroads together?

Final Thoughts

To disrupt current hierarchies and dysfunctional relationships in STEM educational spaces, we need dramatic and systemic changes in the ways that we operate and work together. The HSTEM course model provides an example of a way forward, one seeking to build structures that allow for vulnerability and colearning, empower students to adopt positions of leadership on campus, and foster respect and partnership. We hope that the HSTEM course model and individual inclusive practices we present in this book inspire you. We encourage you to look for ways that the HSTEM process—listening, validating, reflecting, and partnering—can permeate the work that you do at your institution, in your classrooms, and in your laboratories. We invite you to collaborate with your students to devise additional approaches in service of the HSTEM ethos: to empower all students, staff, and faculty to share responsibility for shaping an inclusive and equitable community where all humans can thrive in STEM. Thank you for joining us in helping to support our students, and ourselves, in the process of being our full human selves in STEM.

APPENDICES

APPENDIX A

Selected HSTEM Course Readings and Reflections

Note: This is not an exhaustive list but rather a subset of the resources that we have drawn from, across different iterations of the HSTEM course. We encourage you to consider additional readings and topics that will resonate with your students.

Scholarship Module 1 Readings and Resources: Being Human

Building a Brave Community

Appiah, K. (2018, August 10). Go ahead, speak for yourself. *The New York Times.*

Ross, L. J. (2019, August 17). I'm a Black feminist. I think call-out culture is toxic. *The New York Times.*

Schulman, S. (2016). *Conflict is not abuse: Overstating harm, community responsibility, and the duty of repair* (Introduction specifically). Arsenal Pulp Press.

Tools for Talking Together

Haslam, R. E. (n.d.). Interrupting bias: Calling out vs. calling in. *Seed the Way.* http://www.racialequityvtnea.org/wp-content/uploads/2018/09/Interrupting-Bias_-Calling-Out-vs.-Calling-In-REVISED-Aug-2018-1.pdf

Roberts, H. (2021, June 3). *Use microaffirmations and call out microaggressions to help others.* Nature Careers. https://doi.org/10.1038/d41586-021001498-7

University of Colorado Boulder. (n.d.). *Departmental action teams: Norms of collaboration.* https://www.colorado.edu/project/dat/sites/default/files/attached-files/departmental_action_teams_-_norms_of_collaboration_-_cu.pdf

Being Human in Elite Spaces

Jack, A. A. (2019). *The privileged poor: How elite colleges are failing disadvantaged students.* Harvard University Press.

Westover, T. (2018). *Educated: A memoir.* Random House.

Being Human in STEM

Asai, D. J. (2020). Commentary: Race matters. *Cell, 181*, 754–757.

Barres, B. A. (2006). Does gender matter? *Nature, 442*, 133–136.

Castro, A. R., & Collins, C. S. (2020). Asian American women in STEM in the lab with "white men named John." *Science Studies and Science Education, 105*, 33–61. https://doi.org/10.1002/sce.21598

McGee, E. (2018). "Black genius, Asian fail": The detriment of stereotype lift and stereotype threat in high-achieving Asian and Black STEM students. *AERA Open, 4*(4), 1–16. https://doi.org/10.1177/2332858418816658

Muñoz, J. A., & Villanueva, I. (2019). Latino STEM scholars, barriers, and mental health: A review of the literature. *Journal of Hispanic Higher Education, 21*(1), 3–16. https://doi.org/10.1177/1538192719892148

National Science Foundation. (2019). *Women, minorities, and persons with disabilities in science and engineering report.* www.nsf.gov/statistics/wmpd/

Powell, K., Terry, R., & Chen, S. (2020). LGBT+ scientists give their views on their workplaces. *Nature, 586*, 813–816.

Riegle-Crumb, C., King, B., & Irizarry, Y. (2019). Does STEM stand out? Examining racial/ethnic gaps in persistence across postsecondary fields. *Educational Researcher, 48*(3), 133–144. https://doi.org/10.3102/0013189X19831006

Slaton, A. E. (2013, June 23–26). *Body? What body? Considering physical ability and disability in STEM disciplines* [Paper presentation]. American Society for Engineering Education Conference, Atlanta, GA, United States. https://peer.asee.org/body-what-body-considering-ability-and-disability-in-stem-disciplines

Being Human in Medicine

Goldsby, R. A., & Bateson, M. C. (2019). *Thinking race: Social myths and biological realities.* Rowman & Littlefield.

Vyas, D. A., Eisenstein, L. G., & Jones, D. S. (2020). Hidden in plain sight—Reconsidering the use of race correction in clinical algorithms. *New England Journal of Medicine, 383*(9), 874–882. https://doi.org/10.1056/NEJMms2004740

Student Reflection on Ross (2019)

Ross's opinion piece is an insightful look into the detrimental effects of contemporary call-out culture. The reading really clearly highlights the ways in which the practice, even if well-intentioned, can have the opposite effect. Call out culture can create an environment in which people are too afraid to start the conversations that we truly need for understanding and progress. As someone who has grown up in a less than perfect South Asian cultural environment, I have experienced many instances where the people around me made ignorant and crude remarks. Much of this, influenced by both social hierarchies and post-colonial mentalities, has been ingrained over many generations. As such, breaking down many of these preconceived notions and prejudices is an ongoing process. While it can often be painful, I have realized that it is much more effective to have uncomfortable repeated conversations with people about the beliefs they hold than to simply shun them with the label of ignorance.

Student Reflection on Jack (2019)

Jack's chapter on engaging with professors really resonated with me; coming from public school, the idea that we were just supposed to approach professors was both bizarre and intimidating. I felt this way even with the added privilege of the majority of my professors being my race. . . . I don't think my Chemistry instructors ever learned my name, especially since I was too afraid to go to office hours. I struggled severely in that class and looking back I realized that if I had asked for help, I probably could have understood the concepts a lot better. But, I was so intimidated by the professors and didn't even know how to ask questions that I had. I also felt like office hours were for the smart kids, the ones who knew what they were doing and weren't going to ask "stupid" questions like I was. I held this mindset for years.

Scholarship Module 2 Readings and Resources: Interrogating Ways of Knowing in STEM

Feminist Philosophy of Science

Harding, S. (1992). Rethinking standpoint epistemology: What is "strong objectivity"? In L. A. Alcoff & E. Potter (Eds.), *Feminist epistemologies*. Routledge.

Kuhn, T. S. (1970). The nature and necessity of scientific revolutions. In *The structure of scientific revolutions* (2nd ed.). University of Chicago Press.

Longino, H. E. (1990). *Science as social knowledge: Values and objectivity in scientific inquiry* (pp. 62–82 specifically). Princeton University Press.

Indigenous Ways of Knowing

Kimmerer, R. W. (2013). *Braiding sweetgrass: Indigenous wisdom, scientific knowledge and the teachings of plants*. Milkweed Editions.

Knopf, K. (2015). The turn toward the Indigenous: Knowledge systems and practices in the academy. *American Studies*, 60(2/3), 179–200. https://www.jstor.org/stable/44071904

Tallbear, K. (2014). Standing with and speaking as faith: A feminist-indigenous approach to inquiry. *Journal of Research Practice, 10*(2), Article N17. http://jrp.icaap.org/index.php/jrp/article/view/405/371

Tonino, L. (2016, April). Two ways of knowing: Robin Wall Kimmerer on scientific and Native American views of the natural world. *The Sun Magazine.*

Humanistic Interrogations of STEM and Humanity

Glick, M. H. (2018). Introduction: Toward a theory of infrahumanity. In *Infrahumanisms*. Duke University Press.

Tippett, K. (2021, November 25). Jane Goodall: What it means to be human [Podcast]. *On Being.* https://onbeing.org/programs/jane-goodall-what-it-means-to-be-human/

Student Reflection on Longino (1990)

> This reading dismantled my idea of science. I am a woman in STEM, but I'm only familiar with the field of Mathematics. . . . I've always believed the sciences to be objective. Whatever research was ongoing in any field of science should in theory be objective. Right? Maybe not. Longino says something that resonates with me: "People fetishize the objectivity of science." There are a lot of issues with the way objectivity in science is defined . . . science is a field where there is objectivity, but there is also a lot of subjectivity. And, maybe there are issues with the methods scientists go about reducing subjectivity.

Student Reflection on Knopf (2015) and TallBear (2014)

> After reading both Knopf and TallBear, I was particularly interested in Kim TallBear's reflections on the concept of studying up, studying down, and studying across. In her piece, TallBear thinks about research from a perspective different than one I would guess many are used to (including myself). In her piece, she acknowledges the fact that too often, a binary exists between the researcher and the researched. This ultimately dictates who makes knowledge, and who, what, or where it is extracted from. I find this idea incredibly interesting, particularly in thinking about my own thesis this semester. Too often, specifically in the study of people and communities who have been actively "othered," I think research takes on a linear and transactional form; we (white folks, or those with power) enter spaces that are not our own with a genuine intent to contribute to, or empower the researched, in hopes that we might discover a new perspective or experience in exchange. This dynamic, though characterized by genuine intent, is problematic as it grounds itself in top-down creation of knowledge,

dependent on who owns power in the work and who does not. TallBear highlights this in her differentiation between "standing with" and "giving back."

Student Reflection on Kimmerer (2013)

I am so struck by how beautifully Kimmerer integrates all of the academic readings we've done about Indigenous knowledge, and how it can be integrated into our fields, into her journey in academia, and how that also reflects the ways in which academia upholds colonial systems of power. If there was ever a scientist and a poet in one person, it really is her. I find her so inspiring in how I reflect on my own journey in being a scientist, and hopefully one day a doctor, and a musician, and a theater-maker.

Scholarship Module 3 Readings and Resources: Humanizing STEM

Learning From Plants

Montgomery, B. L. (2020). Lessons from microbes: What can we learn about equity from unculturable bacteria? *mSphere, 5*(5). https://doi.org/10.1128/mSphere.01046-20

Montgomery, B. L. (2020). Planting equity: Using what we know to cultivate growth as a plant biology community. *The Plant Cell, 32*(11), 3372–3375. https://doi.org/10.1105/tpc.20.00589

Creating Inclusive STEM Spaces

Basu, A. C. (2021, March). Are we ready? The future of inclusive excellence in STEM. *The Thinking Republic.* https://www.thethinkingrepublic.com/fulcrum/are-we-ready

Bunnell, S. L. et al. (2021). From protest to progress through partnership with students. *International Journal for Students as Partners, 5*(1), 26–56. https://doi.org/10.15173/ijsap.v5i1.4243

Calaza, K. C. et al. (2021). Facing racism and sexism in science by fighting against social implicit bias: A Latina and Black woman's perspective. *Frontiers in Psychology, 12.* https://doi.org/10.3389/fpsyg.2021.671481

Carlone, J., & Johnson, A. (2007). Understanding the science experiences of successful women of color: Science identity as an analytic lens. *Journal of Research in Science Teaching, 44*(8), 1187–1218.

English, L., & Fausto-Sterling, A. (1986). Women and minorities in science: An interdisciplinary course. *The Radical Teacher, 30,* 16–20.

Jaswal, S. S. (2019, Winter). *Being human in STEM: Moving from student protest to institutional progress.* AAC&U Diversity & Democracy.

Student Reflection on Montgomery (2020)

> I really liked the examples and parallels taken from botany/biology in discussing today's topics; they're very digestible and are definitely helpful for people who come from a STEM background and are trying to understand racial biases in academia and the sciences. Since being home, I have found myself constantly in conversation with my friends and family about the racial inequities I see on campus and in classrooms, etc. For the most part, these conversations are meaningful and productive[;] however, . . . I have come to realize that our conversations can sometimes feel stilted—I think this is because my parents approach these topics with an assimilation-based lens, whereas I have approached them with an environment-critiquing lens. I will be using the botany examples to hopefully get myself and them to see eye to eye on racial biases in STEM and learning.

Student Reflection on Carlone & Johnson (2007)

> I couldn't put down the research article conducted by Carlone and Johnson. This article is a good example of what can be accomplished when you build an objective point of view by collecting opinions and listening to people's stories, instead of just relying on the numbers to tell the whole tale. It also allowed me to reflect on my own experience within the field through their model of science identity.

The remaining appendices are abbreviated versions of the inclusive teaching practice guides detailed throughout the text. Please visit the included link to download the complete version of the Facilitator Guides, which provide step-by-step recommendations and reflective prompts for you to adapt these practices to your teaching and learning contexts.

https://www.routledge.com/Being-Human-in-STEM-Partnering-with-Students-to-Shape-Inclusive-Practices/Bunnell-Jaswal-Lyster/p/book/9781642672299

APPENDIX B

Facilitator Guide: Humanizing the Professor

Access the Full Facilitator Guide

https://www.routledge.com/Being-Human-in-STEM-Partnering-with-Students-to-Shape-Inclusive-Practices/Bunnell-Jaswal-Lyster/p/book/9781642672299

Transparency	Connection	Modeling
Communicate to students that your class is a space that values who they are as whole people and learners, and that you want to get to know them and for them to get to know you. There is a substantial body of literature that suggests that establishing a sense of community and belonging in STEM classes contributes to improved student learning, enhanced student experience, and increased willingness on behalf of students to engage with beneficial learning supports, such as office hours. By sharing your STEM narrative, you are working to build that sense of community.	Share a time when either learning about an aspect of a professor as an individual increased your own sense of connection or willingness to seek support from that person, or when you were better able to navigate the demands of academia because you had the support of someone who recognized the complex nature of your life.	While you will not be asking students to engage in this activity, we encourage you to invite other instructional team members (e.g., cofacilitators, lab instructors, teaching assistants) to share their own STEM journeys with students alongside your own. To increase comfort in doing so, we recommend a preparatory meeting with the full instructional team prior to the class session in which you will implement this activity. During that meeting, you can share your own STEM journey with them. In class, you can share your STEM narrative with the class prior to inviting other instructional team members to do the same.

Supporting References

Freeman, T. M., Anderman, L. H., & Jensen, J. M. (2007). Sense of belonging in college freshmen at the classroom and campus levels. *Journal of Experimental Education, 75*(3), 203–220. https://doi.org/10.3200/JEXE.75.3.203-220

Trujillo, G., & Tanner, K. D. (2014). Considering the role of affect in learning: Monitoring students' self-efficacy, sense of belonging, and science identity. *CBE—Life Sciences Education, 13*(1), 6–15. https://doi.org/10.1187/cbe.13-12-0241

APPENDIX C

Facilitator Guide: Airplane Game

Access the Full Facilitator Guide

https://www.routledge.com/Being-Human-in-STEM-Partnering-with-Students-to-Shape-Inclusive-Practices/Bunnell-Jaswal-Lyster/p/book/9781642672299

Transparency	*Connection*	*Modeling*
The goal of this activity is to create a fun opportunity for everyone to learn each other's names and start learning more about each other. It is designed to help forge a community. And students often report that being known by name to their professor is a key way that they begin to feel included in class. The research indicates that we are more likely to choose friends who are similar to us across a range of dimensions, and yet learning is enhanced when we collaborate across diversity. This activity will hopefully be the launchpad for continuing relationships with each other throughout the semester and the years to come.	Explain why knowing the names of each of your students, and having your students know the names of each other, is important to you. Why does this matter?	Prior to the class in which you will use this activity, fold a paper airplane and write your name and three questions that you will be willing to answer in front of the class. In class, you can show your airplane to the class, read your questions, and answer two of those three questions out loud. Alternatively, you could fly your airplane across the classroom and then ask a nearby student to pick it up and read your questions aloud. You then pick two of the three questions and answer them in front of the class.

Supporting References

Alsagoff, Z. (2015, August 31). *Ultimate ice breaker? Making & flying paper planes!* Edutopia. https://www.edutopia.org/discussion/ultimate-ice-breaker-making-flying-paper-planes

Hong, L., & Page, S. E. (2004). Groups of diverse problem solvers can outperform groups of high-ability problem solvers. *Proceedings of the National Academy of Sciences of the United States of America, 101*(46), 16385–16389. https://doi.org/10.1073/pnas.0403723101

Selfhout, M., Denissen, J., Branje, S., & Meeus, W. (2009). In the eye of the beholder: Perceived, actual, and peer-rated similarity in personality, communication, and friendship intensity during the acquaintanceship process. *Journal of Personality and Social Psychology, 96*(6), 1152–1165. https://doi.org/10.1037/a0014468

APPENDIX D

Facilitator Guide: This I Believe

Access the Full Facilitator Guide

https://www.routledge.com/Being-Human-in-STEM-Partnering-with-Students-to-Shape-Inclusive-Practices/Bunnell-Jaswal-Lyster/p/book/9781642672299

Transparency	Connection	Modeling
This practice is designed to enable students to share information about their background, their concerns, and their hopes for the course with you, so that you have a better ability to fine-tune the course to best meet their learning goals and to continue to build community. Research indicates that the act of reflecting on one's values for their education increases motivation and engagement. This activity is being used by many educators across the country to learn about their students even before the semester begins.	You could provide an example of how a previous instructor helped you better understand a complicated phenomenon by connecting it to a context that mattered or was relevant to you. Alternatively, you could provide an example (either from a past class where you have used this practice or a hypothetical case) in which information that a student shared in their reflection influenced how you presented a particular course topic or the examples that you used in your teaching of that topic.	This is a great opportunity for students to get to know you better and feel more comfortable sharing personal information about themselves with you. Prior to asking students to complete this essay, you could share your own This I Believe essay with your students. Alternatively, if you have their consent to do so, you could share examples of past students' This I Believe essays with the class.

Supporting References

Dewsbury, B. (2018). Teaching as an act of social justice and equity (No. 215) [Audio podcast]. *Teaching in Higher Ed.* https://teachinginhighered.com/podcast/teaching-as-an-act-of-social-justice-and-equity/

National Public Radio. *This I Believe essay writing guidelines.* https://thisibelieve.org/guidelines/

Zimmerman, B. J. (2011). Motivational sources and outcomes of self-regulated learning and performance. In D. H. Schunk & J. A. Greene (Eds.), *Handbook of self-regulation of learning and performance* (pp. 49–64). Routledge.

APPENDIX E

Facilitator Guide: Discussing Class Expectations

Access the Full Facilitator Guide

https://www.routledge.com/Being-Human-in-STEM-Partnering-with-Students-to-Shape-Inclusive-Practices/Bunnell-Jaswal-Lyster/p/book/9781642672299

Transparency	Connection	Modeling
Share with students that your goal is to help them feel included and be successful in this course. One tool to support them in maximizing their experience in the course is being transparent about why the course has been structured as it is and how the different aspects of the course build upon each other to support their learning. You can also point to the research that indicates that when instructors clearly articulate their goals for student learning and how the course design supports those goals, students are better able to navigate and succeed in the course.	There are a number of ways that you might share a personal connection to why discussing class expectations is important to you. For instance, you might describe a past experience that you've had as a student in which you were unclear how the course goals and activities were aligned and how that lack of transparency impacted your learning. Additionally, you may wish to describe why the goals you have set for the course are important to you and to your sense of your role as an educator. What is most important for students to carry forward from this class, and why?	Not applicable.

Supporting References

Fisher, K., Kouyoumdjian, C., Roy, B., Talavera-Bustillos, V., & Willard, M. (2016). Building a culture of transparency. *Peer Review*, 18(1/2).

Harrison, C. D., Nguyen, T. A., Seidel, S. B., Escobedo, A. M., Hartman, C., Lam, K., Liang, K. S., Martens, M., Acker, G. N., Akana, S. F., Balukjian, B., Benton, H. P., Blair, J. R., Boaz, S. M., Boyer, K. E., Bram, J. B., Burrus, L. W., Byrd, D. T., Caporale, N., . . . & Tanner, K. D. (2019). Investigating instructor talk in novel contexts: Widespread use, unexpected categories, and an emergent sampling strategy. *CBE—Life Sciences Education*, 18(3), Article 47. https://doi.org/10.1187/cbe.18-10-0215

Mulnix, A. (2018, November 12). *The power of transparency in your teaching*. Faculty Focus. https://www.facultyfocus.com/articles/course-design-ideas/power-transparency-teaching/

APPENDIX F

Facilitator Guide: Designing Success and How to Achieve It

Access the Full Facilitator Guide

https://www.routledge.com/Being-Human-in-STEM-Partnering-with-Students-to-Shape-Inclusive-Practices/Bunnell-Jaswal-Lyster/p/book/9781642672299

Transparency	Connection	Modeling
Share with students that you believe that all students can succeed in this course. While you have learning goals for them, it is also important that they establish their own definitions of success. Scholarly work in this area indicates that when students are invited to articulate their own goals for their learning, they experience higher levels of intrinsic motivation and greater persistence, especially when faced with challenging material.	You can communicate to students that you value them as individuals and recognize that they have different goals for their education, different skills they want to work on, and different competing priorities. In this task, therefore, you are inviting them to set their own goals for their success in this course and identify specific strategies that they will employ to meet these goals. You may also remind students that they engage in this process of intentional goal-setting and strategy selection in other contexts of their lives already, such as in their athletic or artistic endeavors.	Here you might articulate a specific goal that you have set for yourself this semester, such as enhancing a particular research skill or learning more about a particular topic in your discipline. Share with students why you are focusing on that goal this semester and the strategies that you will engage in order to meet that goal by the end of the term.

Supporting References

Dunlosky, J., Rawson, K. A., Marsh, E. J., Nathan, M. J., & Willingham, D. T. (2013). Improving students' learning with effective learning techniques: Promising directions from cognitive and educational psychology. *Psychological Science in the Public Interest, 14*(1), 4–58. https://doi.org/10.1177/1529100612453266

Elliot, A. J., McGregor, H. A., & Gable, S. (1999). Achievement goals, study strategies, and exam performance: A mediational analysis. *Journal of Educational Psychology, 91*(3), 549–563. https://doi.org/10.1037/0022-0663.91.3.549

Hofer, B. K., Yu, S. L., & Pintrich, P. R. (1998). Teaching college students to be self-regulated learners. In D. H. Schunk & B. J. Zimmerman (Eds.), *Self-regulated learning: From teaching to self-reflective practice* (pp. 57–85). Guilford.

McGuire, S. Y., & McGuire, S. (2015). *Teach students how to learn: Strategies you can incorporate into any course to improve student metacognition, study skills, and motivation*. Stylus.

APPENDIX G

Facilitator Guide: Community Agreements

Access the Full Facilitator Guide

https://www.routledge.com/Being-Human-in-STEM-Partnering-with-Students-to-Shape-Inclusive-Practices/Bunnell-Jaswal-Lyster/p/book/9781642672299

Transparency	*Connection*	*Modeling*
This activity is designed for all members of the class to identify the conditions that will allow them to engage and feel included. Together, the class will construct a set of agreements that it will seek to uphold in their work together. And when moments arise that are inconsistent with these agreements, the class will revisit these goals. The research on community agreements suggests that being explicit about how individuals want to interact with each other allows them to be more cognizant of how they are making and taking space for others. For individuals who tend to be more dominant in groups, these agreements can help them take a step back. For others, these agreements can help to create conditions that allow them to step in and contribute meaningfully.	In this portion of the conversation, you can highlight why developing skills of collaboration and being explicit about how individuals work together are important to the successful doing of science, and thus why you are emphasizing these skills. You may also provide a discussion of a past experience of collaboration that you have experienced, either where a community norms discussion facilitated that work or where the inclusion of such a conversation would have been beneficial.	You too can be an active participant in this activity. At the start of each round, you may choose to provide your response first, before asking students to do the same. On the other hand, you may elect *not* to provide your own responses first, if you sense that in so doing, you may influence the nature of the community agreements that are created.

Supporting Reference

Boyes-Watson, C., & Pranis, K. (2020). *Circle forward: Building a restorative school community*. Living Justice Press.

APPENDIX H

Facilitator Guide: Minute Paper

Access Full Facilitator Guide

https://www.routledge.com/Being-Human-in-STEM-Partnering-with-Students-to-Shape-Inclusive-Practices/Bunnell-Jaswal-Lyster/p/book/9781642672299

Transparency	Connection	Modeling
This activity is an important tool for gathering information about how students are understanding and making sense of the course content, and where they need additional support. Share with students that in addition to gathering just-in-time information about their learning, the research also indicates that by responding to these metacognitive prompts, students are reaping benefits from condensing and reflecting on their learning. Identifying what is confusing will help students recognize where they need to focus their studying or questions to ask in office hours.	Share with students that you value their feedback and want to ensure that your teaching is helping them to process and make sense of the information. Additionally, in line with the community that you are seeking to foster in the class, this activity allows you to share the connections and applications that other peers in the class see to the material.	To model how students might respond to this activity, you could share hypothetical responses to a prompt at the end of a class session that precedes a class meeting in which they will be asked to submit a Minute Paper response. Alternatively, and with student consent, you could share examples of students' Minute Paper responses from a previous offering of the course and discuss how you incorporated those responses into how you approached teaching the next class session.

Supporting References

Angelo, T. A., & Cross, K. P. (1993). *Classroom assessment techniques: A handbook for college teachers* (2nd ed.). Jossey-Bass.

Stead, D. R. (2005). A review of the one-minute paper. *Active Learning in Higher Education, 6*(2), 118–131. https://doi.org/10.1177/1469787405054237

APPENDIX I

Facilitator Guide: Utility Value Writing

Access Full Facilitator Guide

https://www.routledge.com/Being-Human-in-STEM-Partnering-with-Students-to-Shape-Inclusive-Practices/Bunnell-Jaswal-Lyster/p/book/9781642672299

Transparency	*Connection*	*Modeling*
This activity is designed to help students reflect on how the concepts they are encountering in your course connect to their goals and other areas of their lives. The research into utility value writing indicates that when students engage in this practice, especially when they do so at several points over the semester, student engagement, course performance, and retention in STEM increase.	This is a great moment for you to share your vision of the larger purpose of your course, or of higher education, with your students. Why are the skills and knowledge areas that you are discovering together important to pursue? And more than that, why do you think that it's important for students to find meaning and connection between what they are learning in class and who they wish to become more broadly?	You may wish to share a personal skill or area of expertise that you are working on in your own research or professional life, and the value that you see that skill having both as you strive for your professional goals and also for other areas of your life. For example, you may be working to improve your research documentation skills; as such, you could share why this skill is important to your research success as well as the lessons you are learning from honing this skill that are infusing other areas of your life as well.

Supporting Reference

Harackiewicz, J. M., Tibbetts, Y., Canning, E., & Hyde, J. S. (2014). Harnessing values to promote motivation in education. In S. A. Karabenick & T. C. Urdan (Eds.), *Advances in motivation and achievement* (Vol. 18, pp. 71–105). Emerald Group. https://doi.org/10.1108/S0749-742320140000018002

APPENDIX J

Facilitator Guide: Exam Wrappers

Access the Full Facilitator Guide

https://www.routledge.com/Being-Human-in-STEM-Partnering-with-Students-to-Shape-Inclusive-Practices/Bunnell-Jaswal-Lyster/p/book/9781642672299

Transparency	Connection	Modeling
This activity is designed to help students reflect on the strategies that they are employing for learning in your class and the effectiveness of these strategies. Students benefit from making explicit the strategies they are using and from critically examining their efficacy. As the instructor, you also benefit from learning how students are approaching learning in your class and whether you could support them in developing more successful study strategies.	You might highlight for students that as emerging scientists, they can apply the scientific method of developing a hypothesis, making observations, and reflecting on those observations to their own learning. In asking them to reflect on their studying methods using this approach, you are helping them to become better scientists as well as better learners.	Before asking students to complete this activity you may choose to model a strategy or particular set of strategies that you find most helpful to your own learning. When do you use that strategy, and why? Alternatively, if you have used exam wrappers in other courses, and if you have gathered consent from students for this purpose, you could share how previous students have responded to these prompts and give a tangible example of how using this approach helped a previous student achieve better learning outcomes.

Supporting References

Lovett, M. C. (2013). Make exams worth more than grades: Using exam wrappers to promote metacognition. In M. Kaplan, N. Silver, D. Lavaque-Manty, & D. Meizlish (Eds.), *Using reflection and metacognition to improve student learning* (pp. 18–52). Stylus.

McGuire, S. Y., & McGuire, S. (2015). *Teach students how to learn: Strategies you can incorporate into any course to improve student metacognition, study skills, and motivation.* Stylus.

APPENDIX K

Facilitator Guide: Midsemester Feedback

Access the Full Facilitator Guide

https://www.routledge.com/Being-Human-in-STEM-Partnering-with-Students-to-Shape-Inclusive-Practices/Bunnell-Jaswal-Lyster/p/book/9781642672299

Transparency	Connection	Modeling
Gathering midsemester feedback is a process that helps to reinforce community and a collaborative classroom dynamic. Students hold valuable insights into their own learning experience in the class; some of these experiences may not be obvious to you from your position as the instructor. Asking to hear and learn from those insights allows you to make more informed choices about course design, practices, and policies while also communicating that you value students' desires and goals for their learning in your class.	Share with students that you seek to support everyone's learning experience in the class. Hearing what is working for students helps you to decide what to keep or do more of in a class. Hearing what could work better allows you to make more informed choices about the rest of the semester and future semesters. You may also wish to discuss how learning to give and receive feedback is an important professional and interpersonal skill, and that you are helping to support students' development of this skill through this activity.	You may choose to share an example of past student feedback that has contributed to the current design of this course or a different course. You might also choose to model the kind of feedback that would be most useful. What does formative, specific, and productive feedback look like?

Supporting References

Hurney, C. A., Harris, N. L., Prins, S. C. B., & Kruck, S. E. (2014). The impact of a learner-centered, mid-semester course evaluation on students. *Journal of Faculty Development*, *28*(3), 55–61.

Lewis, K. G. (Ed.). (2001). Using midsemester student feedback and responding to it. In *Techniques and Strategies for Interpreting Student Evaluations* [Special Issue] (New Directions for Teaching and Learning, no. 87, pp. 33–44). https://doi.org/10.1002/tl.26

APPENDIX L

Facilitator Guide: Scientist Trading Cards

Access the Full Facilitator Guide

https://www.routledge.com/Being-Human-in-STEM-Partnering-with-Students-to-Shape-Inclusive-Practices/Bunnell-Jaswal-Lyster/p/book/9781642672299

Transparency	Connection	Modeling
This activity encourages students to engage with all students in the classroom, in order to enhance their skills of collaboration and build connections with people they might not otherwise know. Research suggests that we tend to form friendships with individuals who are similar to us, and yet additional scholarship points to the beneficial role of working with diverse groupmates to improve our problem-solving and work as scientists. This activity is designed to help make those connections. Additionally, if you use cards that highlight a wide range of scientists in the field, you are increasing the chance that students will see examples of a successful scientist who holds similar identities to their own.	Share with students why it is important to you that they get to know each other and that they work with folks whom they may not otherwise immediately seek out as lab partners. You can also highlight how these skills of collaboration across diverse others will serve students in many professional roles, such as working in a large company setting, in a health profession, or in education.	You could model finding one's partner by calling out the scientist's name ("Mae Jamison, Mae Jamison") and then model the first steps of the introduction ("Hi, my name is ___. Nice to meet you!") as well as learning more about the information on the trading card ("Wow, I have never heard of ___, but they were involved in ___. Had you heard of them before?").

Supporting References

Goethe, E. V., & Colina, C. M. (2018). Taking advantage of diversity within the classroom. *Journal of Chemical Education, 95*(2), 189–192. https://doi.org/10.1021/acs.jchemed.7b00510

Hong, L., & Page, S. E. (2004). Groups of diverse problem solvers can outperform groups of high-ability problem solvers. *Proceedings of the National Academy of Sciences of the United States of America, 101*(46), 16385–16389. https://doi.org/10.1073/pnas.0403723101

Liberman, Z., & Shaw, A. (2019). Children use similarity, propinquity, and loyalty to predict which people are friends. *Journal of Experimental Child Psychology, 184*, 1–17. https://doi.org/10.1016/j.jecp.2019.03.002

Selfhout, M., Denissen, J., Branje, S., & Meeus, W. (2009). In the eye of the beholder: Perceived, actual, and peer-rated similarity in personality, communication, and friendship intensity during the acquaintanceship process. *Journal of Personality and Social Psychology, 96*(6), 1152–1165. https://doi.org/10.1037/a0014468

APPENDIX M

Facilitator Guide: Community Announcements

Access the Full Facilitator Guide

https://www.routledge.com/Being-Human-in-STEM-Partnering-with-Students-to-Shape-Inclusive-Practices/Bunnell-Jaswal-Lyster/p/book/9781642672299

Transparency	Connection	Modeling
Incorporating this activity into a classroom or laboratory weekly routine allows students to share, and feel valued for, the wide range of skills and interests that they hold as individuals in your class. Sharing the activities that they are engaged in outside of STEM also allows them to make or enrich connections with each other around newly discovered shared interests. The research suggests that students benefit from a larger sense of connection to the campus community; this activity allows them to celebrate that connection and invite others to join them.	We encourage you to share why knowing about who your students are, outside of their STEM identities, is important to you. You might also talk about the kinds of amazing things that students are doing about which you are already aware, and how you hope to learn more through the semester.	This is a great opportunity for students to get to know more about you as a whole person. Share announcements about the events that are happening in your non-STEM communities and invite students, when appropriate, to join these events.

Supporting References

Freeman, T. M., Anderman, L. H., & Jensen, J. M. (2007). Sense of belonging in college freshmen at the classroom and campus levels. *Journal of Experimental Education, 75*(3), 203–220. https://doi.org/10.3200/JEXE.75.3.203-220

Garcia, C. E. (2020). Belonging in a predominantly White institution: The role of membership in Latina/o sororities and fraternities. *Journal of Diversity in Higher Education, 13*(2), 181–193. https://doi.org/10.1037/dhe0000126

Trujillo, G., & Tanner, K. D. (2014). Considering the role of affect in learning: Monitoring students' self-efficacy, sense of belonging, and science identity. *CBE—Life Sciences Education, 13*(1), 6–15. https://doi.org/10.1187/cbe.13-12-0241

APPENDIX N

Facilitator Guide: Group Work Reflections

Access the Full Facilitator Guide

https://www.routledge.com/Being-Human-in-STEM-Partnering-with-Students-to-Shape-Inclusive-Practices/Bunnell-Jaswal-Lyster/p/book/9781642672299

Transparency	Connection	Modeling
This activity helps students to recognize that as they complete collaborative lab activities, they are working on improving their research skills as well as their collaboration skills. Both of these skills are equally important in science, and the research suggests that being explicit about our interactions can help us recognize and improve our approaches to group work. By engaging with students' reflections, you are better able to give them feedback about how they are working together and how they can continue to improve on this learning goal.	Share with students why you think that it's important that they support each other and work collaboratively in the lab, and why you value positive and collegial collaboration in your own work as a scientist. You might choose to share a particular approach to collaboration that you value or a time in your professional work when being explicit about the nature of the collaboration may have allowed it to progress more positively.	Using what is commonly referred to as a "think aloud" approach, you might demonstrate how you would approach an upcoming lab using the prework prompts. You could also, with student consent, share past students' reflections about how their lab partners helped them to succeed in the lab.

Supporting References

Leopold, H., & Smith, A. (2020). Implementing reflective group work activities in a large chemistry lab to support collaborative learning. *Education Sciences, 10*(1), 7.

Scager, K., Boonstra, J., Peeters, T., Vulperhorst, J., & Wiegant, F. (2016). Collaborative learning in higher education: Evoking positive interdependence. *CBE—Life Sciences Education, 15*(4), Article 69. https://doi.org/10.1187/cbe.16-07-0219

APPENDIX O

Facilitator Guide: Telling Your HSTEM Story

Access the Full Facilitator Guide

https://www.routledge.com/Being-Human-in-STEM-Partnering-with-Students-to-Shape-Inclusive-Practices/Bunnell-Jaswal-Lyster/p/book/9781642672299

Note. Part I of this exercise can be implemented as a standalone module. Part II is specifically designed to be completed after your class has engaged with the academic literature around inclusion and equity, and Part III is designed to be completed after students develop their action projects in partnership with campus partners.

General Guidelines to Emphasize to Students

- Have fun! Feel free to get creative. You can write something, draw something, use graphics, images, magazines, newsprints, or whatever other media helps you capture your story.
- Your representation does not need to be fully self-explanatory, as long as you would be able to walk someone through your story in a way that makes sense to you.

- Please spend no more than 1 hour on this assignment. We want you to capture how you conceptualize your journey in STEM to this point but recognize that it will not be a perfect or complete picture of who you are.

Part I: Your HSTEM Story (Past) Prompts

- What role has STEM played in your life so far? What experiences, both positive and negative, stick out in your memory? All of you, whether currently engaged in STEM or not, have engaged with STEM through your education and have been touched by STEM methods, knowledge, technologies, and culture. How has that impacted who you are now?
- What about STEM do you find most engaging or enjoyable? What aspects of STEM do you think are most important or relevant to your future?
- What STEM topics do you hope to learn about during your undergraduate studies?
- Looking ahead, what is your sense of how you will intersect with STEM in the future (e.g., what is your envisioned career trajectory and/or life)?

Part II: Your HSTEM Story (Present) Prompts

- Please revise and expand on your HSTEM Story (Past) or construct a new HSTEM Story (Present). What new understanding do you have about your journey and role in STEM, based on our work together so far?
- Please identify at least three sources from the course that have influenced how you are currently thinking about your HSTEM story. Explain the connections that you see between these sources and how you are currently thinking about your journey in STEM. You do not need to agree with the sources. Instead, be sure to discuss how they made you think differently about your story, perhaps by revealing gaps in your experiences, by introducing new concepts or frameworks through which you have reconsidered aspects of your experience, or by challenging your ideas.
- Again, please spend no more than 1 hour on this activity.

Part III: Your HSTEM Story (Future) Prompts

- Now we are asking you to envision your future self in STEM. In this iteration of the assignment, we ask you to consider what you want to be doing in 5 years and how you want to be connected to STEM at that point in your life. Further, we want you to consider who you want to be as a human in STEM. How will you stay connected to our HSTEM community and to what we have learned together in order to develop into that aspirational future human in STEM?
- Spending no more than an hour on this activity, you can either revise a previous version of your HSTEM story or construct a new representation of your HSTEM Story (Future).
- Please be sure to address the following questions in the construction of your story:
    - Who would you like to be as a human in STEM in 5 years?
    - What HSTEM practices and principles will you incorporate to help you achieve your future HSTEM self?
    - How can the HSTEM community support you as you move toward that aspirational self?

ABOUT THE AUTHORS

Sarah L. Bunnell

Sarah L. Bunnell has been actively involved in scholarship of teaching and learning research, and mentoring others in SoTL, since 2006. She has published multiple articles and chapters on SoTL, including in the *Journal of Faculty Development, International Journal for Students as Partners, Case Studies in the Environment, Teaching and Learning Together in Higher Education*, and the edited volumes *Threshold Concepts in Problem-Based Learning* (Brill, 2018) and *Ethics and the Scholarship of Teaching and Learning* (Springer, 2022). She served as president of the International Society for the Scholarship of Teaching and Learning (2021–2022) and served in elected positions on the ISSOTL board for 10 consecutive years prior to moving into the presidential position for the society. As the associate director and STEM specialist for the Amherst College Center for Teaching and Learning, her work focuses on providing faculty with the frameworks and support that they need to impact student learning and a sense of community in their classrooms and laboratories. Her contributions to the HSTEM Initiative include assessment, helping faculty design and implement HSTEM practices across the curriculum, and connecting the work of the HSTEM network with other national and international efforts toward inclusive STEM education. Sarah received her BA degree in neuroscience from Middlebury College and her MA and PhD in developmental and cognitive psychology from the University of Kansas.

Sheila S. Jaswal

Sheila received her BA in German and biochemistry from Mills College, where her experiences in women-only classrooms and laboratories provided an opportunity to learn and lead in science settings in the absence of gender-based implicit bias and stereotype threat. While earning her PhD in biochemistry from the University of California at San Francisco, she co-led a middle school girls' science club for a year through the NSF-supported "Triad Project" of the Science Education Partnership. Under the tutelage of

Liesl Chatman, Kimberly Tanner, and colleagues, she experienced the transformative power of experiential and active learning coupled with metacognitive reflection on the part of the learners and the educators. As a professor in the Chemistry Department and Program in Biophysics and Biochemistry at Amherst College, she partners with a team of undergraduate researchers to study the interplay between protein stability, dynamics, and function using a combined biophysical and computational approach. She has published this work widely, in journals such as *Protein Science* and the *Journal of Physical Chemistry*. Sheila is the director of the "Being Human in STEM" (HSTEM) initiative. She cofacilitates the HSTEM course in collaboration with students, staff, and faculty colleagues; organizes campus and regional HSTEM events; gives talks and workshops at colleges, universities, and conferences nationwide; oversees a growing HSTEM network and collaborators at other institutions; and shares curricular and other HSTEM resources at www.beinghumaninstem.com.

Megan B. Lyster

Megan Lyster has supported students, faculty, and staff in designing and implementing project-based learning experiences since 2007. She taught courses in design, social entrepreneurship, and women in business at Hampshire College, and served as the codirector of the Hampshire College Social Venture Fund and Advisory Network from 2010 to 2013. Megan then transitioned to supporting faculty as the instructional designer for experiential learning in the Amherst College Center for Community Engagement, where she facilitated community-based and project-based learning initiatives inside and outside the classroom. While at Amherst, she developed and facilitated the Design Thinking Challenge, an intensive program in which small teams of students grappled with and identified potential solutions for campus-based challenges. She also partnered with Sheila (and later, Sarah) to codevelop the Being Human in STEM initiative from its inception in the spring of 2016, and served as a codesigner and coinstructor for seven iterations of the HSTEM course, with a specialized focus on the development and implementation of student-led projects. In her current role as the assistant director in the Wurtele Center for Leadership at Smith College, Megan supports students, faculty, and staff to cultivate the creativity, courage, and collaborative capacity to facilitate positive change in the world. Megan received her BA in 2002 from Hampshire College, and her MA in 2009 from Prescott College.

INDEX

academic literature, connecting lived experiences with, 152–154
action projects, student-led
  campus change through, 28–32
  campus community involvement within, 31–32
  example of, 49
  feedback regarding, 49
  grounding within current institutional landscape, 155–156
  lessons learned from, 158
  overview of, 33
  planning for, 29–31
  process of, 49, 154–155, 168–169
  sharing with campus community, 157–158
  student individual growth through, 121–122
  themes of, 30
  topic selection for, 155
active listening, 20, 59–60, 64, 108, 169
admissions policy, 2–3
advisee, partnership role of, 43
affective empathy, 55–56
agency, for change, 166
Airplane Game, 73, 76
Amherst College, 3, 120–125, 142, 145, 157
Amherst Uprising
  as case study, 3–9
  effects of, 36, 52, 121, 165
  introduction to, 1
  photo of, 4
  responses to, 9–12, 13
Angelou, Maya, 112
Asian Americans, 2

assessment
  challenges with, 111
  of courses, 113–114
  ethic of inquiry within, 129–131
  of faculty, 113
  within HSTEM course, 34
  of inclusive classroom climate, 136
  question types within, 130–131, 139
  of science identity, 136
  as systematic, 128
assumptions, 170

Being Human in STEM website, 18, 69
Being Human module (HSTEM course), 23–24
believing approach to readings, 22
belonging, measurement of, 135–138
Black Alumni Weekend, 121
Black Lives Matter movement, 4, 165
Blacks, 2, 3
BOOM! event (Mount Holyoke College), 157–158
Bradtmiller, Louisa, 146
Braiding Sweetgrass (Kimmerer), 153
brave space, 19–20, 45–46
Brown, Michael, 4
Brown University, 32
burnout, 118

"call in" action, 64, 157
campus stakeholders, partnership with, 48–49
Center for Race, Ethnicity, and Human Rights (REHR) (Soka University of America), 147

215

change
    allies and accomplices for, 116
    case studies regarding, 120–125
    within community, 154–158
    faculty-focused, 124–125
    institutional readiness for, 138–139
    intentional, backward design approach to, 44
    lack of resources as barrier to, 117–120
    lack of shared consensus about the need for change as barrier to, 114–116
    lack of shared value or direction as barrier to, 113–114
    overview of, 111
    possibility of, 116
    process of, 112–120, 125–126
    psychological support for, 118–119
    requirements for, 117–120, 125–126, 166
    structural support for, 117–118
    success regarding, 116
    translational support for, 119–120
    wishes regarding, 112
Chatterjea, Devavani, 146
Chávez, Victoria C., 148, 154, 161
Chemistry AntiRacism Advisory Committee (CARAC), 124
class expectations, within HSTEM course, 77–78
cofacilitators, 24–25, 37, 46, 47–48, 50, 150
cognitive empathy, 55. *See also* empathy
cognitive wrappers, 83–84
Cohen, Phoebe, 161
colearning, trust-building through, 46
collaboration, for DEI work, 118
collective growth, 167–169
commitment, to change, 166
commonality, identification of, 55
community
    building of, 150–151
    change envisioning within, 154–158
    creation of, 118
    HSTEM, 19–20
    meaning-making within, 107–108
    within STEM courses, 71–81
    transformation of, 169
community agreements, 20
Community Agreements activity, 79–81
Community Announcements activity, 87–88
compensation, for student participation, 117–118
cost, of undergraduate degree attainment, 3
course materials, student growth through engagement with, 120–121
courses, evaluation of, 113–114
cross-disciplinary cofacilitation, 47
cultural capital, within low socioeconomic backgrounds, 8
curricula, STEM, 7–8, 122
curricular practices handbook, HSTEM, 68–69

Dandridge, Katyana, 3–4, 6, 116
data, institutional, 114, 155–156
Davidson College, 142, 145, 151
Dean, Cornelia, 32
deep teaching model, 56
De Grandi, Claudia, 148, 161–162
DePauw University
    action project lessons within, 158
    HSTEM course history within, 145–146
    institutional profile of, 142
    peer mentoring within, 156
    student feedback within, 160
    timeline of HSTEM course offerings, 145
    virtual learning within, 151
Designing Success and How to Achieve It activity, 78–79, 83
Dewsbury, Bryan, 148, 162

direction, lack of, 113–114
Discussing Class Expectations activity, 77–78
diversification, 2–3
diversity, 3, 21–28, 100–101
Dudle, Dana, 145, 158, 161

educators, medical practitioners *versus*, 57
emotion, 55, 56
emotional validation, 39
empathy
 activation of, 59–60
 active listening exercise, 59–60
 affective, 55–56
 cognitive, 55
 entangled, 63–64
 function of, 169
 importance of, 167
 limitations of, 63–64
 in the medical field, 57–58
 Meta-Reflections exercise, 61–63
 overview of, 54, 55–56, 64–65
 requirements for, 54
 in teaching, 56
 teaching strategies regarding, 58–63
 When Have You Felt Included? exercise, 61
engagement, classroom practices for, 81–86
entangled empathy, 63–64. *See also* empathy
ethic of inquiry, in inclusive teaching, 129–131
Exam Wrappers activity, 83–84
expectations, for change, 112

facilitators, 37, 46, 47, 69–70
faculty
 change by, 124–125
 diversity lack within, 8–9
 evaluation of, 113
 feedback about change from, 115
 HSTEM impact on, 160–163
 humanizing of, 72–73
 partnership feedback from, 51
 partnership with, 40, 44
 protest opinions of, 13
feedback
 action projects, 49
 from cofacilitators, 50
 within DePauw University, 160
 from faculty, 51, 115
 function of, 168
 HSTEM course, 126, 159–160
 within Macalester College, 152, 160
 Midsemester Feedback activity, 84–86
 noninclusive spaces, 114–115
 partnership, 50–51
 within Soka University of America, 154
 STEM department (Amherst University), 7
 within University of Rhode Island, 154
flexibility, 70–71

Garner, Eric, 4
gatekeeping practices, 134
goals, 78–79, 83, 123, 168
Greenland, Kristen, 48
groundskeeping practices, 134–135
Group Work Reflections activity, 88–90
guiding questions, 170–171

hack session, 138
Henderson-Stull, M. Nidanie, 147–148, 158, 162
high school science, preparation lack within, 9
Hispanic Americans, 2
HSTEM Central Dogma, 38
HSTEM course
 adapting core pillars of, 150–151
 assessment within, 34, 136–137
 Being Human module within, 23–24
 benefits of, 163

building of, 16–19
case studies regarding, 120–125
core readings within, 21
effects of, 36
empathy teaching strategies within, 58–63
faculty impact from, 160–163
features of, 19
feedback regarding, 126
goal of, 123, 168
Humanizing STEM module within, 26
Interrogation of Ways of Knowing in STEM module within, 24–25
lessons learned from, 166–167
model for, 18
modifications to, 154
national and institutional context of, 122–124
network impacts of, 158–163
"new conceptual frameworks" questions within, 134–135
overview of, 16, 33–34
process model of, 37–41
ritual within, 20
topics regarding, 17
unfamiliar terms within, 25
"visions of the possible" questions regarding, 132
website for, 18, 69
"what" works questions regarding, 131–132
HSTEM curricular practices handbook, 68–69
HSTEM Salon, 28, 31–32
HSTEM Summit, 32–33
human-centered design, 48
humanities department, 12
Humanize the Professor exercise, 72–73
Humanizing STEM module (HSTEM course), 26

ideation, within human-centered design, 48
identity, 99–100, 166–167
implementation, within human-centered design, 48
imposter syndrome, 27
inclusion, 3, 21–28, 86–90
inclusive classroom, 3, 135, 136, 167
inclusive teaching, ethic of inquiry within, 129–131
individual growth, 167–169
inspiration, within human-centered design, 48
interpersonal-level risk of students, 40
Interrogation of Ways of Knowing in STEM module (HSTEM course), 24–25

Kharel, Savan, 149
Kim, Sally, 60

lab-based practices
  assessment of impact of, 90–91
  Community Announcements activity, 87–88
  Group Work Reflections activity, 88–90
  for inclusive and collaborative research spaces, 86–90
  lab partner formation within, 86–87
  Scientist Trading Cards activity, 87
lab partners, 86–87
Latino Americans, 2
leaky pipeline, 133–135
learning enhancement, classroom practices for, 81–86
listening, 38–39, 59–60, 64, 108, 169
lived experiences, 26–28, 152–154
Lom, Barbara, 145, 159, 160

Macalester College, 142, 145, 146, 152, 157, 160
marginalized groups, 115
Markley, Michelle, 146, 159, 162
Martin, Treyvon, 4
medical field, empathy within, 57–58
medical practitioners, educators *versus*, 57

mentee, partnership role of, 43
metacognitive equity, 81
Meta-Reflections exercise, 61–63
Midsemester Feedback activity, 84–86
Minute Paper exercise, 82, 195–196
Miranker, Andrew, 149
Mochrie, Simon, 149
money, as change resource, 117
Mount Holyoke College, 143, 145, 146–147, 154, 157–158
Murphy, Cullen, 6

network modeling approach to organizational change, 139
"new conceptual frameworks" questions, 130, 134–135
nonbelonging, 99–100
noninclusive spaces, student feedback regarding, 114–115

Packard, Becky Wai-Ling, 147
partnership
  with campus entities, 156–157
  with campus stakeholders, 48–49
  cofacilitator feedback regarding, 50
  collaboration comparison with, 42–43
  defined, 45
  early days of, 41–49
  expanding ways of knowing within, 47–48
  faculty feedback regarding, 51
  listening within, 38–39
  overview of, 36–37, 52
  partnering within, 41
  reflection within, 40–41
  risk within, 40
  student feedback regarding, 50–51
  testimonials regarding, 50–51
  validating within, 39–40
peer mentoring, 156
persistence, measurement of, 133–135
police violence, timeline of, 4
Poturovic, Selma, 145, 158

privileged poor, 23–24, 153
The Privileged Poor (Jack), 23–24, 152–153
protests
  criticism of, 13
  discomfort regarding, 13
  effects of, 165
  examples of, 4–5
  faculty responses to, 13
  responses to, 9–12
  See also Amherst Uprising
psychological support, as change requirement, 118–119

Race & Gender in the Scientific Community course (Brown University), 32
"Racism Lives Here" rallies, 4–5
Ramos, Rona, 155, 158, 160, 161
readings, 21–22, 47
reciprocity, 46
reflection
  development of, 20
  of educational journey, 102
  empathy and, 59
  importance of, 90–91
  overview of, 40–41
  to reading response, 21–22
  self-interrogation within, 151
  structure of, 29
  "3-2-1 Reflection Assignment," 151–152
research assistant, partnership role of, 43
research spaces, within lab-based practices, 86–90
retention, 133–135
Rice, Tamir, 4
rigor, 113–114
ritual, importance of, 20
Roberts, Jackie, 156

Salon, HSTEM, 28, 31–32
Sandstede, Björn, 32
scaffolding, 31

Schmalzbauer, Leah, 47
science, high school, preparation lack within, 9
science field, 100–101, 112
science narratives, 98–101
scientific model, 167
Scientist Trading Cards activity, 87
Scott, Walter, 4
self-efficacy, 135–138
self-interrogation, 151
self-knowledge, 101
self questions, 131
self-reflection, 40–41, 90–91, 151
self-worth, 99–100
shared experience, emotional connection through, 55
shared ownership, 44
Sheppard, Kelly, 147
ShutdownSTEM movement, 123
skeptical approach to readings, 22
Skidmore College, 143, 145, 147, 156–157
socioeconomic backgrounds, cultural capital within, 8
Soka University of America, 143, 145, 147–148, 154, 155
stakeholders, campus, partnership with, 48–49
STEM course
   Airplane Game within, 73, 76
   building community within, 71–81
   Community Agreements activity, 79–81
   Community Announcements activity, 87–88
   Designing Success and How to Achieve It activity, 78–79, 83
   Discussing Class Expectations activity, 77–78
   engagement practices within, 81–86
   Exam Wrappers activity, 83–84
   facilitator guides for, 69–70
   flexibility within, 70–71
   Group Work Reflections activity, 88–90
   Humanizing the Professor exercise, 72–73
   learning enhancement practices within, 81–86
   Midsemester Feedback activity, 84–86
   Minute Paper exercise, 82
   Scientist Trading Cards activity, 87
   This I Believe essay assignment, 76–77
   Utility Value Writing activity, 82–83
STEM department/STEM classroom
   career choices within, 134
   diversity lack within, 8–9, 24
   empathy strategies within, 58–63
   female representation within, 98–99
   inclusion and diversity within, 21–28
   leaky pipeline within, 133–135
   lived experiences within, 26–28
   protest response from, 12–13
   representation importance within, 27
   student feedback regarding, 7
   surviving *versus* thriving within, 137–138
   training phenomena within, 133–134
stipends, for student participation, 117–118
Story activity
   evolution of, 104–106
   example of, 104–106
   format of, 102
   future assignment within, 102, 103–104, 105–106
   genre of, 102
   goal within, 107
   implementation of, 152
   iterative process within, 108
   meaning-making within, 107–108
   overview of, 95–98, 109
   parts of, 101–104
   past assignment within, 102, 103, 104
   present assignment within, 102, 103, 104–105
   principles regarding, 106–108
   reflection within, 102, 106
   sharing within, 107–108

structural support, as change
    requirement, 117–118
student-led action projects
    campus change through, 28–32
    campus community involvement
        within, 31–32
    example of, 49
    feedback regarding, 49
    grounding within current
        institutional landscape, 155–156
    lessons learned from, 158
    overview of, 33
    planning for, 29–31
    process of, 49, 154–155
    sharing with campus community,
        157–158
    student individual growth through,
        121–122
    themes of, 30
    topic selection for, 155
student loan debt, 3
student partner, 42, 44, 45–46
success, operational definitions of,
    132–138
Summit, HSTEM, 32–33
sustainability, requirements for, 117

Takarimbudde, Sanyu, 3–4, 6, 116
teaching assistant, partnership role of,
    42
Teffo, Lerato, 3–4, 6, 116
theory-of-mind (ToM), 55
third space, 45
This I Believe essay assignment, 76–77
"3-2-1 Reflection Assignment" (Yale
    University), 151–152
translational support, as change
    requirement, 119–120
trust, 39, 46, 135
tuition, 3

undergraduate colleges and universities,
    changing demographics within,
    2–3

undergraduate degree, costs regarding, 3
United States, demographic changes
    within, 2
University of Colorado-Boulder, 2–3
University of Missouri-Columbia, 4–5
University of Rhode Island, 143, 145,
    148, 152, 154
University of Utah, 143, 145, 148–149,
    151, 153–154, 156, 160
Utility Value Writing activity, 82–83

validating, 39–40
values, 113–114, 166
virtual learning, HSTEM adaptation
    for, 151
"visions of the possible" questions, 130,
    131–132, 162
vulnerability, 46, 165–166

Watkins, Ruth, 156
"what is" questions, 130, 138
"what works" questions, 130, 131–132
When Have You Felt Included? exercise,
    61
white Americans, 2, 3
Williams College, 144, 145, 149
women, in STEM fields, 98–99
written reflection, 21–22

Yale University
    action project lessons within, 158
    action project themes within, 155
    HSTEM course history within, 149
    HSTEM Summit at, 32
    institutional profile of, 144
    reflection assignment within,
        151–152
    student-led discussion at, 160
    student protests at, 5
    survey within, 156
    "3-2-1 Reflection Assignment"
        within, 151–152
    timeline of HSTEM course offerings,
        145

For Product Safety Concerns and Information please contact our EU
representative GPSR@taylorandfrancis.com
Taylor & Francis Verlag GmbH, Kaufingerstraße 24, 80331 München, Germany

www.ingramcontent.com/pod-product-compliance
Lightning Source LLC
Chambersburg PA
CBHW051610230426
43668CB00013B/2059